ONE NIGHT OF
MADNESS

Best wishes,
Stokes McMillan 11/20/09

STOKES MCMILLAN

Oak Harbor Publishing of Houston, TX

ISBN: 0-9825291-0-4
ISBN-13: 9780982529102
Library of Congress Control Number: 2009906653

Author photograph by
J. Pamela Photography, Houston, TX

Visit www.booksurge.com to order additional copies.

Oak Harbor Publishing of Houston, TX

For Teresa

Contents

Preface

Writing a book can be difficult, all-consuming work; it grasps an author's mind and wrings it dry of the outside distraction commonly known as "normal life." What would make an otherwise sane person take on such a task? There are nearly as many answers to that question as there are books, but in the case of the one you now hold in your hands, the answer is simple: a scrapbook.

In 1950 a small-town Southern newspaper photographer snapped a once-in-a-lifetime photograph of the capture of two killers. Taken in a farmyard setting deep in the heart of Mississippi's pine forests, the photo exudes activity and danger. Two men are being frisked as they lie on their stomachs spread-eagled in the dirt. Between them, a rough-looking character in convict's striped pants stands guard with a pistol in each hand, a bloodhound at his side. Months after this dramatic picture first appeared in a low-circulation, country weekly newspaper, it garnered the prize as America's best journalistic photograph of 1950 by the prestigious National Press Photographers Association, beating out six hundred entries from newspapers around the country, including the biggest and richest. This award-winning photo is on the cover of this book.

Naturally, the honored photographer's wife, who also happened to be the daughter of the newspaper's editor and publisher, was duly proud of her husband's major accomplishment. She decided to build a scrapbook about the photo. Her scrapbook would contain the blue-ribbon picture and the story behind it: a story of mayhem, murder, posses, and trials as recorded by articles from several national newspapers and shown by numerous 8 x 10 black-and-white glossies taken by her husband. When the material she gathered outgrew the grossly undersized family album, she pasted everything into a 30 x 30 inch behemoth normally used for page layout at her father's newspaper.

Perhaps you've guessed it, but the woman who assembled the scrapbook was my mother, and the photographer was my father. As a little boy, I occasionally pulled the scrapbook from its storage spot beneath my parent's bed and gazed over its collection of photographs, but I had no thought of reading the accompanying newspaper articles. My parents told me the rough details of the story, and that was good enough for me.

Decades passed. Eventually, I inherited the scrapbook. Like my mother, I kept it beneath my bed, but took no interest other than to pull it out a few times to show the pictures to my children and to share with them what little of the background story I remembered. Then I tucked it back under the bed and relegated it to the back of my mind.

Things changed as the 2001 Christmas season approached. Our middle child, then a college sophomore, stated that his gift wish was to have a poster made of his grandfather's award-winning photograph. He wanted to hang it in his apartment. A great idea, I thought, so I made posters of that photo and one other from the scrapbook for him and his two brothers. So that I might provide my family with more interesting details behind the photos, I decided to take the time over the holidays to read the scrapbook's newspaper clippings.

I laid the large scrapbook out on a table and turned to its first page. A headline from the January 29, 1950, *St. Louis Post-Dispatch* blared "Murder in Mississippi" in bold print. I began to read, and time melted away as a story of violence, fear, race, love, revenge, politics, and courtroom drama captured me. When I finally closed the cover, I knew that the story of this 1950 event deserved more than to be secreted within the pages of an old scrapbook—it deserved to be told, and ownership of the scrapbook made me the one to tell it.

Nobel Prize–winning author Toni Morrison laid down my challenge: "If there's a book that you really want to read but it hasn't been written yet, then you must write it." Well, dear reader, here is the book that I wanted to read after perusing the slowly degrading pages of my mother's old scrapbook. The result of years of research, dozens of eyewitness interviews, and multiple site visits, this story is a true account of actual events as best as I could sort them out.

The conundrum I faced was not only that participants' memories fade and change over a half century but that newspaper accounts of the time did not always agree. Where there was a conflict, I chose the version that enabled the action to flow in the most logical and realistic manner. In order to deliver a more human and readable tale, I took literary license by adding some otherwise unknowable details to the story's events—in effect, colorizing the scrapbook's black-and-white photos and discolored newsprint. It is a literary genre known as creative nonfiction, first popularized in Truman Capote's classic, *In Cold Blood*. Know that each person mentioned in my story is real; many are still alive.

While researching the story, I was sometimes shocked and frustrated by the slow pace and weak effort apparently exhibited by certain people in responding to crisis situations where a "normal person" today would react more hurriedly. In some instances, they seemed almost to dawdle during dire emergencies. But I came to see that these traits were trademarks of life in the rural South sixty years ago, where less populated regions often lacked telephones and electricity, most roads were unpaved, mule-drawn wagons were common, and life in general was slow. Certainly there was no EMS, no 9-1-1. Even with this realization, I still found some of the characters' attitudes to be inexplicably casual. Rather than attempt to sooth the modern reader's sensibilities by fictionalizing a justification for their actions, however, I chose simply to describe what happened.

Stokes McMillan
June 29, 2009
Houston, Texas

Prologue

This is the true account of a tragic affair that briefly drew the notice and concern of the nation at the midpoint of the twentieth century. Like many such episodes, it was small to history but devastatingly large to those affected. It culminated in one night—one horrible night of madness in Attala County, Mississippi.

The land that is now central Mississippi was once occupied by the Choctaw Indian nation. White settlers replaced the Choctaws early in the nineteenth century and divided the land into counties. Attala County, named after a then-popular book's account of a heroic and beautiful Mississippi Indian princess, lies at the geographic center of the state.[1] In a coincidence that serves as a perpetual reminder to Attala's citizens of their land's Indian heritage, historical and geographic factors sculpted the county into the shape of a broad stone arrowhead pointing northeasterly toward the origin of its white pioneers.

Nestled in gentle rolling hills, amid woods of mixed hardwood and pine where "the Magnolia, raising its motionless cone, surmounted by large white buds, commands all the forest," Attala County is sheltered from the outside world, a tranquil place where life proceeds at a slow pace.[2] Its seat and largest town is Kosciusko. With a population of 6,753 in 1950, Kosciusko was the biggest municipality within sixty miles.[3]

Attala County is divided politically into five beats, with Beat 4 occupying the southwest portion. Within Beat 4 lies the small village of Newport. In 1950 its two country stores and several churches served the hundreds of black and white residents scattered throughout the surrounding land. Except for a few white landowners descended from the area's pioneers, most were poor dirt farmers or sharecroppers with little education. Blacks and whites shared the same living conditions, the same socioeconomic status, and in a few rare instances, the same families.

The dawn of a new decade, January 1950, ushered in the chance for a fresh start. Americans were relieved to leave behind the 1940s, and the national trauma of World War II. People were ready to turn their attention to other matters. They did not have to wait long.

Only days into the new year, an incident occurred in Attala County, Mississippi, that captured the national spotlight. Unfortunately, it started the decade off on a sorrowful note. But thankfully, it was brief. Although the light of attention would soon pass and the event fade into history, the matter helped bring to America's awareness a subject that would come to dominate the nation's consciousness for the next two decades: civil rights.

Generally considered to have begun with the *Brown v. Board of Education of Topeka* Supreme Court decision of 1954, which struck down the "separate but equal" notion in outlawing school segregation, the civil rights era was actually the culmination of long years of often violent, always demeaning oppression of minorities, especially against African Americans in the South. The acts of racial violence and discrimination had been mostly local events little known to the rest of the country. Only with twentieth-century improvements in mass communication were they able to attract widespread attention.

Part 1

All lands have stories, but few are worth remembering. Most are bland, monotonous tales lacking the interest or notoriety to be passed from generation to generation. Like smoke, they soon drift away. Some stories, however, in particular those tales containing deeds of both good and evil—virtues established not by ground or sky or plants or buildings but by the men and women that tread the soil— sweep over a territory like a consuming fire, branding the hearts and minds of their listeners, and become part of the heritage of a region. They live on.

So it was in a small patch of central Mississippi in the middle of the last century. A diverse group of characters, each bringing to the mix his or her own history and morality, left to mingle for decades, created a recipe of human ingredients that would provide the land with yet another story—one with a taste bitter to the palette, but not soon to be forgotten.

Chapter 1

The Turners

He felt it coming. Long before his ears heard the sound, his body sensed it—a faint tingling on the skin, a gentle drumming inside the chest.

Nineteen-year-old Archie Levy strolled slowly along a dirt road deep in the woods of the central Mississippi hills. The road's red clay surface—scarred when wet with deep ruts from wagons and trucks—made walking treacherous for the hurried. But Archie didn't hurry; he ambled, slowly, hands in his coat pockets, eyes locked on the ground a few feet ahead, his mind either lost in a thought or devoid of one.

Tranquility surrounded him. Only the throaty *caw, caw* of a distant blackbird interrupted the sound of the breeze flowing through the nearly naked trees on this chilly December day in 1949.

Now the wind carried a barely perceptible noise to Archie's ears. Slowly the sound grew into a distant, clamorous rumble—the sound of a pulpwood truck. In a few more moments, Archie recognized the auditory fingerprint of his father's pulpwood truck approaching from behind.

Six steps later he heard the high-pitched squeaking of the old truck's springs, tortured by ungreased years carrying countless logs over the washboard roads of Attala County's remotest areas. The '34 Chevy flatbed still did the job, but it made a hell of a racket.

Archie nudged closer to the berm of dirt, rocks, and leaves at the edge of the road. He tugged his wide-brimmed hat down tighter onto his curly black hair and glanced behind him, the whites of his eyes contrasting with his light brown skin. A thin mustache below a narrow nose highlighted his face. His ragged clothes revealed poverty.

The truck topped a hill a quarter mile back and came into view, kicking up a cloud of dust; it was barreling toward him. "Leon," Archie mumbled. He was the only person that drove so recklessly on this road. "Things sho' has changed since he come back." The rumble and squeaks crescendoed into a roar. The truck weaved left and right around big ruts and fallen limbs in the road. Archie could now make out its skeletal profile: a scratched white grill in front of the rounded hood; no cab—only a seat with a cracked windshield in front; and four thin metal stanchions sticking up at the corners of the truck's bed.

Archie stopped walking and stared—arms at his side, fists clenching and unclenching—at the approaching menace. The truck straightened its path, and he could clearly see the driver. It was a white man, staring right at Archie, laughing. Archie held his gaze firmly on the truck and backed up to the road's edge. He crouched slightly, ready to jump if need be into the protective wall of trees lining the road.

With a frightening clamor, the truck suddenly skidded and headed straight at him. At the last moment, it veered left and came to a sliding halt with the passenger door, had there been one, an arm's length away. The trailing dust cloud caught up with and obscured the truck for a few seconds, then slid past the bumper and dispersed into nothing.

The driver let out a loud rebel yell and pumped his right fist in the air. He was a big, dirty white man, roughly twice Archie's age, with curly brown hair spilling from a filthy hat and days-old stubble on his face. And an enormous grin.

He brought his right hand down to his waist and quickly thrust it in the air again, this time holding a pistol pointed skyward. Two loud shots rang out. "Hey, brother," the man yelled. "You shit in your pants or somethin'?"

Archie tried to act nonchalant, but his heart was racing. This wasn't the first time the man had got his goat. It seemed like whenever he was around there was excitement. Archie liked him. "Leon, how come you got Pappa's truck?"

The driver spit and answered, "Been down to Thomastown. Daddy done said I could borrow it. Hop on, Bug. I'll take ya home."

Archie, nicknamed "Bug," climbed up onto the truck's rusty metal frame. As he grabbed the cold steel of the front right stanchion, the truck shot forward. Archie held on for dear life with his right hand and clamped down his hat with his left, grinning broadly.

For miles they sped, through thickly wooded hills where the road lay atop the ridgeline like a stripe of reddish-tan paint; past areas of treeless flatlands, some filled with rows of white cotton stubble left from the recent crop, others overgrown with briars and sedge; past cemeteries where old gravestones stained dark with mildew proudly proclaimed in eroded letters: "C.S.A."—Confederate States of America. A narrow wooden bridge across a small stream startled the landscape with a noisy *bumple-umple-umple-lump* as the truck hurried across its warped wooden planks.

They finally came to a lone cabin, set off the road in a small clearing surrounded by leafless trees. Leon swerved right onto a makeshift driveway leading to his and Bug's home.

The four-room shack was constructed of wide, vertical planks of assorted shades of silvery gray; some even hinted at an ancient coat of white paint. A crooked front porch ran the width of the house. A trickle of smoke rose from a lone stovepipe protruding above the roof of uneven tin sheets of rust and silver. Littered about the yard of bare earth and dead grass were old rags, rotting pieces of cardboard, empty cans, and a useless truck tire. Out back, a drafty, one-hole outhouse stood in solitude.

Several people mingled outside, a usual occurrence when the weather permitted. Bug's younger brother, Hop, was at the woodpile gathering pieces of split pine. Next to him stood another brother, Junior, with outstretched arms holding several pieces of the wood.

A hen burst from behind the house, flapping its wings and clucking in panic as it frantically changed directions to avoid the grasps of the boy chasing it, ten-year-old Rat. He was the youngest member of the family.

The pulpwood truck skidded to a stop in front of the shack, and Bug leaped down. Joe, the family's mongrel dog, ran up to Bug with tail flailing and received a vigorous rub behind the ears. When Leon came out of the truck, Joe eyed him sidelong and stopped wagging his tail.

Standing on the porch with arms crossed, watching the truck's reckless arrival with furrowed eyebrows, was Bug's seventeen-year-old sister, Ape. Wearing a ragged sweater and a knee-length dress, she hovered close to a wrinkled old woman sitting in a chair. Ape's olive-colored skin stood out against the white skin of her grandmother, Elvira.

Bug, Hop, Junior, Rat, and Ape: five mulatto siblings with the last name of Levy shared the small shack with their Caucasian family members, the Turners: Leon, the half-brother nearly a generation older than the five; Howard, the father of them all; and Howard's mother, Elvira.

Eighty-year-old Elvira Rutherford Turner sat motionless in the porch chair with hands folded in her lap, clutching a dirty white handkerchief. A long black dress, stained and filthy, covered her thin body. Unbrushed white hair tumbled over humpbacked shoulders to her waist. Her eyes stared blankly into the distance from beneath the brim of a weathered black hat.

· · ·

Elvira was the matriarch of this unusual family—a poor family of two last names and two races. Her background would not have predicted her current status, for she was born to privilege in one of the region's first white families.

Her great-grandmother Elizabeth, the daughter of an officer in the American Revolutionary War, was a Tennessee pioneer woman. In 1812, twice widowed, Elizabeth had gathered her household items and her ten-year-old son, Franklin Rutherford, into a two-horse wagon and headed south.[1] For weeks they traveled along an old Indian trail called the Natchez Trace into what was then the young nation's southwest frontier, the Mississippi Territory.[2] After crossing the Yockanookany River in land that was to become Attala County, Mississippi, the pair settled on Bolatusha Creek, a few miles east of the present community of Newport.[3]

Over the ensuing decades, Franklin and his children prospered, acquiring large tracts of land around Newport. The Rutherfords were a prominent family in the area.

Thus, Elvira Rutherford, Franklin's granddaughter, was born in 1869 to a youth of relative prosperity. She was a pretty Southern belle as a young girl, but beneath her well-heeled upbringing and high social stature was a spirit of independence and stubbornness inherited from her great-grandmother.[4] In addition to acquiring the skills of cooking, sewing, music, and other feminine subjects of the day, Elvira learned to handle a gun.

Around 1890 Elvira married Nirum Samuel Turner, of another leading Attala County family.[5] Deep in the backwoods of southwestern Attala County, they built a dogtrot cabin on land given to Elvira by her parents.

Their marriage was rocky from the start. Elvira labored hard to establish her household, spending hours each day working the crops and the land, shooting varmints with her ever-present pistol. Samuel, for his part, was not prone to arduous toil. He preferred the genteel life of a Southern gentleman landowner; his wife could take care of the mundane matters dealing with home and farm.

Elvira gave birth to a blue-eyed son, Clarence Howard Turner, on April 2, 1893, but only months afterward, marital tension came to a climax.[6] Elvira was laboring in the fields when her husband came out to discuss a matter with her, leaving the baby alone in the cabin. They fought, and she stormed away to the house. Samuel followed, and Elvira shot the hat off his head.[7] The event marked the source of a nickname Elvira would live up to the remainder of her life—"Miss Hellfire." It also marked the end of their marriage.[8]

The Rutherfords' divorce—a social stigma among the well-heeled—was viewed as a dishonorable act by Elvira's family, who ostracized the headstrong woman. Subsequently, she and son Howard led a relatively isolated life on their farm. Never attending school, Howard had little contact with other children. His day consisted of accompanying his mother as she plowed fields, hoed weeds, chopped wood, gathered eggs, milked cows, churned butter, scrubbed floors, and sewed clothes. For goods Elvira couldn't produce, they walked or rode a wagon on primitive roads to the country stores at Newport, four miles north.

Working the land alone, Elvira and young Howard slid into economic hardship. By the early twentieth century, their living standards had become depressingly low. Elvira's appearance changed drastically: her face acquired a tanned-leather appearance; her hands became tough and calloused; her teeth, those left of them, showed the decay of neglect as well as the stains of the snuff she dipped and the strong coffee she drank. Her gaunt frame was perpetually covered by full-length black dresses, and her long black hair was covered with a sweat-stained, masculine hat when she was outdoors.

At the age of fifteen, Howard Turner captured the affections of thirteen-year-old Effie Powell, but he was unsuccessful in winning the approval of her family. Effie decided she could not live without Howard, so she snuck away to his home. Her brother soon came looking to retrieve her, but Elvira, in a reappearance of Miss Hellfire, met him at the door with squirrel gun in hand and ran him off.[9]

A week later, the two youngsters, accompanied by Howard's mother, traveled to the Attala County Courthouse to be married. Because Howard was a minor, Elvira penciled a letter of consent, verbatim:

Aug. 20 1908 This is my son that wishes to marry this girl. She is an alphan with-out any kindred her and knows not the where-abouts of any of his kin. She is at my house and has been for a week. While they are both under age but I have no objichives w his marrying the girl.

Elvira Turner[10]

Howard and Effie married that day and lived in Elvira's house.[11] They had a son on August 3, 1911.[12] He was a big child with a shock of curly brown hair. They named him Leon. No middle name—just Leon. Leon Turner.

For a few years, the Turners lived a normal, rural existence. Elvira and Howard did the farmwork; Effie tended to little Leon and the house chores.

Howard began supplementing their income by logging. The central Mississippi logging industry flourished in the early 1900s, and several peckerwood lumbering operations opened in the woods of Attala County. Howard joined in the boom by hauling felled trunks in his wagon behind two oxen named Logan Red and Spottin' Red.[13]

Negroes were a part of normal life for the Turners. Seeing, dealing with, and talking about them were as ordinary a part of everyday life as crops, weather, or horses. Howard and his family were practically as poor as their black neighbors, but the social structure put whites over blacks. Howard and Effie reflected this in everyday speech by making derogatory comments about blacks. Leon Turner's earliest years were spent listening to his father and mother casually speak of Negroes in this demeaning, disrespectful manner.

When Leon was three, his mother became ill with "the consumption." Tuberculosis was a savage disease of the poor and unsanitary that spread easily from person to person, striking fear into the lives of those it contacted. To avoid its spread, Howard and Elvira isolated Effie by moving her into the backyard corncrib, passing meals to her beneath a closed door. Young Leon was kept away, only rarely hearing the voice of his mother behind the impersonal walls. Suffering in that lonely corncrib, Effie slowly wasted away until she died.

Howard devoted himself as much as possible to his now motherless child. He took Leon hunting and taught him to shoot a rifle and a pistol. He trained his son to know the land and to be independent, to rely solely upon himself for survival. Leon looked to his father as his rock. Their bond was strong.

As Leon grew older, Elvira tried to introduce into his life the education his father lacked. But Leon wasn't an interested student. The boy rebelled against having to sit still and learn; he preferred the outdoors and took to spending more time away from the house. Since Howard didn't seem to care, Elvira stopped bothering.

Leon's best friend was his cousin Parvee Rutherford, who was two years older. The son of one of Elvira's younger brothers, Parvee was fun-loving, adventuresome, and wild. He and Leon played together almost every day after school. But while his cousin was at school, Leon roamed the hills practicing with rifle and pistol. By age ten he was a skilled marksman.

Leon and his father continued to be close, but their time together decreased as the years passed. Leon preferred cavorting with friends, primarily Parvee. Howard also preferred being with someone else.

Howard had been in his early twenties when his wife died. For a time afterward, his need for companionship was satisfied by the presence of his young son and aging mother, but his sexual need was unfulfilled. No interesting, available white women lived within courting distance. However, another group of local young women was plentiful—black women.

Throughout the South, a veil of silence surrounded sexual relationships between the black and white races. Although prohibited legally and frowned upon socially, interracial sexual trysts, both forced and voluntary, had been occurring clandestinely since the earliest days of slavery.[14] One result, naturally, was children. Nearly 10 percent of slaves listed in the 1860 census were classified as "mulatto." Due to the secrecy surrounding such racial intermixing, this percentage "was undoubtedly an undercount."[15]

Mississippi imposed many laws dealing with miscegenation.[16] An 1865 statute imposed life imprisonment for any freedman, free Negro, or mulatto who intermarried with any white person. While this law was removed during Reconstruction, it was reinstated in 1880 when marriage between white persons and persons with one-quarter or more Negro blood was declared "incestuous and void." In 1890 the state constitution was amended to prohibit marriages between whites and those of one-eighth or more Negro blood. Asians were included in the list of unacceptable partners for whites with the enactment of a new statute in 1906 prohibiting intermarriage between a white and an Asian or person of one-eighth or more "Mongolian" blood.

Regardless of laws, sexual relations between the races continued to occur in the early 1900s, whether commercially, exploitatively, or casually.[17] By being discreet, the participants avoided offending the sensitivities of society. Left over from the days of a master's total domination over his female slaves, it was quietly accepted—particularly among white men— that a white man might have an incidental affair with a black woman.[18] To have a visible, open relationship, however, was not socially tolerable.

Hattie Levy was a very dark-skinned, slightly cross-eyed Negro woman. Born in 1903, she lived with her family in a small cabin not far from the Turners'.[19] In 1922 Hattie birthed a son she named Curtis. The identity of Curtis's black father was uncertain, and no man claimed him.

Hattie and Howard Turner had crossed paths for years on the roads of Beat 4. Being ten years older, Howard had at first paid her no attention; she was merely another young black girl. But as she grew into womanhood, Howard began to take notice. Not long after Curtis's birth—years since the death of Howard's wife—the acquaintance of Hattie and Howard took a more meaningful turn. Perhaps it started when Hattie was hired to help out around Howard's house taking care of his aging mother; before long Hattie and Howard became lovers. Eventually, Hattie and her son moved into Howard's home.[20]

Elvira and Leon were suddenly thrust into a socially radical circumstance. Not only was there a new woman and child in the house, but they were Negroes—people whom the Turners had heretofore kept separate from their lives. Elvira accepted the situation with the patience of age. After all, the young woman her son had chosen would be helpful with household chores.

Leon, however, saw his preteen world turned upside down. His father had accepted into his home, into his very bed, a woman of the race he had previously maligned. Furthermore, Hattie's young son had intruded upon the scene and was being treated in the special manner of all babies. For the first time in his life, Leon was no longer the center of attention. He did not adjust well to the situation. Anger and rebellion surfaced. He treated Hattie with disdain and Curtis with intimidation. This forced Howard to be harsh with his son. Leon withdrew, spending more time away from home, alone and with Parvee, roaming the woods and hills, shooting his father's guns. He became the best marksman in the area.

In July 1924, after little more than a year, a midwife delivered Howard and Hattie's first child, Annie Mae. Three years later came Joe D., and Joseph the following year. All had light brown skin, curly—not kinky—black hair, thin lips, and narrow noses. Since their parents were not married, following the custom of the day the children were given their mother's last name—Levy.[21]

A common practice among Negro families of the area was to give children nicknames. Accordingly, the mulatto Levy children were labeled: Annie Mae was called "Sugar Gal," Joe D. picked up "Kook," and Joseph was known as "Lice."

The growing family lived in the dirt and clutter of Elvira's aging cabin, where dogs, goats, and chickens freely roamed. The weather-beaten structure began showing its years. Ill-fitting boards covered missing windowpanes. When it rained, pots, pans, tin cans, and buckets were scattered about the floor to compensate for the leaky roof.

Hattie grew dissatisfied living in Elvira's house. Her young children were always picking at rotten wood or getting scratched by an exposed nail, and they were constantly sick in the winter from the drafts and leaks. Worst of all was Leon's unrelenting meanness. When he was around, Hattie spent half her time trying to protect her children from him, or calming them after Leon's torments. Even Howard and Elvira were unable to stop Leon's bullying.

Eventually, Howard built a house for Hattie on his mother's land. It was another plain, tin-roof shack, but it was in better condition than Elvira's house; and it was separated from Leon.

Hattie and her children now lived across a pasture from the Turners. For Leon's sake, Howard remained in the house where he had been raised. The children came and went freely between both houses; a well-worn dirt path soon linked them.

The one family in two houses lived in their own isolated world. Their farm was self-sufficient, with a vegetable garden and cows, goats, and chickens providing adequate, but not abundant, food. Cash crops of cotton, corn, and sugarcane brought in a few meager dollars, along with Howard's work hauling pulpwood.

Elvira Turner was a wonderful grandmother. She loved all of "her" children and was very kind and devoted to them. Never did she display any hint of racial intolerance; she seemed to totally accept Hattie and the children.

Leon, by contrast, had little to do with his half-brothers and -sister. Being so much older than them, he did not participate in their play. He helped his father and grandmother with farmwork during planting and harvesting seasons, but otherwise shied away from the labor of growing season. Mostly, he stayed away from home.

At fourteen or fifteen, Leon began to work with his father lugging timber. Manhandling the heavy logs into Howard's wagon produced powerful muscles on the teenager, and Leon's height grew along with his strength. By age nineteen, he was six foot and a hard two hundred pounds—large for that time.[22] Unfortunately for those around him, his temper grew right along with his size, with bouts of explosive rage that often translated into physical violence. And with this violence came a reputation: all who knew Leon realized that he was bad news and one to be avoided.

The volatile situation between Leon and his siblings was resolved in 1931 when he married a young white girl, Leslie Hutchins, and moved out.[23] Although Leon's departure removed a major irritant for Howard and Hattie's family, their troubles were far from over.

Mississippi, as did the entire South, had an unwritten rule of racial interaction that said members of one race were not to socialize with the other race. Casual friendship was accepted; but except for visits of business, charity, church affairs, or the like, citizens of one race were not to have close, sustained contact with those of the other. Nearly all members of both races silently conformed to these principles.

Not the Turners.

In this small enclave of Attala County's Beat 4, where everyone's business was everyone's business, Howard and Hattie's highly visible relationship and family were the talk of the area. Whites and blacks alike disapproved of their lifestyle, and as a result, neighbors shunned the family. It was as if they belonged to neither race. One contemporary said of Howard Turner, "The people of Newport did not think of him as being white. In a sense, it was as though he had forfeited that privilege."[24]

The primary form of entertainment in such rural settings was socializing. People stopped over at other people's houses, sat a spell, and gabbed. But no one visited the Turners, and they in turn visited no one.

Getting together was especially important to women, who primarily stayed home all day taking care of the children and elderly parents. They looked forward to stopovers by other women as a reason for inviting them in, relaxing over a piece of sweet potato or pecan pie, and catching up on community gossip.

Elvira, now an old woman called "Miz Elvira," made extra money peddling churned butter and garden vegetables from house to house. The ladies who answered the door were friendly to her, but they did not invite her into their homes. Worse, perhaps, was that Elvira's brothers and sisters and their families stopped having anything to do with her family.

Hattie's experience resembled that of Elvira: former friends and family ostracized her. As a result, the only grown woman she talked to was Howard's mother; but Miz Elvira spent most of her time walking to Newport's stores, selling vegetables, or taking care of her own house. With a house full of young children, Hattie became chained to her home.

And the children kept coming.

Archie Levy was born in 1930, and a second daughter, Addie Bea, in 1933. Then came a child that would die as an infant—the only one of Howard and Hattie's children that failed to reach adulthood. Next came three sons: T.J., Howard Jr., and Frankie, the youngest, born in 1939.[25] Like their older siblings, these children acquired nicknames: Archie was "Bug"; Addie Bea, "Ape"; Howard Jr., "Junior"; T.J., "Hop"; and Frankie, "Rat." In all, Howard and Hattie had eight surviving children, all physically and mentally normal except for Junior, who was mildly retarded.

Like their parents, the children of the Turner-Levy household were socially alienated. Other children of the area would have nothing to do with them, a hurt that remained with the Levy children their entire lives. Even as an old man, Bug lamented, "We were hated by both races of people."[26]

The 1930s saw Miz Elvira walking. Now in her seventh decade, she roamed miles each day. Time stole away her straight-back posture, and the elder of the Turner clan became stooped over; but that didn't stop her. Using a walking stick to steady her gait, she continued to stroll often and far.

Wearing a pair of Howard's old work shoes, she hiked to and from surrounding towns, even as far away as Kosciusko, sixteen miles northeast. Dressed in a threadbare, flowing black dress with long, unwashed white hair beneath a faded black hat, she was a frequent sight on the roads of southwest Attala County. Occasionally, she caught a ride with the morning milk truck or a kind townsperson; but mostly, she walked in solitude.

While pregnant again in 1942, Hattie Levy became ill. Her worn body, weakened by years of toil and poverty, struggled to cope with growing a baby and fighting an illness. It was a losing battle. She died at age thirty-nine.

Hattie's loss was very difficult on the family. Howard was left with twenty-year-old Curtis and seven other children, ages fifteen to three—Sugar Gal had married and left home. He moved into the children's home rather than having them move into Miz Elvira's house, which was now a half century old and literally falling apart. With Elvira unable to perform housework at seventy-three and with the only other female being Ape, age nine, the domestic attributes of the house gained a largely masculine bent. Those typically feminine aspects that make a house a home declined drastically.

Family meals, in particular, suffered from the loss of Hattie. Until, that is, Howard discovered canned pork and beans. After that, pork and beans became a staple of the family's diet.[27]

In spite of the austere conditions, Howard remained a devoted father. On occasional Saturdays, he carried his youngsters to the big city of Kosciusko in a 1934 Chevrolet pulpwood truck he had bought.[28] The children marveled at the hustle and bustle of the town of 4,500, with its white-columned courthouse sitting on a manicured green lawn in the center of the town square. Surrounding the square were a colorful variety of stores, where merchants and customers knew each other by first names. Howard strolled the busy sidewalk with his mulatto children noisily tagging along a few steps behind. Sometimes Miz Elvira accompanied the group. The sight of this unorthodox family was memorable enough that more than fifty years later, many of Kosciusko's older citizens still recalled them vividly.

A year after Hattie's death, Howard moved his family two miles north. Salvaging the least-rotting planks from Hattie's home as well as a few sound pieces from one of the two cabins of his mother's dogtrot house, he built a four-room shack on land belonging to one of his uncles.

Still headstrong and independent in her mid-seventies, Miz Elvira chose to remain by herself in her dilapidated home. She rarely bathed; her dingy black dress was worn and threadbare. Numerous sores from a half century of sun exposure now afflicted her face and neck. These swollen, wartlike protuberances continually oozed, causing her to dab her face often with a disgusting white handkerchief.[29]

Miz Elvira was tenacious in providing for her family. Almost every Saturday when the weather allowed, she walked to Kosciusko carrying a gunnysack. Making the rounds of local businesses' garbage cans, she collected anything that could be of use to her family, including rotting bananas and other discarded delicacies from grocery stores.[30] Slinging the sack of goodies over her shoulder like a black-robed, stooped Santa Claus, she trekked the roads back to Newport with her walking stick, pausing occasionally to wipe her sores.

By 1949 Curtis, Kook, and Lice had married and settled elsewhere. Elvira's old home had become too unsafe for her to live in alone, so she had moved into Howard's house. There she spent hours sitting on the porch, gazing out on the world. Howard still hauled logs; he had even managed to buy an additional truck, a 1935 model.[31] Bug, who at nineteen was the oldest of Hattie's sons at home, worked with his father. Ape, Hop, Junior, and Rat also lived with the family.

One other child of Howard's was now living in the house. Ever since Leon Turner had left the household in the early thirties, he had drifted in and out of trouble. His marriage had failed; he had become a troublemaker, a crook, and a womanizer; he had made money solely by thievery, gambling, and moonshining. Eventually, he had committed a violent crime that earned him a lengthy prison sentence. After being released in 1948, he had moved back home. Actually, Leon wasn't home all that much; he was usually out and about.

• • •

As a cold breeze hinted at the coming 1949 Christmas season, Bug jumped off the pulpwood truck and greeted his dog, Joe, after the wild ride with Leon. Bounding up the two steps onto the rickety cabin's porch to join Elvira and Ape, Bug didn't even try to figure what Leon had been doing earlier that day; it simply wasn't anything worth wondering about. He just knew that things had changed since Leon got back, 'cause "Leon was always into something."[32]

Howard Turner, 1950.

Some of the Levy children, 1950. L to R, front row:
Hop, Ape, Bug with Joe the dog; back row: Rat, Junior.

The shack where the Turner/Levy family lived.

Chapter 2

Leon

Bug was right. Leon Turner was "always into some-thing," and most of the time that something was trouble. It had been that way practically his whole life. The history of Leon Turner was a history of turmoil.

During his first dozen years, Leon was an only child. Then his widowed father became involved with another woman, a black woman; suddenly, several children were afoot, children that Mississippi law and Leon classified as Negro.

When Leon responded to his young half-siblings, it was usually with roughness. The growing teenager saw the fear in the children's eyes; he learned how he could dominate the weak ones around him, how bullying and intimidation pro-duced the results he desired. The seeds of belief in his domi-nance and superiority, especially over blacks, were planted.

Leon's attitude of supremacy was reinforced by his excep-tional skills with guns. There was always a pistol stuck in his belt, and often he carried a rifle as well. This was not at all unusual—most of his neighbors carried a firearm. What was uncommon about Leon was his ability to use them. He had a natural talent for marksmanship. It was said he could hit a nickel from thirty yards.[1] He was quick to show off his skill.

Fighting was something else the boy mastered. When local white boys ridiculed Leon's father for being involved with a black woman, Leon fought to defend his old man. Over time, his fighting ability grew along with his tem-per. He battled with ferocity and an astonishing ability to take punishment that few could overcome. Total victory was his aim.

Leon Turner wanted others to know that he was the best and to acknowledge him for it. People that gave him the proper respect for his abilities could get along with him. Those who challenged him in any area, however, were apt to find the issue decided right then and there in a full-blown brawl.

He liked to be in control. Things had to be his way, and they had to be his way quickly—he was not patient. This applied even to animals: rather than ignore a dog barking at him, Leon would simply shoot the offending canine.

Leon also wasn't concerned with the law. Whatever struck his fancy is what he did, whether or not it was legal. One illegal activity in which he dabbled involved alcohol. With national Prohibition in effect during the 1920s, there was black market money to be made by those willing to risk an occasional run-in with the law. It was predictable that Leon and his best friend and cousin, Parvee Rutherford, gravitated toward this business. They learned the process of making moonshine—a harsh, clear whiskey with high alcohol content. Setting up a still deep in the woods near Leon's house, the boys made moonshine—at first only for themselves, but as they honed the craft, they made larger batches for sale. Backcountry distilling turned out to be another activity for which Leon had a natural bent.

When Parvee graduated from high school, his daddy bought him a fancy new car and sent him off to the University of Mississippi—Ole Miss—over a hundred miles north of Newport. Parvee's college career proved as colorful as the boy himself. He quickly mastered the social aspect of university life and gained a reputation as a big partier and a big spender.

Unfortunately, he placed little emphasis on academic endeavors. After only a few semesters, his money supply reached comparability with his grades— low—and he moved back home to Beat 4.

Now with wheels and with Prohibition ended, Leon and Parvee expanded their carousing west into Holmes County, where they could find the type of nightlife that they craved.

The shared Attala-Holmes county line ran down the middle of the wide, murky Big Black River. Paralleling the Big Black just inside Holmes County was U.S. Highway 51, a paved two-lane highway connecting Memphis and Jackson. Within the county, spaced about ten miles apart along this major road, were the small towns of Durant, Goodman, and Pickens, running north to south. These three little communities were peaceful and quiet during the day, but at night, they woke up. Located outside their incorporation limits along Highway 51 were several beer joints and nightclubs catering to a wide range of clientele. The ones for whites were called honky-tonks; those for blacks, juke joints.

Leon and Parvee spent many nights at the Highway 51 honky-tonks. Booze, brawling, girls, and gambling—all of Leon's favorite activities—were there for the taking, and he took them to the fullest. His favorite bar was the Rainbow Garden, the wildest, sleaziest, roughest honky-tonk around, located just north of Durant. It was a particularly active place for gambling. Many a sunrise saw Leon playing high-stakes cards, or betting big in his preferred game of craps.[2]

On occasion, he got into fights with other customers out in the club's parking lot. More than once he spent the remainder of the night cooling off in the Durant City Jail.

At age twenty-four, Leon was a strikingly good-looking man with a tall, muscular body, a full head of wavy brown hair, a tough but handsome baby-face, his daddy's blue eyes, and good teeth. Matching his size was his sexual appetite. Leon liked women—all women, black and white alike—and spent much of his time and energy pursuing them.

Living in the area was a pretty young white girl named Wilma Leslie Hutchins. Endowed with flowing dark hair and an ample bosom, Leslie was an outgoing and adventurous girl. The prominent event of her social calendar occurred on Saturday nights, when there was usually a dance at somebody's house.

These shindigs were a main source of mixing and entertainment for many locals. Amateur musicians supplied the music, and alcohol, typically of the homemade variety, flowed freely.[3]

It was at these Saturday night dances that Leslie Hutchins and Leon Turner got together. Never boring, Leon was a welcome relief from the dullness of everyday life to the young girl. After a brief courtship, the couple decided to make their party permanent. They married on December 30, 1931.[4]

Trouble arrived quickly, for Leslie soon learned that Leon was stuck in party mode. He continued his wild ways—leaving his wife at home while he went drinking and gambling with Parvee.

Another problem for Leslie was income, or rather, its source. Being an honest farmer or laborer wasn't Leon's style. He preferred earning money by means of his lucrative moonshine business. In fact, he enlarged his still to increase production capacity and recruited local men, mostly black, to sell—bootleg—the whiskey for him.

Leslie frowned on Leon's coarse activities and took it out on her husband. Resentful of anyone trying to control him, Leon fought back. Their marriage became a loud, stormy misadventure.

By the end of their fourth, childless year, Leon was openly carousing with other ladies. Leslie's application for divorce even stated that he "brought black girls to their home."[5]

Leon seemed to have no regrets about the divorce. If anything, his excessive lifestyle and lawlessness ramped up. Contributing to Leon's unbounded behavior was a new acquaintance, a man well established in illicit activities.

Tillman Branch was ten years older than Leon. Born to a prominent Attala County Beat 4 family, he was a big, mean fellow rumored to have been involved in moonshining, prostitution, bribery, and bootlegging. He had killed at least two men through the years and had served time in the state prison.[6] Twice married to white women, Tillman also kept black mistresses in a house trailer off Highway 51 near Goodman. One of the wives, fed up with these extramarital affairs, kidnapped her husband's favorite black mistress and sent her packing to Detroit. Tillman found his lover and returned her to the trailer.[7]

Beneath his unsavory aspects, Branch was a keen businessman. His most lucrative business was located just south of the Goodman city limits, where Tillman owned one of the most popular juke joints around.

Although the white bars along Highway 51 were unruly, disorderly businesses of unrestrained debauchery, none of them could compare to the sheer, uninhibited wildness of Tillman's juke joint, the Blue Flame. Also called "The Spot" by locals, the Blue Flame had it all: boozing, dancing, fighting, gambling, cockfighting—and an occasional shooting to keep things lively.

Tillman worked the bar in his joint and was the only white person there, but he was bad enough that no one messed with him. He ruled the Blue Flame with a blue-steel snub-nosed .32 caliber pistol whose trigger guard was bent from pistol whippings of unruly patrons.[8]

Leon Turner and Tillman Branch somehow met, and being two of a kind, they formed a relationship of mutual interests and respect. Tillman, a successful entrepreneur with money, power, and prestige, was a role model to Leon. The men got along, but at a distance—they were too alike to fraternize closely.

Branch's Blue Flame did a brisk business selling moonshine. Tillman owned several local stills to supply this commodity; he also bought from independent operators like Leon.

As the years passed, Leon's recklessness increased. When angered or threatened, he tended to shoot his ever-present pistol without deliberation.

Leon and Parvee set out to steal a chicken one day at the shack of a black schoolteacher. Leon snuck to the chicken coop in the back of the house while Parvee stood watch out front, leaning lazily against the unpainted shack, smoking. When Parvee heard the sound of panicky chickens, he grew curious and walked toward the back.

Leon was chasing a plump hen around the backyard when he glimpsed movement at the corner of the shack. In one easy motion, he drew his pistol and fired. Parvee was struck in the hip. Though the wound was serious, he eventually recovered; but poor Parvee walked with a limp for the rest of his days.[9]

Residents of Beat 4 knew about Leon's shenanigans, but his size and temper kept anyone from challenging the behavior.

In reality, most Newport residents were afraid of Leon. As a result, they avoided him, but they didn't snub him. When seeing Leon on the road or in a store, they acknowledged him with a greeting, for to ignore Leon Turner was to invite trouble. As one former neighbor recalled, "If you saw him, you talked to him. You were sort of afraid not to."[10]

Although Leon was a threat and a bully to those he considered weak or inferior, he was calm, polite, and helpful to those he recognized as authority figures. One such local figure was Judge John Franklin Allen, a man who rose from adversity to become a major influence on the residents of Newport.

John Allen had been born soon after the Civil War and orphaned by age twelve along with his three siblings. At fourteen he took over managing the family's 120-acre Newport farm at a time when the nearly destroyed economy of Mississippi was struggling through the post-Reconstruction period. Under his purview, the farm succeeded and grew.

Along the way, he graduated from Ole Miss Law School, served in the Mississippi House of Representatives, and was elected judge for Mississippi's Fifth Circuit Court, which included Attala County.[11]

Throughout his career, Judge Allen continued to build his farming operation. He eventually owned a 7000-acre cotton plantation. The judge and his wife resided in a modest, white, single-story house two miles west of Newport on Highway 14, a dirt road running east–west through Newport. Also living on the land were fifty families of sharecroppers.[12]

The manager of the large plantation was Pat Smithson, a local farmer who had married the judge's daughter. A lean, competent man who feared no one, Smithson was the silent type. He carried a whip to do his talking as he roamed the plantation on horseback.

Judge Allen and Pat Smithson knew Leon Turner well and treated their volatile neighbor respectfully but carefully. Leon, in turn, caused them no significant trouble, but there were incidents of strength testing strength.

One afternoon, Pat Smithson was inspecting a fence line along a pasture that bordered on Highway 14. Nearby was a white wooden gate at the entrance of an access road onto the property. An automobile came speeding down the highway and, barely slowing, turned onto the access road. Instead of stopping before the closed gate, however, it crashed through the barrier and then skidded to a stop amidst the rubble of splintered white wood.

Smithson spurred his horse to the car and saw that the driver was Leon Turner.[13] He looked around at the damage then back at Leon and calmly asked, "Big boy, why did you tear the gate down? Why didn't you open it?"

Leon stared at him wild-eyed and shouted, "Goddamn you! Don't call me no big boy, you son of a bitch."

Smithson merely looked down at him in silence and rode off.[14]

By the late 1930s Leon Turner's reputation among the citizens of Newport was firmly established—and it was not complimentary. An egocentric, unreasonable, dangerous man, he was uncaring of the thoughts of others, unyielding in his disregard for rules, and uninterested in anything beyond his control.

He liked to attend black baseball games; and if he found out about a Negro social gathering, he would be there selling moonshine. Leon's arrival energized the young folk; but older black citizens disliked having him around, for his presence meant that someone was likely to get hurt, lose money, or find himself with a problem—either with the law or with

Leon. Despite their concerns, if Leon showed up, he was not asked to leave.

1940 was a pivotal year for the Turner/Levy family. Annie Mae (Sugar Gal) Levy was sixteen, beautiful, and restless. At an age when many of her peers were already married, she seemed trapped in an endless obligation to her home, helping her mother take care of children. Never did she complain; it was her duty, after all, as oldest child. But Sugar Gal wanted a life of her own.

She had been seeing J. D. Whitcomb for some time and she was in love. The couple wanted to marry, but both families were against the relationship. Her father felt that J.D. was too old for Sugar Gal, was lazy, and was a reputed drinker. As for Annie Mae, J.D.'s mother saw her as half-white trash from an outcast family.

It was the classic romantic dilemma for the two young lovers. Ironically, Annie Mae's father had been in a similar situation over thirty years before when the family of his love interest objected to him. As Howard had solved his problem in 1908, so did his daughter in 1940: Annie Mae and J.D. ran away to get married. Neither of the elopers had a car, so they literally ran—and they hid.

They hid because Leon was fanatical about his half-brothers and -sisters obeying their father and grandmother. He was mightily devoted to these elders, and he could not abide the slightest disobedience by his siblings—he took this as disrespect. Annie Mae now feared what Leon might do when he learned that she had defied their father by running off with J.D.

Leon had been out when Annie Mae ran away. He arrived home hours later to find his grandmother upset and his father furious. Upon learning that his half-sister had eloped with J. D. Whitcomb against her father's wishes, Leon flew into a rage and charged out the door.

He scoured the area searching for Sugar Gal, checking every trail, inspecting every abandoned shed, visiting every house, demanding to know if anyone had seen his sister. Eventually, he wound up at J.D.'s house, where J.D.'s mother, Sallie, lived with no husband. Leon forced his way in and loudly threatened to kill her son when he found him. Sallie feared for J.D.'s life—she knew Leon's temper and knew he was capable of doing anything when in such a fury. She also knew of Leon's weakness for women. Using that knowledge, she distracted him from the search.

The extra hours gave Annie Mae and J.D. enough time to clear the area and get married. In time, the two families accepted the situation.[15]

By mid-1940, Leon was twenty-nine, unmarried, living at home, and without a "respectable" job. He continued his life of excesses and was frequently at the edge of the law. Despite several minor skirmishes with the sheriff and an occasional night in jail, he had never been in major trouble. That changed one sweltering summer evening.

A Saturday night house dance was in full swing in Sallis, a small community six miles north of Newport. Leon was there with his pistol and a jug of moonshine when a brawl broke out. Buddy Gowan, a tough local boy, was on the floor beating the tar out of another man. Someone dared him to stop the fight, saying that Buddy was so bad not even Leon could separate the fighters.

Leon Turner didn't care which way the fight went, but he couldn't refuse a dare, particularly when there was a crowd of people watching. He pulled his pistol and yelled over the roar of the party, "I didn't start this fight, but I'm gonna end it." With that, he pointed his weapon at the two men tumbling on the floor and fired twice, seriously wounding Buddy Gowan.[16]

Up to now, the consequences for Leon's uncurbed actions had been relatively minor. But this senseless attack was almost murder. Leon was arrested and taken to jail in Kosciusko. Buddy Gowan ended up in the hospital, where he experienced a slow recovery.

Turner was charged with assault with intent to kill and tried September 12, 1940, in the Fifth Circuit Court of Mississippi. Court was held in the Kosciusko courthouse with Leon's neighbor, Judge John F. Allen, presiding. Having a trial under Judge Allen should have been in Leon's favor, but a newly elected district attorney offset any advantage. James Plemon "J.P." Coleman was an uncommonly smart and talented young attorney out to make a name for himself. He performed his prosecutorial duties with zeal and rigor. A jury quickly found Leon guilty and sentenced him to ten years hard labor at the Mississippi State Penitentiary at Parchman.[17]

Despite her oldest grandchild's incarceration, Miz Elvira remained supportive of Leon and, along with Howard, visited him every few months. A year after Leon's conviction, she submitted a request for parole to Governor Fielding Wright. The townspeople were not ready for Leon's return, however; several wrote their objections to the governor, and Leon was denied parole.[18]

Elvira's attempt to have Leon released had been mostly for sentimental reasons. She still had Howard, Hattie, and their brood for company and for help when needed. Then Hattie died, and Howard moved away with his children.

Although Elvira chose to stay in her old house, she soon discovered that she did not like living alone. Besides the loneliness, she had difficulty tending to the household by herself. Deciding that things would be better if Leon were back in her home, the old woman concocted a plan to make it happen. Her first action was to walk about another petition among Beat 4 residents supporting Leon's release. She told the citizens how prison had straightened Leon out and how much she needed him. Most people took pity on Miz Elvira and signed the paper.

The stage was set for her second action.

Dawn promised a beautiful spring day on April 13, 1943, as seventy-four-year-old Elvira Turner set out on foot from her home deep in the woods of Attala County. Wearing an old pair of men's work boots, she carried only a walking stick and a large black purse containing the petition, a few dollars, a jar of water, a bite to eat, and her pistol. She walked north to Newport, and then west along Highway 14. All day she trudged onward, pausing at times to rest at the side of the road, nibble at her food, and sip from her water jar. Twenty miles later, Elvira Turner arrived at Goodman and made her way to the bus station on Highway 51.

The sight of this stooped old woman dressed in a tattered black dress drew stares from passengers waiting to catch the day's last bus to Memphis. They watched as she slowly shuffled to the ticket clerk and inquired about a bus to Jackson. After the clerk informed her that the next one was the following morning's early run that arrived in Jackson shortly before 7:00 a.m., Elvira reached deep in her bag and pulled out her money. With ticket in hand, she then settled her old frame into one of the wooden benches inside the small terminal, finished eating the meager remains of her day's meal, and waited.

Through the long night, Elvira sat there, sleeping fitfully, the room's only occupant. Early the next morning, a clerk gently shook her awake, and she boarded the southbound bus for the two-hour trip to Jackson.[19]

When Governor Paul Johnson's staff arrived for work in the State Capitol Building that morning, they were surprised to find a disheveled old woman sitting on the marble floor outside the governor's office suite. In a weak voice, Elvira told them her story; she begged to see the governor. The staff escorted her into the suite's waiting area, settled her into a comfortable leather chair, and brought a cup of strong, hot coffee. Shortly after 10:00 a.m., Elvira Rutherford Turner was ushered into the office of Governor Johnson.

Upon seeing his poverty-stricken constituent, the governor rose from his desk and helped her sit at one end of his office couch. Governor Johnson sat at the other end, his nose as well as his eyes informing him of her journey's difficulty. He listened patiently as Elvira explained her solitary living condition and her need to have Leon back at home. Pleading with the governor to release her grandson, she promised that he would reform if let out of prison.

"Leon will never touch whiskey again," she implored. "He has learned a lesson—he promises to come home and take care of me."[20] She pulled out her petition with Newport residents' signatures showing their approval of Leon's release. Finally, she used the success of her long walk as divine proof of Leon's intention to straighten out, adding, "If the good Lord didn't believe my boy was good now, he would have placed stumbling rocks in my path."[21]

Governor Johnson could not let Elvira's amazing feat be for naught. He granted her wish, stating that she would not have to wait long before her grandson came home.

Someone gave her lunch money, and she left. As one newspaper wrote, her "shoulders seemed less stooped, her face was wreathed in smiles, her red-rimmed eyes sparkled on the verge of tears. Her voice was high-pitched with excitement as she inquired the direction to the local bus station, and began the trip back" to Newport.[22]

True to his word, the governor pardoned Leon the next day. The State Pardon Board's recommendation of release imposed two conditions on Leon: the suspension of sentence would only last "pending good behavior and on condition that he abstain from drinking or handling liquor in any way."[23]

The remarkable story of Elvira's journey to the governor's office made newspapers all over Mississippi, and beyond. In a letter to his wife, one Attala County World War II soldier wrote that he had seen the story about Elvira in the military newspaper *Stars and Stripes*.[24]

Rewarding his grandmother's sacrifice, Leon lived in her house after his release from Parchman Penitentiary. But he did not straighten himself out; to the contrary, he quickly returned to his former ways.

He was loudly welcomed back at the Holmes County nightclubs. Realizing that Leon was going to be short on money for a while, club owner Tillman Branch gave him a job operating a still in the Newport area. While most of its whiskey was sold at the Blue Flame, Leon was allowed to sell some of the product he made, splitting the proceeds fifty-fifty with Tillman. This temporary arrangement was safer for Leon than operating his own still, for should word of the distillery get to the sheriff, ownership would trace back to Tillman. Leon was untouchable so long as he wasn't caught at the still.

During winter, when the biting wind rolled unimpeded over barren cotton fields, Leon wore a blue denim long coat, its big pockets stuffed with half-pint bottles of freshly brewed product. He was a walking whiskey store, selling hooch for a dollar to all comers.

In late 1943, at a Kosciusko five-and-dime store, Leon met Alma Reed, a rosy-cheeked, full-figured single woman five or six years older than he. Alma was immediately attracted to the strong, handsome fellow with curly hair. Over the next few months, the two saw each other often. Owning the couple's only automobile, Alma routinely drove to Newport to pick up Leon.

Their rendezvous were times of intense passion. Sometimes while driving, they pulled over and made love among green rows of cotton.[25]

At last, Leon's future was growing brighter. Had this period of Leon's existence been allowed to continue, Alma may have rewritten the remaining chapters in his life story. Sadly, their romance lasted only a single, short season.

Leon continued to operate a still for Tillman Branch near Newport, but the men's business relationship soured. While Tillman demanded to call the shots, Leon fought being controlled by anybody. The growing tension between the two came to a head one Friday night at the Blue Flame juke joint. Leon, drunk, rode his horse to the parking lot and sat in the saddle cursing at the crowded establishment. Black patrons scattered as the wild-acting white man waved a pistol in the air. Leon called Tillman out, slurring, "You think you're bad.

You done run up against another bad fellow. If you bad, just make your move."[26]

Danger was nothing new to Tillman Branch; it came with owning a place like the Blue Flame. Still, he knew better than to go gun to gun with Leon Turner. He stayed inside and avoided a confrontation.

This no-win situation cost Tillman face, something he could not allow in his rough world where survival required a ruthless reputation. Branch realized it was time to rid himself of Leon. Weeks later, after arranging for Leon to be at the still on a particular day, Tillman tipped off the Attala County sheriff. The sheriff raided the still and caught Leon red-handed. It was a direct violation of the conditions set for his parole over a year before.

The state revoked Leon's suspended sentence on February 25, 1944.[27] He was returned to the penitentiary to complete the ten-year sentence imposed for shooting Buddy Gowan.

Alma Reed was devastated. The man she loved was going away to prison for an unbearable number of years. Her misery multiplied when she found out that she was pregnant. Alma grew bitter at Leon for throwing away their future. She decided never again to lay eyes on him.

On October 1, 1944, Leon Turner's only child was born, a girl her mother named Suzie Lee Reed.[28]

Leon's imprisonment meant his grandmother could no longer live by herself. Elvira left the house built when she was a newlywed and moved in with her son and grandchildren. Her old home eventually rotted away; no trace of it remains.

Leon served out the remainder of his sentence uneventfully. For five years, he caused no trouble within the often brutal Parchman prison; he merely survived. On September 3, 1948, with time credited for good behavior, thirty-seven-year-old Leon Turner completed his sentence and went home.[29]

The Leon Turner that returned to Beat 4 was only slightly changed physically from the one who had left. His body had filled out slightly, but he was by no means fat. His full head of wavy brown hair now bore a tuff of gray at the hairline above his forehead.

His biggest change was mental. Prison had hardened Leon and made him even less compatible with the ways of the outside world. He went in an angry man; he came out angrier.

Newport had changed little. The same families lived in the same houses, went to the same churches, traded in the same stores. Every now and then, Leon heard of a place that had burned down a while back, but mostly his old stomping grounds were intact.

In the people who had formerly touched his life, however, major changes had occurred. Alma Reed was history. Curtis, Kook, and Lice had married. Judge Allen had retired from the bench. Parvee Rutherford had been in a fight where someone blindsided him in the head with a piece of lumber. In addition to leaving a large crease at the bald crown of his head, the impact affected his health, producing slower movement, hesitant speech, and other physical ailments.[30] He was now in the care of his family.

Even the place Leon called home changed, for his entire family had moved north of his grandmother's land. Leon now lived in a small shack crowded with Elvira and Howard Turner and five of Howard's children. These youngsters were now nearly strangers. When Leon first went to prison in 1940, Bug had been ten, Ape seven, and Hop, Junior, and Rat even younger. During Leon's brief period of parole, he had kept away from them. Now, after years of the structured routine of prison, Leon was thrust into the undisciplined, chaotic world of teenagers.

Bug wasn't bad. At nineteen, he was older than many men who had served time with Leon. Bug took a lot of responsibility running the household.

Ape was a pretty sixteen-year-old who did most of the cooking and housework. To Leon, she was far and away the most unpleasant member of the family. Moody, testy, and impulsive, she treated him like an unwelcome intruder into her life. Since this attitude did not set well with Leon's need for respect, the two clashed often.

Hop, Junior, and Rat—ages fourteen to ten—were always together and always rowdy. They hardly knew and didn't particularly like Leon. Having quickly learned that he was easy to anger, they avoided him as much as possible.

For the first few weeks after leaving prison, Leon tried logging with his father and Bug. But, reminded of the years of chain-gang labor in prison, Leon soon became fed up with the hard work. He quit logging and returned to an easier activity. Assembling a still on a small creek not far from his grandmother's original house, Leon resumed making and selling moonshine. He found two or three black men to bootleg his whiskey.

The outrageous partying that Leon maintained as a young man was now but a memory. None of Newport's young adults wanted to hang around this legendary old troublemaker. On occasion, he hooked up with other undesirables and rode around drinking or going to his old Holmes County honky-tonks. But the spark of wild, uninhibited revelry of his younger years was gone. Mostly, Leon spent his time alone.

He got around either by foot or by an undersized old mare that Leon pushed mercilessly. On Sundays when his father didn't work, Leon borrowed one of the pulpwood trucks; he drove it as hard as he did the horse.

More than ever, Leon drank. He wandered the roads and trails of Beat 4 in solitude, drinking from an ever-present jug of moonshine.

Leon was an anomaly around Newport. The community, as well as life, had passed him by during his years in prison. Where the end of World War II had ushered in a modern era, Leon's ways were stuck in the past. He had become a loner who came and went like the cool breeze that signaled the approaching end of 1949.

A Thanksgiving tradition at one of Newport's white churches was to hold evening hayrides for youth. Kids whooped and hollered and sang and flirted as a preacher-driven tractor pulled a hay-filled wagon along remote county roads. One crisp night, as a crescent moon cast its gray light on the ghostly landscape, the tractor's headlights illuminated a lone figure walking in the distance. Wearing a hat and a long coat, the apparition seemed to be staggering toward them, following a nonexistent crooked path in the road. As the wagonload of noisy kids drew closer, some recognized the darkly dressed phantom as the mysterious Leon Turner. They all knew of him. Drawing within hailing distance, the group quieted a bit. They could see that Turner's left hand was cupped at his forehead, shielding his eyes. Grasped in his right hand was a jug.

From the driver's seat, the preacher shouted a warm "Hello, Mr. Turner."

Over the sound of the tractor engine, the group heard a mumbled reply: "If y'all don't turn that damn light out, I'm gone shoot it out."[31]

Newport entered the last weeks of 1949 with a lighted fuse in its midst. Far from mellowing in middle age and becoming a part of his community, since coming out of prison Leon had become more volatile, more unpredictable, and more detached from normalcy than ever. Although they witnessed this change for the worse, none of the residents who had known Leon all his life foresaw the tragic turn he would take. The real tragedy, however, was that Leon's path would run through the most innocent of people—people simply trying to survive in peace among the cotton fields and wooded hills of Attala County.

Leon Turner, 1950

Chapter 3
The Harrises

In the early twentieth century, schools for African Americans in Beat 4 were simple one- or two-room wooden buildings where all children learned side by side, regardless of grade. The schools covered grades one through eight. Education beyond the eighth-grade level was difficult, for black high schools were located only in larger towns. Since few poor families owned automobiles, the daily commute was impractical. Earning a high school diploma required a rural black child to live with relatives in town during the school year. Most kids began first grade, but few made it all the way through the eighth. Only the truly ambitious graduated from high school.

One particularly smart little girl from Newport who seemed destined to achieve this level of education was Mary Ella Roby. Little Mary Ella was one of her teacher's best students. As a preschooler, she had tagged along to class with her older brother and sisters, soaking up knowledge. Once she reached school age, she conquered any subject presented to her.

Mary Ella was born in July 1915, the fourth of her parent's six children and the youngest of three girls. A sickly little switch of a girl, her nickname was "May Baby." Her family were sharecroppers living in poverty on Judge Allen's plantation. Her father, a huge, deep-voiced man who ruled his family with a firm hand, allowed no dissent to his authority.

He was quick to discipline the children, but never abusively. A stern look was usually all he needed to keep his children in line. Mary Ella both loved and feared him. She was especially fearful when he was drunk.

Like many men of the area, her father was a gambler and a drinker. When he drank, he was totally unpredictable and sometimes violent. Whenever he staggered home, Mary Ella hid and cried.

Her mother, Mary, was as gentle as her husband was not. Blessed with a positive outlook and a forgiving attitude, she provided a warm environment for her family. Mary taught her daughters that the best a woman could do in life was to marry and raise a family.

Mary Ella was a subdued child who hated to be scolded by her parents. She learned that the best way to stay out of trouble was to keep quiet. Even when she didn't like something, she held her tongue.

As an intelligent teenager, she was independent and self-confident. Combined with her tendency to internalize her emotions, these traits produced a strong stubborn streak. Except for her teacher and parents, she took correction and direction from no one, silently ignoring anyone who attempted to control her. This characteristic made her appear to some as arrogant.

Having lived all of her life within walking distance of Newport, Mary Ella knew everyone in the area, including the white boy Leon Turner, who was four years older. She didn't like him. To her, he was a blowhard and a braggart who thought too highly of himself and his color, especially considering that he was just as poor as she and less educated. Furthermore, Leon drank and gambled, the two vices that Mary Ella particularly frowned upon.

Leon was a randy young man always on the prowl for sex; and Mary Ella, getting shapelier every day, gained his attention. His wooing style utilized crude sexual innuendos, an unappealing approach to Mary Ella's sense of superiority over him. When he made such advances, she turned her back to him.

As Leon roamed about on foot or horseback, he would stop at the nearest black family's shack and ask for food whenever he became hungry. When Mary Ella was fourteen, she and her sister were jabbering in the kitchen as they cleaned up after lunch. They heard the sound of heavy boots walking on the porch to the kitchen door, which was open wide to allow a breeze to blow through. Out of the corner of her eye, Mary Ella saw Leon Turner standing right outside the door with a cocky sort of look, waiting for them to jump to his service. Leftover food was in plain sight, and the girls knew that he wanted something to eat. Without skipping a beat, the sisters chatted louder than before, all the while pretending not to see Leon.

After a few moments of teasing, the girls finished cleaning the dishes and walked off into another room out of Leon's sight. They waited until they heard the sound of boots shuffling off, and then glanced out a window to see Leon skulking away. Hugging each other, they laughed loudly at his back.

At sixteen, Mary Ella was an attractive young woman with a pleasing figure and a thin face with high cheekbones, wide eyes, and full lips. She continued to excel in school and was almost at the point of transitioning to the eighth grade. While most of the children that had begun first grade with her had dropped out, closing the door on any opportunity to escape poverty, her chance for a better future seemed bright.

She was dating twenty-one-year-old Eli Thurman. The relationship was important to her, but she wasn't yet interested in marriage. Her two older sisters were still single, so it was not a concern.

Then her mother, Mary, became seriously ill and saw her own death approaching. She feared that Mary Ella's self-sufficient, stubborn nature would hinder her marriage prospects, foreclosing what she saw as the only way for a girl to erase the uncertainty of the future. She told Mary Ella that it was her wish to see her get married. Only by knowing her child's future was secure could she truly rest in peace.

Mary Ella married Eli Thurman on March 12, 1932, and dropped out of school.[1] One month later, her mother died.

The glow of new marriage quickly dimmed, but it wasn't because of Eli's drinking. Mary Ella had known about this habit when she married. What she had not known was Eli's meanness.

A year and a half after marrying, Mary Ella bore William Henry Thurman.[2] By this time, Eli was physically abusing her.

Sober or drunk, Eli flew into frightening rages during which he mistreated his wife. For the next four years, he made her life a living hell, sometimes beating her severely. Mary Ella endured the abuse in silence, for she did not want anyone to know that she was being brutalized by her husband but yet was remaining with him. Even after Eli once struck her across the bridge of the nose with a piece of kindling wood, Mary Ella refused to leave him. Divorce became even less of a consideration when a daughter, Verlene, was born in June 1935.[3]

In April 1937 Mary Ella was again pregnant and expecting to go into labor at any moment. She sat in a rocking chair one cold night holding Verlene, who was sick with pneumonia, when Eli announced that he was going out. Mary Ella wouldn't let him. Emotion overcame caution, and she yelled that he better stay sober and available until the baby came. Eli snapped. Grabbing a razor blade, he held it to her throat, and with his angry eyes inches from hers, he threatened, "You don't know who you're foolin' with. I'll cut your goddamn head off."

Verlene screamed and struggled. Mary Ella was about to lose her grip, sending Verlene crashing to the wood-plank floor, when Eli backed off. Shaking with terror and hatred, Mary Ella clutched her baby and struggled to stand. Minutes later, she walked barefoot to her father's house. She was alone, for Eli had not let her take either child.

The next morning, Mary Ella's brother came to fetch the children. Eli allowed Verlene to go, but not four-year-old William. Never again did the boy live in his mother's home.

Twelve days later, Mary Ella gave birth to another son, Frankie C. Thurman.[4] Eli did not try to gain custody of Frankie.

Now separated from Eli, twenty-one-year-old Mary Ella was left with two small children. She found it ironic to think back on her mother's dying wish that she marry in order to have someone to take care of her. In reality, marriage had only resulted in little ones totally dependent on her.

For the next several years, Mary Ella struggled with severe poverty. She and the children moved from relative to relative, living in crowded cabins. To maintain some degree of self-respect, she helped with household duties and farm-work. She even mastered plowing behind a mule.

Eventually, Mary Ella began seeing other men, but marriage was out of the question. Out of these relationships came two children. The first baby died after birth in 1939. The second, Mary C. Burnside, was born in December 1941. Mary Ella called her "May C."[5]

In 1942 Mary Ella and her three children were living with her father when he died. She then moved in with an older sister, but this resulted in a most unpleasant situation as her sister treated them poorly. It was a dreadful period in Mary Ella's life.

During this time, a man whom Mary Ella had known his whole life came into the picture. She actually remembered when Thomas Harris was born—she had been seven at the time. Now Thomas was a handsome nineteen-year-old, and he was pursuing her. At twenty-six, Mary Ella didn't think of Thomas in a romantic way, but the same could not be said of him. He was enamored with the older woman. He wooed her with a doggedness she could not dismiss.

Thomas Harris had the reputation of being an unusually talented farmer, which for poor Mississippians was an invaluable trait in a man. No matter how dire the times, a good farmer could always provide food.

Mary Ella and Thomas eventually developed a passionate relationship. He found her mature and mysterious; she found him hopeful and energetic. Even her children liked him. He surprised her by proposing, but marriage was a step she wasn't yet ready to take again. Rather than give Thomas an answer, she tiptoed around the question so as to avoid ending up engaged but also to keep the relationship going.

Being dogged in his pursuit of Mary Ella, Thomas was battling more than her hesitance of the heart; he was also defying his mother and father, who didn't think the older woman with three children was good enough for their son. But Thomas would consider no other; his infatuation was unquenchable.

Thomas Harris's persistence finally paid off when Mary Ella decided that living with her unpleasant sister was unsatisfactory. Realizing that the younger man who cared deeply for her would be able to provide for her and the children, her attitude about marrying him changed to the affirmative. But a roadblock prevented her from accepting his proposal—she was still legally married to Eli Thurman, and his whereabouts were unknown.

The situation languished for months with no solution in sight; and then, surprisingly, Eli came to her. He had been drafted into the army and was now living at Ft. Hood, Texas. Like Mary Ella, he was eager to remarry and thus also needed a divorce.

In September of 1943, six years after their separation, Eli Thurman abruptly filed for a divorce from Mary Ella. He sought custody of both William, who was living with Eli's father, and Verlene, who was living with Mary Ella. To impugn Mary Ella's character, Eli denied paternity of Frankie, who had been born days after the marriage-ending razor incident.[6]

Mary Ella was served a subpoena to appear in the Attala County Chancery Court, which put her in unfamiliar legal territory. Wisely, she sought help from Judge John Allen, the longtime landlord of Mary Ella's family.

As a good steward of his land and people, Judge Allen kept track of his workers and their families through the years.

He knew of Mary Ella's troubled marriage to Eli and her current relationship with Thomas Harris. The judge was keenly
interested in Thomas, for word had it that the young Negro
was an excellent farmer. Disappointingly for Judge Allen,
Thomas farmed with his father, a sharecropper on someone
else's land. Because the judge stood to gain financially if he
could get Thomas to sharecrop on his plantation, Mary Ella
found the elderly, white-haired magistrate to be in a particularly receptive mood when she asked for his help in obtaining
a divorce. The pleased judge volunteered the services of his
sons, both of whom were lawyers.

The divorce ending the eleven-year marriage of Mary
Ella and Eli Thurman was granted on December 14, 1943.
Custody of William Thurman was awarded to his father, while
Verlene and Frankie Thurman remained with their mother.[7]

Nine days later, Judge Allen took great satisfaction upon
hearing that Mary Ella and Thomas Harris had married. The
judge wasted no time recruiting Thomas Harris to work for
him. He gave the new Harris family a small, three-room
house and put Thomas in charge of several acres of fertile
plantation land.

The next March, Judge Allen welcomed at his home
Thomas Harris and dozens of other men who were his sharecroppers. They were there to borrow cash to enable their families to live until crops were harvested and sold in the fall.
With the sale's profit, God willing and weather holding, they
would repay their debts to the judge and have enough money
left over to get by until the next March, when they would
again be back at the judge's house seeking another advance.
They called this day when they drew a loan "draw day."[8]

With borrowed land and cash now in hand, Thomas set about raising his first cotton crop. Mary Ella, Verlene, and Frankie all pitched in to help. To the amazement of his mother and stepfather, Frankie, who was just turning seven, was a diligent worker in the fields. When he wasn't at school, he was outside helping Thomas. He worked so hard, like a man, that he was given the nickname "Sonny Man."

Verlene also worked the fields, but she complained about the labor. In truth, Verlene complained about almost everything. At ten years old going on twenty, she was a headstrong, independent girl—a remake of her mother at that age. She was so crabby and bossy to her two younger siblings that Mary Ella often fussed at her to stop telling them what to do.

In spite of the challenges of raising his first crop on his own land, Thomas succeeded. The following months saw his cotton fields transformed from the wet green of spring to the dry olive-drab of summer to the sun-lit white of fall as the fluffy cotton bolls opened.

Late fall produced a flurry of urgent activity. Acres and acres of cotton needed to be picked before the seasonal rains began. Each day's sunrise found Mary Ella, Thomas, and the children in the fields with burlap sacks slung on their shoulders, plucking each seed-laden ball of fiber out of its boll and into the sack in one fluid motion. It was skin-tearing, back-breaking work, but eventually the task was done. Thomas hauled the gathered cotton to a gin, where the seeds and husks were removed and the fluffy fibers were compressed into bales, which were then sold.

The fall of 1944 was good for the Harris family. Sale of their cotton allowed them to pay back the judge's draw money and still have a tidy sum left over—an event that sparked a joyous celebration.

Sadly, trouble accompanied the money from that first crop. Thomas now seemed to think he could do as he pleased. With the winter lull in farming activity, he began leaving the house at night and coming back drunk hours later. He openly told Mary Ella that he was gambling with friends. She didn't condone her husband's behavior and let him know it in no uncertain terms. But she put up with it, for Thomas was an adequate provider who never abused her.

In January 1946 Mary Ella gave birth to her first child by Thomas Harris, Ruby Nell.[9] His daughter's arrival brought an increased sense of family to Thomas. He was especially close to Nell, as the little girl came to be called.

The baby changed the dynamic between Mary Ella and Thomas's mother, who was known as Big Momma. Having never accepted her son's choice for a wife, Big Momma had forever been cold to Mary Ella. With Nell's birth, however, she began to soften—not because Nell was her son's first child, but because Big Momma was a superstitious woman— and Nell had been born with a "veil" over her head.

The amniotic sac, or amnion, which holds the fluid in which the human fetus is immersed, usually sloughs off the baby at birth. Sometimes, however, a baby is delivered with the amnion covering its head like a veil.[10] Such was the case with Nell. Big Momma, who maintained her ancestral notions of voodoo, believed that Nell's being born under the veil was a sign that the girl would be clairvoyant.[11] She took pride in her granddaughter's special birth. Her first visit to her daughter-in-law occurred soon afterward. Frequent offerings to babysit followed.

Life settled into a normal pace for the Harris family for the next two and a half years. During this time, the judge moved them into a slightly bigger house with more land on the north side of Highway 14 a half mile east of his own house. The new place was a four-room shack with a covered front porch and electricity. Mary Ella was content with her new home.

Verlene was now thirteen, and her hormones were raging. Mary Ella tried to discuss sexual matters with her, but the two headstrong women were too much the same to communicate successfully. Their attempts to talk often resulted in a clash of wills with Verlene leaving in a huff to a nearby friend's house.

Frankie, on the other hand, had a calm demeanor. Tall for his eleven years, he was a responsible, good-natured boy who spent his time playing or doing farmwork. Like his stepfather, Sonny Man displayed a distinct knack for farming, although he did not want to be a farmer when he grew up. He had found another interest.

Frankie was enthralled by stories of the Tuskegee airmen. The valiant exploits of these brave World War II Negro fighter pilots trained at the airfield in Tuskegee, Alabama, thrilled him and captured his dreams. Mary Ella encouraged her son's skyward vision and even bought him an aviator's cap. With wings of the U.S. Army Air Corps sewed on its front, the hat became Frankie's most prized possession. He wore it constantly during the day. At night, it hung from a nail by his bed so he could put it on first thing in the morning.

Seven-year-old Mary was sensitive and shy, with huge, happy eyes. May C., as she was called, was a very feminine little girl who liked to dress nicely, usually wearing a small, pink bow in her hair. Meticulously neat, her school shoes were carefully placed side by side each night beneath her bed.

In September 1948 Mary Ella and her family unknowingly entered a downward spiral that would change their world. Triggering this transition was Leon Turner's release from prison.

Mary Ella had not dealt meaningfully with Leon since 1940. Following his parole in 1943, she had only seen him in passing a few times. Then she had heard the stories about his being returned to Parchman Prison after being caught red-handed at a still. Now Leon Turner was once again out of prison and living two miles from her place.

Leon's return did not immediately concern Mary Ella. He was far enough away that his presence wasn't felt, and she was too busy with children to think of him. There was simply no connection in their lives.

Unfortunately, the connection was soon made. It came in the person of "Aunt Rilla." Rilla Meeks was the sister of Thomas Harris's mother. Born Rilla Sallis, she had married young to an older man named Meeks, who died shortly thereafter, leaving her childless. Remarrying would have been easy for the attractive widow, but she enjoyed her unattached status.

The lady whom Thomas called Aunt Rilla was tall, dark-skinned, and nearing forty. Wire-rim glasses and an erect posture gave her the stately look of a schoolteacher or librarian; but that's where the similarity to respectability ended. In reality, Rilla was wild. She smoked heavily, cussed shamelessly, and drank profusely. Independent, vivacious, and uninhibited, she was a vivid character unafraid to speak her mind.

Her unbridled, in-your-face attitude endeared her to the younger generation, including Thomas, but made her an object of uncertain suspicion to "responsible" adults like Mary Ella. While Thomas enjoyed the company of Rilla, Mary Ella maintained her distance. This arrangement satisfied Rilla, for she had never cared for Thomas's wife and had wasted no effort to befriend her.

Although Rilla Meeks lived alone, she wasn't a loner. To the contrary, she enjoyed the company of men and usually had plenty. There was no shortage of fellows dropping by.

Within months of his release from prison, Leon Turner operated a still hidden in the woods south of Newport near Ousley Creek, close to the remains of Miz Elvira's abandoned house. Using his past brewing skills supplemented by tips picked up from "experts" in prison, he produced a particularly potent moonshine. Word spread of its kick.

Among the locals who heard about Leon's whiskey was Rilla Meeks. Rilla was three or four years older than Leon and had never dealt with him, but that changed in early 1949. They were approaching each other while walking on the dry side of a muddy road. Leon carried several half-pint bottles of a recent batch of 'shine stuffed in the pockets of his long coat. After the two struck up a conversation, Rilla ended up buying two bottles from Leon.

So began an alliance of kindred spirits. Despite being on opposite sides of the racial divide, they had much in common: neither had a spouse or child; both were fiercely independent; each struggled with a fading youth. Rilla continued to buy Leon's whiskey. Eventually, she began selling his moonshine for a portion of the take. For the first time in her life, Rilla was a bootlegger. This unlawful activity excited her.

The excitement turned into attraction for the man that provided it. In the end, Rilla and Leon became lovers.

Their trysts were for gratification, not romance. They did not hide their relationship, for neither cared about the approval of others. Rilla began visiting Leon's house with its comfortable, multiracial environment. In time, she developed a close friendship with Howard Turner.

Thomas Harris came to know Leon Turner through his Aunt Rilla. Initially, Thomas and Rilla shared an occasional bottle of Leon's moonshine. Then Thomas accompanied Rilla to Leon's shack. Thomas began buying from Leon and eventually became another of his bootleggers. Sometimes Leon brought the whiskey to Thomas's home.

Thomas also began gambling, drinking, and driving around with Leon and his small circle of white friends. Like Rilla, Thomas became friends with Howard Turner. Other blacks criticized Thomas for being too "white."

Mary Ella Harris was not at all happy with this turn of events. With her lifelong knowledge of Leon, she feared that any connection of her young husband to the older, explosively violent man could only lead to trouble. She insistently told Thomas how she felt, but her warnings went unheeded.

Nearing the end of another pregnancy in May 1949, Mary Ella was huge, hot, and uncomfortable. Her irritability was high and her patience low. After being away from home one Saturday morning, she returned to find the children playing outside and her husband nowhere in sight. Waddling up the steps onto her porch, she entered her bedroom. Conversation was coming from the rear of the house, so she continued into the kitchen. Before her lay a scene she was not prepared to handle. Rilla Meeks and Howard Turner were sitting at her kitchen table, and Thomas was at the stove cooking a pot of turnip greens. The three were talking and laughing—obviously having a pleasant visit. Mary Ella spoke no words, but her expression said everything when the threesome noticed her. She turned and walked out.

Sitting on the edge of her bed, she seethed about the intrusion into her home by those two people. Within seconds, Thomas came to her. Instead of soothing his wife, however, he went on the attack, loudly fussing that she was being rude, that she had better mind the way she treated people. Mary Ella sat still with hands clasped in her lap and her jaw set, gazing straight ahead, silent.

Rilla, Howard, and Thomas talked for a while in subdued voices. The visitors left after they had eaten the simple fare that Thomas prepared.

When they were gone, Mary Ella's frustrations and discomfort boiled over in a rant against her husband. He was keeping too much company with a bad group of people, she complained. Rilla was leading him down a dangerous path. She didn't trust Leon or Howard in the least, and neither did other blacks. "There's plenty of black folk that don't allow them to come to their house, but you let them come to yours," she scolded.

She warned that riding around with those white boys was only going to bring him trouble. "You think they're going to think more of you than they do the others that will not associate with them. I tell you what—whenever they take a notion to mark a black family, the family they know is the family they get."

Thomas ignored Mary Ella's words. Even after Mary Ella gave birth on June 2 to James Edward Harris, he continued his ways.[12]

Whereas Howard treated Thomas as a friend, Leon's attitude was one of merely tolerating his bootlegger. He did not hesitate to threaten or bully Thomas when the feeling arose. Nor did he hide his interest in Thomas's women.

Leon had always been sexually interested in Mary Ella, who remained quite attractive. Though she had repeatedly rejected his overtures through the years, Leon's desire had not abated. He still sought her, and she still rebuffed him, but now it was in plain view of Thomas. Thomas took a passive role, not intervening in this cat-and-mouse game.

Complicating the mix was Leon's growing desire for Verlene, who was now fourteen. Leon made crude advances to her, but Verlene gave him the same cold shoulder as her mother.

On an autumn day in 1949, as the Harris family was in a field tending to their cotton, Leon Turner rode up on his horse to Verlene. The young teenager rudely turned her back to him and continued working. Looking down from his horse, Leon quietly said something to her, but Verlene ignored him. After again trying unsuccessfully to talk to her, Leon raised his voice in exasperation, "You treat me like a dog. I ain't no dog."

Verlene grunted, "Uh huh," and walked off to her house. Without looking back, she went inside, loudly slamming the door shut.

Leon cursed and rode off.

Though Verlene retreated to her own home, she may have longed to go instead to a nearby house on the other side of Highway 14. There lived the family of Isaac Roby, the uncle of her natural father, Eli Thurman. The several Roby children who lived there were Verlene's second cousins and lifelong playmates. Among them was her cousin Buck. Buck was twenty-five. Verlene wasn't aware of it at the time, but she was newly pregnant with his baby.

Little Nell, born nearly four years ago with a veil over her head, began having prognostic dreams on the Fourth of July, 1949, after several families had assembled for their annual holiday gathering. Nell saw one of her brother's friends playing there, a boy named Fleming.

The following morning, while Mary Ella lay in bed before arising for the day, she overheard Nell tell Verlene that she had dreamed Fleming was dead. The words of her superstitious mother-in-law flashed into Mary Ella's mind at the time, but she gave no further thought to Nell's dream—not until she heard days later that Fleming had been killed in an accident.

In the ensuing months, Nell was thrice visited by nightmares. The first time, she awoke crying in the middle of the night. As Mary Ella held her tightly, Nell sobbed that she had dreamed of her own death. Mary Ella could only hold her child close and whisper that it wasn't real.

Nell had the vision twice more.

The approaching end of 1949 found thirty-four-year-old Mary Ella, her twenty-seven-year-old husband, and their children with a future plainly visible: a life of backbreaking work to maintain a livable poverty. They had a shelter and food on the table, but very little else. Sharecropping was not going to improve their situation.

To make matters worse, Thomas saw troublesome signs that made him wonder if he could even rely on sharecropping. Cotton farming was beginning to change. Powerful new machines that did the work of many laborers were coming to the fields of the South. As it turned out, his suspicions were correct. Tractors, mechanized cotton pickers, and the like would soon bring down the institution of sharecropping.

In the end, however, farming methods were not to matter in Thomas's destiny. His future, as well as that of his family, was soon to be unwillingly changed.

Chapter 4

The Sheriff

Roy Braswell didn't grow up intending to go into law enforcement. He only knew that he wasn't interested in following in his father's footsteps.

Born in 1917, the youngest of three children, Roy was raised on a farm near the northern Attala County community of Shady Grove. His father owned four hundred acres—a slightly small holding by local standards. Each family member worked hard in the fields growing cotton and corn and helped take care of the chickens, cattle, and hogs. Roy dutifully did his share of the chores and, through it, developed a healthy work ethic; but he knew this was not his life's passion. Quiet and pensive, he liked to dabble with numbers.

It was uncommon then for Mississippi farm kids to attend college, but Braswell was an ambitious sort. After graduating from high school in the mid-1930s, he kissed his mother goodbye and went north—all the way to Memphis—where he enrolled in Draughn's Business School. He lived in a boarding house and performed odd jobs to pay his way.

Following business school, Roy moved back to Attala County and took a job as a bookkeeper with the local Gulf Oil Company distributor. Now twenty years old, he was of medium build, clean-shaven, and mature. He preferred pressed slacks and shirts to the overalls worn by many young men in the area. With his education and good job, he was one of the area's most eligible bachelors.

One Saturday night a house dance was held in Shady Grove. Roy enjoyed these get-togethers with friends, cousins, and schoolmates. Rarely was there a new face in the crowd. This particular night, however, an unfamiliar girl attended— a pretty brunette in a green dress. Roy couldn't keep his eyes off of her.

Eighteen-year-old Inez Bailey, from Kosciusko, had been invited by one of her girlfriends. Wearing a dress her mother had sewn for the occasion, Inez garnered much attention, including that of Roy Braswell. Their initial meeting began awkwardly. Roy asked her to dance; but the group was square dancing and she didn't know how, so she declined. Roy stayed, and the two stood and talked. Hitting it off right away, they kept in each other's company the entire evening. At the end of the party, they agreed to go out.

Days later, Roy received a surprise when he came calling at Inez's home, for his date lived under slightly unusual circumstances.

The oldest of four children, Inez lived with her family in a house atop a small hill a block from downtown Kosciusko. The house itself was normal—a small, wood-frame dwelling slightly overdue for a coat of white paint. A ground-level front porch looked out on a toy-scattered yard beneath a gigantic oak tree. Viewed on its own, the home was unremarkable. But just ten feet away on the same lot, loomed another, larger building, institutional and imposing—the Attala County Jail.

The jail was a two-story structure with an exterior of sun-bleached red bricks. Patches of white plaster dotted the exterior wall—remnants of past jailbreaks. Spaced evenly along three of the structure's walls were narrow, barred windows, each with a massive steel-plate, hinged at its top, as an awning. The building was topped with a tin roof forming a weathered silver pyramid with a brick-faced clerestory jutting from the center of each side. Kosciusko's newspaper, the *Star-Herald*, may have best described the old jail, calling it "an architectural monstrosity."[1]

As if a tornado had ripped a plain working-class home off its foundation and dropped it intact next to a random jailhouse, the juxtaposition of the small white house and its large brick neighbor could not have been more striking. They were joined by an enclosed passageway that connected the jail's kitchen to the house's dining room. Thus, the jail didn't need a room for entertaining visiting sheriffs and other dignitaries, and the home didn't need a kitchen.

Inez Bailey lived in the house adjoining the jail because her parents were Chief Deputy Sheriff Everett Bailey and his wife, Gladys, the county jailer. It was because of Gladys's job that the family lived where they did.

Attala County's jailer was responsible for all matters relating to the lockup—including admitting prisoners—and had to be available day or night. Accordingly, county officials had long ago built a house connected to the jailhouse where a single jailer could reside, thus enabling him or her conveniently to attend to his or her duties, similar to a lighthouse keeper. The house came rent-free with the job—an important inducement to meagerly paid county law-enforcement officers.

Attala County elected a new sheriff every four years, with no consecutive terms allowed.[2] The incoming sheriff designated who would live in the jailer's free home. Sometimes, a cash-strapped sheriff chose his own family to live there.[3] Since other duties prevented him from constantly being at the jail, the job of jailer fell by default to his wife. More often than not, the sheriff selected one of his deputies to live in the house, and the deputy's wife became jailer.

Such was the case in 1937. Sheriff David F. Sallis, a dentist, had taken office the previous year.[4] He already owned a nice country home, so he authorized Deputy Sheriff Everett Bailey to move into the white house. Gladys Bailey became jailer.

In this unusual household setting, bookkeeper Roy Braswell courted Inez Bailey. Inez was fun and energetic, witty and outgoing, the perfect complement to Roy's serious, reserved attitude. Their dates typically consisted of spending time at her house, playing Rook in the living room or talking on the front porch, away from Inez's siblings. The evening ended promptly at ten o'clock with a sweetly delivered pronouncement by Gladys: "Roy, it's time for you to go on home."[5]

As the romance of Roy and Inez grew, so did Roy's closeness with her parents. Gladys Bailey showed him the jail, familiarizing him with the old building and how she ran it. Deputy Sheriff Bailey shared some of the details of his work with this likeable young man courting his daughter. Roy listened with interest.

Roy and Inez married in October 1937.[6] They moved into a small house not far away from the jail and Roy's work; in Kosciusko, nothing was far away from anything. A year later, Roy Jr. was born.

Roy Braswell's first taste of politics came when his father-in-law ran for sheriff in the November 1939 election. Roy actively stumped the county seeking votes. Spreading the

"Bailey for Sheriff" message at all the small country stores, he became intimately familiar with the tiny communities dotting the countryside. Roy Braswell liked the world of back-slapping, good-old-boy country politics. Furthermore, the people of Attala County liked him.

Everett Bailey won the election. One of his first actions as sheriff was to hire Roy as deputy sheriff in charge of the county's revenue, for the full title of Bailey's new office was Attala County Sheriff and Tax Collector. The department's staff—Sheriff Bailey, Roy Braswell, another deputy, and three ladies associated with tax collection—occupied an undersized office on the first floor of the courthouse crammed with old wooden desks, tables, ashtray stands, coat trees, filing cabinets, and walls of ceiling-high bookcases stuffed with tax record books.[7]

Although Braswell had a good job at the courthouse office, it was not glamorous by any means. He was eager to experience the more exciting aspects of being a lawman. An opportunity arose the next summer.

Roy and Inez had finished supper with her parents in their jailer's house when the phone rang. Answering it, Sheriff Bailey was told about a shooting at a house dance in the nearby community of Sallis. Sheriff Bailey needed to respond quickly, and he wanted a deputy with him; so he recruited his son-in-law. Roy jumped at the chance.

The two men hurried west to Sallis and found a group of people hovering over seriously wounded Buddy Gowan. Someone told the sheriff how Gowan and another man had been fighting, and how Leon Turner had shot Gowan. Leon was still there, leaning against an upright piano with a jug in his hand and a hangdog look on his face. The sheriff arrested Turner, then he and Deputy Braswell hauled Leon to jail in Kosciusko. Leon was subsequently tried in Judge Allen's Fifth Circuit Court and sentenced to ten years in prison.

This episode marked Roy Braswell's first encounter with Leon Turner. It was not to be his last.

Roy enjoyed this adventure with his father-in-law. Wanting to experience more of the "Sheriff" part of the Office of Sheriff and Tax Collector, he began to accompany Sheriff Bailey on county patrols. Eventually, Roy was allowed to make the rounds by himself.

During this time, Roy lost most of his hair and began wearing a hat. In the summer, he wore a straw hat; in the winter, a gray felt Stetson. Roy liked hats and regularly bought a new one from Thornton's Men's Wear or Leonard's Department Store, both on the square.[8] He also began smoking inexpensive Roi-Tan Blunts cigars that he bought by the box at a nearby pharmacy.

World War II only briefly interrupted Roy's job. He received a draft notification early in the war and reported to Camp Shelby, an army post in southern Mississippi. A physical revealed that he had flat feet, a condition rendering him ineligible for service. Roy returned home to his deputy sheriff duties.

His foot condition actually benefited the Attala County Draft Board, which was required to meet an annual quota of draftees. Every year, they sent a draft notice to Braswell and counted it toward their allocation. Roy would make the trip to Camp Shelby, be rediagnosed with flat feet, and then return to Attala County, only to repeat the process the following year. He was never inducted into the army.

November 1943 saw J. M. "Boss" Weatherly elected as the new sheriff. By this time, Roy Braswell had firmly established himself in the department, so Sheriff Weatherly retained him as deputy.

Once again, the occupants of the jailer's house changed. Everett and Gladys Bailey retired and moved out after eight years of residence. With the new sheriff's wife having no interest in being the jailer, Roy and Inez Braswell ended up moving into the house they already knew so well. Inez replaced her mother as jailer.

Roy gained an exceptional amount of on-the-job training during the next four years. Boss Weatherly lived several miles from Kosciusko in an area of the county where telephone lines had not yet reached, so there was no way to quickly contact him in the evening after he had gone home. Consequently, Deputy Braswell received any after-hours emergency calls. When the nighttime operator received a request for "The Sheriff," she knew to transfer it to Deputy Braswell at telephone number "5-2."[9]

The role of jailer fit Inez Braswell like an expensive dress. Neither afraid of nor intimidated by the prisoners, she treated her charges humanely. She did her best to make the jailhouse if not clean, then at least bearable. It had too much history to be clean.

As were all aspects of life throughout the South during this period, the jail was racially segregated. Black prisoners occupied the first floor and white inmates the second. While living conditions on the second floor were dreadful, those on the lower floor approached insufferable due to an unintended, and unremedied, result of the building's construction. A giant plate of welded steel sheets served as the ceiling of the first story and the floor of the second. A gap between the edge of the plate and the exterior brick walls improved ventilation throughout the building. Unfortunately, it also provided a convenient place for white prisoners to urinate. Particularly on Saturday nights, when the jail was heavily populated with drunks, walls of the black men's first floor cells glistened with smelly wetness, and pools of urine formed on the concrete flooring. Decades of such practice had left the facility with a permanent stain and an overpowering stench.[10]

In 1944, Roy Braswell had his second encounter with Leon Turner. The previous year, Braswell had been astonished to learn of seventy-four-year-old Elvira Turner's arduous journey to Jackson to petition the governor for release of her grandson. He had been more surprised that the governor granted her request. Leon's return to Newport was of major concern to the lawmen of Attala and surrounding counties. Sheriff Weatherly and Deputy Braswell talked to people in Beat 4 and learned that Leon was reverting to his old ways of drinking, gambling, and moonshining. But authorities were unable to catch Leon doing anything illegal, so they could not arrest him. All they could do was keep a distant eye on the parolee and wait for a lucky break.

That break came early in 1944. The Holmes County sheriff called Sheriff Weatherly to say he had received a tip—no doubt from nightclub owner Tillman Branch—that Turner was making moonshine at a still near Newport. The tipster even told when Leon would be there.

On a cold February evening, Boss Weatherly, Roy Braswell, and other lawmen hid in the woods while Leon Turner cooked up a fresh batch of white lightnin' at Tillman Branch's still. Leon was sitting on a log in front of the hot fire sampling his brew when raiders suddenly sprang out of hiding with guns drawn. Completely surprised, Leon gave up without a fight.

A few days later, Leon's parole was revoked and he was sent back to prison. He would not resurface for years.

In 1945 a tragic event occurred in downtown Kosciusko that would have a major impact on Roy Braswell's career. It was a quiet Tuesday morning, two days before Thanksgiving. The holiday was going to be particularly meaningful: the nation's first Thanksgiving at peace since Pearl Harbor. Thousands of war-weary veterans, having returned home, were in the process of transitioning sanely and stably back to civilian life; but, for some, the adjustment to peacetime was not easy. Such was the case of Edward Wilkins, a twenty-eight-year-old ex-soldier who had recently returned to his Attala County roots after spending the last part of the war in a veterans' hospital. Wilkins had psychological difficulty leaving the fighting behind.

Deputy Braswell was in the sheriff's courthouse office doing routine paperwork when a commotion erupted outside the office. It sounded like two men in a heated argument. Roy hurried into the courthouse foyer and saw a flustered young man walking rapidly in circles, arms gesturing, yelling incoherently at a uniformed policeman. Roy recognized that the frantic civilian was Ed Wilkins. The policeman ordered Wilkins to stop and tried to grab him by the arm, but Wilkins only grew more agitated.

Knowing of the veteran's disturbed condition, Braswell walked up and, in a quiet, reasonable voice, tried to calm him. Wilkins merely spun around and dashed out of the courthouse.

The two peace officers ran after him. Darting across the street, they caught up with Wilkins in front of Allen's Drug Store. The three men skuffled, then Wilkins broke free and ran into the nearby Firestone Store. He emerged brandishing two axes and began stumbling down the sidewalk, ranting incomprehensibly. The lawmen, accompanied by a growing crowd of spectators, followed Wilkins around the square, keeping their distance as the ex-soldier wildly swung the axes at unseen enemies.

Kosciusko's chief of police, E. C. Hall, came out of the nearby police office and saw the turmoil. Hall walked toward Wilkins, drew his pistol, and told Wilkins to drop the axes. When the deranged man didn't respond, Hall fired a shot into the air and another into the ground.

The gunfire took Wilkins back to the battlefield. He responded by throwing an ax at the shooter. Under attack, Chief Hall fired at Wilkins. Wounded, the veteran charged toward his adversary and threw the second ax, hitting Hall in the side. Hall pumped several bullets into the crazed man, but Wilkins kept coming. He reached the chief and fought feebly. After a brief struggle, Hall threw Wilkins to the pavement. The young veteran did not get up.

Chief Hall was in anguish over the shooting. He cried out to the man lying at his feet, "Look what you've made me do!"[11]

An ambulance rushed Edward Wilkins to the hospital, but his wounds were too great to survive.[12]

E. C. Hall was briefly treated at the hospital and released. Although his physical wound was minor, the psychological damage was serious. A highly patriotic American, he was shaken to the core by killing a war veteran. Hall turned to alcohol to ease his anguish.

As the November 1947 election neared, Roy Braswell was worried about his job. The primaries had whittled the sheriff's race down to two men, Police Chief E. C. Hall and Willie Blanton, a farmer who had been sheriff from 1932 to 1936. It was rumored that Blanton, should he win, intended to select his brother to be deputy sheriff in Roy Braswell's place.

Roy didn't particularly like or trust E. C. Hall, but he did not want to relinquish his job. Roy had ambitions for the sheriff's office—he had tested the waters in the past primary—and knew that being out of law enforcement for at least four years would dampen any chance of being elected. Thus, he approached candidate Hall with a deal: he and his father-in-law, popular former sheriff Everett Bailey, would work the county to influence people to vote for Hall if Hall would retain Braswell as deputy when he won. Hall accepted the proposition.[13]

Braswell and Bailey actively canvassed the county touting the attributes of Mr. Hall, arguing for new blood in the office rather than electing a man who had been sheriff over a decade before. Their campaigning was effective: Hall won the election.

Sheriff E. C. Hall honored his word, and Braswell stayed on as deputy sheriff. Roy and Inez had to move out of their house next to the jail, however, because Sheriff Hall selected his nephew, Quitman Harris, as county jailer.

One duty of the sheriff was to attend courthouse sessions of the Mississippi Fifth Circuit Court.

Whereas the court had been the domain of Newport's Judge John Allen for nineteen years, January 1948 had witnessed his retirement. Now, two months later, Judge Allen's newly elected replacement was about to make his first appearance as judge in Attala County. This fledgling magistrate was J. P. Coleman, who, as a young district attorney, had prosecuted Leon Turner in 1940. While the last years of the elderly Judge Allen's court had been slow, relaxed, and informal, the proceedings of thirty-three-year-old Judge Coleman were expected to be different. Coleman had campaigned on efficiency and speed for his Circuit Court—something Attala County had not seen in decades, if ever. It was into this new court environment that recently inaugurated Sheriff Hall was to show up for his first session.

With the morning proceedings due to start in minutes, Judge Coleman was in his chamber adjoining the courtroom. In the spectators' gallery, Deputy Sheriff Roy Braswell sat in the first of many rows of wooden benches, casually chatting with someone sitting behind him. Scattered about the room were a few other citizens—slightly more than the normal handful of regular court aficionados—here to witness Judge Coleman's first appearance. Their conversations created a low murmur throughout the room.

The side door to the high-ceilinged room opened, and Braswell looked its way. His eyes widened as he saw Sheriff Hall entering the courtroom.

Hall's tie was loose and crooked; a conspicuous shaving nick adorned his chin. He walked in a slow, stiff, deliberate manner from the door to the railing that separated the spectators' area from the bar and grasped it with his left hand. Pausing, he took a deep breath before advancing to a nearby chair back, which he held while again hesitating. In such a manner, the sheriff advanced from object to object, haltingly making his way toward Braswell. Roy could see that Hall's eyes were glazed.

Conversation, interspersed with quiet chuckles, picked up throughout the courtroom.

Hall finally worked his way to a position next to Braswell and lowered himself in a controlled collapse into a bench seat. From three feet away, Roy noted a strong smell of alcohol. The two men conversed briefly, and Roy could tell the sheriff was liberally drunk. After a moment, Braswell rose and made his way out the chamber's side door. He dashed into a nearby office and called the jail.

When Quitman Harris answered, Roy told him that his uncle was at the courtroom drunk. He urged Harris to come get him before the judge entered. Luckily for Hall, Quitman made it to court and retrieved the sheriff before Judge Coleman ever saw him in his condition.

But the damage was done. Word of the event carried to the mayor and the County Board of Supervisors. These men agreed that this sort of embarrassing behavior could not be tolerated, though they hoped the incident was an anomaly. They gave Sheriff Hall another chance.

The other shoe dropped a year later.

A county resident died of natural causes one night in early 1949. Procedures specified that the body not be removed until the county coroner came to the scene and provided a preliminary ruling on the cause of death. This particular evening, however, the coroner was unavailable; so, again per procedures, the sheriff was called to perform the inquiry.

It took an abnormally long time for E. C. Hall to arrive. And when he did, it was plain that he was "full to the back teeth" drunk. Staggering around while conducting the investigation, the sheriff made a laughable spectacle of himself. Deputy Braswell was eventually summoned to take care of the situation and get his boss home.

In a furor, county leaders decided that Sheriff E. C. Hall had to go. Hall was summoned to a closed-door meeting and given the choice to either resign or be impeached.

On March 10, 1949, fifteen months after taking office, Sheriff Hall submitted the following letter to the Board of Supervisors:

> For the past several months I have been under a very severe physical strain. My health is and has been very poor. I have had a serious rectal operation and I am now suffering considerable physical pain.
> I consider it advisable under the above circumstances to tender my resignation as sheriff effective immediately.[14]

The board accepted Hall's resignation and appointed Chief Deputy Sheriff Roy Braswell to fill in as acting sheriff. Furthermore, they scheduled a special election in two months to permanently fill the position. Braswell immediately announced his candidacy, as did four other men.

The special election was held May 10, 1949. Roy Braswell received 1,567 votes, while former sheriff Willie Blanton pulled second place with 1,121.[15] And so it was that twelve years after marrying a sheriff's daughter and nine years after becoming a deputy sheriff, the thirty-two-year-old bookkeeper became Attala County sheriff and tax collector.

Braswell held modestly the position that many throughout the county called "High Sheriff." Rather than a uniform, his usual mode of dress was khaki pants and a white dress shirt—with or without a tie. The only visible display of his office was a sheriff's badge clipped to his belt. The official sheriff's car was a four-door 1947 Ford that he and Inez had bought two years earlier. Since Attala County didn't furnish its sheriff with an automobile, occupants of the office used their own vehicles. He kept a black-handled, .38 caliber pistol in his car's glove compartment along with a pair of handcuffs. He wore the weapon holstered on his right hip only when there was a possibility of trouble. Always he wore a hat, and always he carried a cigar.

Since Braswell was elected to fill the unexpired term of E. C. Hall, he would have the job less than three years. He chose to keep Quitman Harris as the jailer. Roy and Inez would remain in their small, cozy house on East Adams Street, where they had moved when Hall became sheriff.

The young sheriff set out to make a quick impact by concentrating his department's efforts on an illegal activity that had become more widespread in the years since the war—moonshining.

Attala County's natural environment was ideal for making moonshine: plentiful springs; weather suitable for year-round outside operation; and, critically important, abundant vegetation to conceal the activity from prying eyes. Despite the limitless number of potential hiding places in his jurisdiction, Sheriff Braswell gained impressive results busting stills right away. It seemed that he had an uncanny ability to find them, no matter how remote or well concealed they were. This success was attributable to two factors: first, Braswell's familiarity with the county's web of back roads gained during his periods of campaigning for Sheriffs Bailey and Hall, and second, a secret weapon to which he had special access—Inez.

Following Sunday church services, Roy and Inez enjoyed taking leisurely afternoon drives, like many of the area's citizens. The Braswells' weekend excursions, however, covered much more territory than was typical of other Sunday drivers. They explored remote county roads that few traveled. Enjoying the unspoiled air of Attala County, they motored through lush timberlands covered by the wide, green leaves of the kudzu vine that blocked off views as effectively as a curtain. The purpose of their Sunday afternoon outings was not merely to enjoy the beauty of nature; they toured these isolated regions of Attala County in search of a unique smell.

Roy drove slowly, chewing on an unlit cigar. Inez sat on the passenger side with her window open, nose turned outward. Although years of cigar smoking had killed her husband's sense of smell, Inez's olfactory capacities were excellent. As they drove, Inez sniffed for the dank, sour smell of mash.

Mash—a mixture of cornmeal, yeast, sugar, and water—is first boiled over a fire in an open barrel and then left to sit for days. It ferments as it sits, turning sugar into alcohol and carbon dioxide. The gas causes the mash to bubble, creating a distinctive odor that carries far on the wind. Commonly, wild animals such as raccoons or opossums would investigate the smell, climb into the open barrels, and drown.

When Inez Braswell smelled this unmistakable scent, Roy stopped the car and walked upwind into the surrounding thicket. A few minutes of searching revealed one or more barrels of mash sitting next to a still. By observing the amount of bubbling in the mash, the sheriff's experienced eye could tell how far along the fermentation process had progressed, allowing him to estimate when the batch would be ready for the final, cooking step that produced moonshine. Before that time, Roy and his men would raid the still to destroy it and hopefully nab the moonshiners.

During regular working hours, when Sheriff Braswell wasn't putting stills out of business or doing office chores, he patrolled the roads of the county. If he saw Elvira Turner as she strolled around Newport, he made a point of pulling over to chat with her for a few minutes. Sometimes he gave her a lift to Kosciusko during her Saturday forays into town. They talked about her health, Newport, and her grandchildren, particularly Leon. This was one method Braswell used to keep tabs on the troubling ex-convict.

Roy had known of Turner's release from Parchman in September 1948. Reports since then had been worrisome, revealing a man different from the one Braswell had helped return to prison five years before. Leon seemed now to be a loner, a wanderer without a steady job, a man with time on his hands—a dangerous combination of traits in such an explosive man. But there was nothing the sheriff could do other than be wary of the threat lurking in Beat 4.

At the end of 1949, Sheriff Roy Braswell was making his mark catching moonshiners. Soon, however, he would have the opportunity to make a much larger catch, one that would provide the ultimate test of his experience, his character, and his drive to succeed.

Attala County Jail alongside the jailer's home.

Sheriff Roy Braswell.

Chapter 5

Hogjaw

Most of the businesses and residences of Natchez, Mississippi, sit on a bluff high above the shoreline of the Mississippi River. Only a small cluster of buildings huddled around Silver Street occupies the thin strip of land reaching from the riverbank to the base of the escarpment.

The section of town sitting atop the bluff has historically been called Natchez On-the-Hill. With a population defined by a wealthy planter class living in stately antebellum mansions, Natchez On-the-Hill was perched above the lower part of the city, Natchez Under-the-Hill, whose residents were somewhat less refined.

Under-the-Hill had long been considered the unseemly part of Natchez, a place where proper people did not tread. Women of the night, liquor, and gambling in bountiful quantities provided wallet-busting entertainment for river travelers disembarking at the city's busy port or those journeying northward by land on the Natchez Trace. During its heyday in the 1800s, the Under-the-Hill district gained a notorious reputation, one that remained even after the mighty Mississippi had eroded away most of the tenuous sedimentary land on which the nefarious businesses stood.

In 1940 Natchez Under-the-Hill's disreputable past continued to taint its residents; or so it seemed to the district's sprinkling of inhabitants, including the free-living souls who lived in shanty boats moored along the shoreline. It appeared that the good citizens living on the bluff literally and figuratively looked down on them.

Such was the case with one of the boat residents, a ne'erdo-well young man named Clarence B. Grammer. People had looked down on him his whole life. Grammer claimed he had never caught a break in his twenty-two years. Growing up poor in Greenwood, Mississippi, he had a difficult childhood; and his troubles had carried over into adulthood. At eighteen he was sentenced to two years in the Mississippi State Penitentiary at Parchman for grand larceny.[1] Now free, he was on the run as a draft dodger from Louisiana's Concordia Parish, located on the opposite side of the river from Natchez.[2]

At five foot eight and 148 pounds, Grammer was as mean as one of the mongrel dogs that scrounged about "under the hill" looking for scraps of food, fighting with others over the tiniest morsel.[3] Clarence had a fierce temper that was easily triggered; and when it was, he fought viciously. A strong sense of self-preservation, a low consideration for the well-being of others, and an above-average intelligence fortified by a tenth-grade education also helped him survive.[4]

He lived on a homemade shanty boat, a small wooden shack built on top of a barely larger barge. It was cramped, leaky, and smelly; but it was home—a home that could be easily relocated should bad fishing or onshore troubles so dictate. In mid-October 1940 Grammer had floated his houseboat to its present location off Natchez Under-the-Hill, tying up alongside several others. Living with Clarence was his girlfriend, Mildred Davis, who months before had left a boring existence and a boring boyfriend in the Delta in search of adventure in the unrestrained environs around Natchez.

Clarence and Mildred could usually be found in attendance whenever there was a boxing match in town. Two-bit promoters occasionally brought in two-bit fighters to exchange fisticuffs at local lodges or fairgrounds before packed houses of wildly cheering spectators. Clarence loved the fights. He had boxed a little in his hometown and had once even aspired to be in the ring professionally, but his all too frequent bouts with the law had foiled that ambition.

Still, he wasn't about to let the fact that he wasn't really a boxer stop him from making people believe that he was. Whenever anyone brought up the subject, he loudly boasted of his prowess in the ring, claiming his pugilistic career was cut short by injury.

Clarence had a knack for telling tall tales about himself. His stories were an imaginative combination of unfulfilled dreams, colorful fictions, and fanciful accounts of other inmates he had heard about in prison, with maybe a smidgeon of truth thrown in so he couldn't be accused of outright lying. Bragging about his own "adventures" was commonplace in the mangy speakeasies he frequented with Mildred.

Somewhere along the way, his blowhard stories attracted an admiring hanger-on, a skinny nineteen-year-old Polish boy named Wallace Silkowski who had been in the country a little over three years.[5] Wallace spoke heavily accented, broken English. Each morning at dawn, he paddled across the Mississippi in a canvas kayak to make money picking cotton on a Louisiana plantation.[6] At the end of the day, he came back to Natchez Under-the-Hill and spent the earnings partying with his crazy American friends.

When Clarence Grammer had moored his shanty boat, he ended up adjacent to one belonging to an elderly fisherman named Frank Leche. Leche had lived at that site for quite a while, quietly fishing from one of the two motorboats he kept tied alongside. Not much for socializing, Leche was a cantankerous old coot who just wanted to be left alone. Something about him didn't sit well with Grammer, and the feeling was mutual. They were like two chemicals that remained under control while separated but produced a violent reaction when brought together. Their intense dislike for each other came to a head on the afternoon of Friday, October 25, 1940, when they had a huge argument, the subject of which is lost to history.

The following Wednesday, two fishermen recovered the body of Frank Leche from the river. An autopsy revealed that he had been shot with a squirrel gun, stabbed at least twice, had his head bashed in with an ax, and then, still breathing, thrown in the river with iron weights strapped to his legs. Neighbors reported to the Adams County sheriff that they had heard a single shot last Friday afternoon, and that Frank Leche had not been seen since. Furthermore, his two motorboats were missing. Also missing were Clarence Grammer, his girlfriend, and the Polish youngster.

A huge two-state manhunt was mounted.[7] The sheer brutality of the murder made front-page headlines in the *Natchez Democrat* newspaper. Residents of surrounding counties became aware that two men and a woman were on the loose, probably in motorboats.

After killing Frank Leche, Clarence Grammer had waited until night to board Mildred into one of Leche's small boats. He persuaded Wallace Silkowski, who had been picking cotton in Louisiana at the time of the murder, to get into the other. Under cover of darkness, the three pushed off, started the Evinrude motors, and headed south.

The trio was on the run with no destination in mind and no timetable to get there. They traveled along the shore of the mighty river, stopping along the way to beg for or steal food. After a few days, they pulled up on the eastern riverbank near the southwestern corner of the state of Mississippi. Grammer wanted to leave the boats and take his chances traveling on land, but Silkowski insisted on pressing further south to a river island he knew. The fugitives parted ways.

Eight days after the murder, Clarence and Mildred found themselves hungry and exhausted, asking for food at a farmhouse outside Fort Adams, Mississippi. After being given something to eat, Grammer casually inquired if the farmer had heard anything about a murder committed in the area recently. The farmer said no, but in fact, he had seen the newspaper's report of the murder. Suspicious, he notified the Wilkinson County sheriff.

Meanwhile, Clarence and Mildred made their way into Fort Adams. There, a fisherman who had taken special interest in the Natchez death of a fellow fisherman noticed them. He recognized the description of the bedraggled couple walking through town. Boldly, he drew a gun on them, then proceeded to tie them up with a rope and hold them at gunpoint until the sheriff arrived.[8] The pair was taken to Natchez, where Grammer blamed the murder on his nineteen-year-old Polish acquaintance. He ratted that Wallace Silkowski could be found on Turnbull Island, Louisiana.

Not long afterward, Silkowski was sitting on the porch of a poor family's shack on Turnbull Island devouring a donated sweet potato, when the sheriff of West Feliciana Parish drove up. Wallace was arrested and promptly transported to Natchez.[9]

That Silkowski had been in Louisiana at the time of the murder was easily established. He was soon released. Similarly, Mildred Davis was exonerated of any wrongdoing. Legend has it that her old boyfriend rode to Natchez on a bicycle and carried her back home to Greenville.[10]

Clarence Grammer, on the other hand, was guilty as sin. He confessed and was sentenced to life imprisonment. Parchman Penitentiary admitted him for the second time on December 7, 1940.[11]

In many ways, Parchman in the 1940s was more like a plantation than a prison. Its 20,000 acres were spread out over forty-six square miles of flat, rich Delta soil in Sunflower County, ninety miles south of Memphis. Parchman was a town in itself, complete with a brickyard, machine shop, cotton gin, canning plant, dairy, sewing shop, slaughterhouse, laundry, and railroad depot.[12]

The penitentiary's nearly 2000 men and women prisoners were segregated along racial and gender lines into smaller groups of 100 to 150 inmates living in their own field camps.[13] Fifteen of these camps were spread out at least a half mile apart across the vast prison land. At each camp, convicts slept and ate in a long, single-story dormitory called a "cage." A sergeant, a prison employee who reported directly to the prison superintendent, ran each camp. Black convicts called their sergeant "da Main Mos' Man"; to whites, he was "The Man."[14] Maintaining control was primarily the job of trusties—long-term inmates whom prison authorities trusted to act as security at the camp.

Barbed-wire fences, placed more to delineate boundaries than to prevent escapes, surrounded each camp. The primary deterrent to breakouts was trusties who patrolled on horseback armed with Winchester rifles. Called "shooters," they were given an incentive unique among the nation's prisons: should a trusty kill or injure an escaping prisoner, a quick pardon by the governor was assured, regardless of reason for incarceration.

In the event that an escaping inmate made it past the shooters undetected, Parchman had two groups of dogs to take care of them. First were the "sniff dogs," trained to follow the trail of a long-gone escapee; second were the "kill dogs," guaranteed to permanently and horribly end any possibility of a convict's future escape.

The bloodhounds, beagles, and German shepherds that made up Parchman's canine corps were bred, trained, and handled by the men of Camp 5.[15] Inmate dog handlers were known as "dog boys." They were presided over by a single trusty called the "Main Mos' Dog Boy."[16]

Obviously, if one had to be a prisoner in Parchman, then being a trusty was the preferred way to go. This position allowed the most control over one's own life, as well as the lives of regular inmates in the camp.[17] All inmates with lengthy sentences aspired to be a trusty.

Since Clarence Grammer's 1940 return to Parchman Penitentiary was his second incarceration there, he knew the pecking order and how things worked. His first sentence had been a short two years; he had merely concentrated on doing his time, not attempting to climb the ladder of Parchman's hierarchy. This second time, he was in for good. Consequently, he set about to improve his quality of life by improving his prison status.

The primary attribute needed to thrive at Parchman was toughness. Inmates respected the hardest fighters, the meanest men. The man named Clarence Grammer didn't have such status, and acquiring it as a new arrival could mean years of fighting his way to the top. Instead, he took a short cut by changing his identity.

As a youth, Grammer had watched several bouts of Curtis "Hogjaw" Mullen, a talented boxer from his hometown. Mullen gained renown throughout northwestern Mississippi by winning the state's 1928 welterweight championship at age eighteen.[18] He had long since left the ring and dropped out of sight.

When Clarence Grammer arrived at Parchman, he told fellow prisoners that he was former boxer Hogjaw Mullen. Clarence told elaborate stories about some of Hogjaw's real matches, and then made up tales of even more exciting bouts. Somehow, he pulled it off. Whether most inmates had never heard of Hogjaw, or prison sentences had skewed the sensibilities of those familiar with the name, or Grammer beat any doubter into believing, Clarence was accepted as who he said he was. To the Parchman inmates, the unfamiliar murderer Clarence Grammer didn't exist; instead, respected boxing champion "Hogjaw Mullen" was in their midst.

As he matured and gained weight, Hogjaw became harder, meaner, and more formidable. He fought anyone, anytime, and he won. Within a few years, Hogjaw Mullen had the reputation as the South's "toughest convict."[19] He said of himself, "I'm one scary son of a bitch."[20]

His toughness and nasty disposition favorably attracted the attention of his camp's sergeant. In Parchman's system, each sergeant chose his own trusties. Because trusties maintained order among violent criminals living in brutal conditions, their selection was based largely on the ability to use force to intimidate and control others.[21] Hogjaw made it a point to demonstrate this desired quality from the start, and within a relatively short period, he became a trusty.[22]

For the first time in his life, the former Clarence Grammer had real authority over men.

To go with it, he now had the look of a trusty. All male inmates wore shirts and pants with wide black and white stripes, but there was a difference between the stripes of regular prisoners and those of trusties. Ordinary convicts wore their stripes horizontally—prison slang called the outfits "ring-arounds." Trusties, on the other hand, wore "up-and-downs" with vertically running stripes.

Coveted by the lucky men who wore them, vertical stripes allowed a generous freedom of action and, most important, elevated their owner above other convicts. But they did not make the wearer all-powerful. The prison superintendent demanded strict accountability from trusties. Any trusty who beat or killed an inmate without a justifiable reason faced demotion to "ring-arounds." This meant returning the ex-trusty to the ranks of those fellows he had brutalized and letting nature take its course. This unthinkable scenario encouraged trusties to rein in abusive behavior, for, as one prisoner recalled, "only idiots risked their up-and-downs."[23]

Besides becoming a trusty, Hogjaw was also assigned the highly desirable dog-handling job. He moved to Camp 5 and became a "dog boy" training under Kennie Wagner, Parchman's legendary Main Mos' Dog Boy.

Working with the dogs was possibly the best thing ever to happen to Hogjaw Mullen. As a trainer, he excelled—it was as though he instinctively understood the personality of each animal under his care and could bring out its best ability.

Hogjaw's specialty became tracking people with "sniff dogs." Controlling his hounds with thick leather leashes as they loped near full speed in pursuit of a hot trail, he felt what the dogs were sensing. Watching their movement as they sniffed the ground, hearing changes in their bays as they picked up a scent, Hogjaw guided his animals quickly to a quarry. His low, powerful body proved ideal for dashing through vegetation at full speed. Ever one to sing his own praises, he boasted of being the only man who could keep up with dogs in a chase. He even claimed that he and his hounds could outrun a horse.[24]

Hogjaw came to know Leon Turner through his boss, the Main Mos' Dog Boy. Kennie Wagner was Parchman's most famous criminal in residence at the time. A Virginia-born killer, jailbreaker, and handsome romantic adored by scores of females nationwide, Wagner had once been a trick-shot artist.[25] There was only one other man at Parchman known to have as fine an aim: Leon Turner. Their occasional shooting contests drew large crowds of prisoners and prison dignitaries. By assisting Wagner at these matches, Hogjaw dealt with Turner and learned to respect his shooting ability.

Hogjaw attained every trusty's dream in the spring of 1947 when he legitimately killed a prisoner trying to escape and thereby earned a pardon.[26] Following his release, he moved east to Columbus, Mississippi. He continued to go by the prison name that had served him so well.

Hogjaw took a job at a local machine shop, where his wild tales both entertained his coworkers and earned him the reputation of being careless with the truth. On the side, he bought some bloodhounds from Parchman and ran them for anyone willing to pay for his services.[27]

A decent-looking man with a steady job and a gift of gab, Hogjaw was prime marrying material at age twenty-eight if a girl was willing to overlook a few faults. Connie Ruth Long, an unsophisticated lass from the poor side of Columbus, was, and she didn't take long to snatch him up. At twenty-seven, Connie Ruth was on the upper end of a country girl's marrying age. She was a pretty blonde a little on the hefty side, or so explained her mother when showing a picture of her daughter "taken when she was not so fleshy."[28]

Their marriage, while not exactly made in heaven, proved adequate. Hogjaw, after so long in prison, was glad to have a woman; and Connie Ruth, after simply so long, was relieved to have a man. The bride's new husband was kind to her except for the few occasions he roughed her up a bit when he was drunk. But even then, said her mother, Connie Ruth "probably brought some of it on herself, because she, too, was high-tempered."[29]

For well over a year, Hogjaw made it in the outside world. But like a boiling pot of grits, his temper could only go for so long before spilling over and making a mess. He was drinking with some of his old Parchman buddies in Minter City one night when he got into a fight with a black man, threatened several others with a shotgun, and resisted arrest. The State of Mississippi, which frowned on such antics from a paroled murderer, expeditiously revoked his pardon and returned him to Parchman in December 1948.

Two major factors made this prison term more tolerable than the previous one. The first was Connie Ruth.

Although Parchman Penitentiary could hardly have been described as a progressive penal institution, it was America's first prison to institute the practice of conjugal visitation. Each camp had a rustic wooden shack, called the "red house" or the "tonk," that contained several small rooms to accommodate sexual interludes.[30] Other inmates were very cooperative in this regard, even babysitting when necessary. In the early 1900s, intimate visits were allowed only on the fifth Sunday of those months that had more than four Sabbaths. Due to popular demand, the visitation schedule was changed in 1946 to two hours every Sunday and the entire afternoon every third Sunday.[31]

On that eagerly anticipated visitation day, a special train brought wives and girlfriends to the inmates. Because the train started its journey from the Jackson depot at 12:05 a.m. on Sunday morning, it was called the "Midnight Special." The Midnight Special pulled several coach cars all through the night as it traveled north, stopping at small towns along its route to pick up female passengers bound for their man. It arrived at Parchman Station around dawn.

Inmates accustomed to hard labor and even harder overseers eagerly awaited the arrival of "Rosie"—their slang term for all women—on Sunday morning. In the quiet before the dawn of those blessed days, the black inmates of Camp 1 lay awake in their bunks straining to hear the wafting sound of a locomotive's distant whistle. Upon hearing it, they crowded around the barred windows of their cage, staring out beyond the floodlit grounds into the darkness beyond, seeking a glimpse of the train's headlight. It was Parchman lore that any man whose face was illuminated by the Midnight Special would have on board a woman visitor carrying a gubernatorial pardon.[32]

One former inmate, Huddie "Leadbelly" Ledbetter, "King of the 12-String Guitar,"[33] immortalized the train in his song "Midnight Special":

Yonder come little Rosie . . .
Piece of paper in her hand

Goes a marchin' to the Cap'n
Says I want my man.

Oh, let the Midnight Special
Shine her light on me
Let the Midnight Special
Shine her ever lovin' light on me.[34]

Connie Ruth Mullen was among those women who spent Saturday afternoons at the beauty parlor followed by hours in front of a mirror primping and preening for the visit to her man. After Hogjaw had been sent back to Parchman, she had moved to Greenwood, about thirty miles from the prison, and hired on as a waitress at the Alice Café. According to her approving mother, "She never misses a Sunday goin' to Parchman to see him."[35]

Connie Ruth had bragging rights over the other visiting females, whose fragrance from liberal splashes of perfume combined with thick cigarette smoke to give the prison's waiting room a unique and memorable aroma. For Hogjaw had become a prison big shot—the second major improvement in his prison stay.

Kennie Wagner had escaped the prior March. He walked right out the front gate carrying a .45 caliber machine gun, and then evaded the very bloodhounds he had trained.[36] Camp 5's sergeant wasn't happy with Kennie's successor— after all, he had been unable to track down the escapee—so when Hogjaw showed back up after only a year and a half's absence, the camp boss promptly promoted him to Main Mos' Dog Boy.

Hogjaw was in his element. As the prison's chief dog handler, he had authority over dozens of men; he had a pearl-handled revolver in a strap-on holster to wear during manhunts; he had all the food he wanted; and he had Connie Ruth on Sundays. Parchman was where he belonged; the one place in the world where he fit in perfectly.

To top it off, Hogjaw was with the state's best team of tracking dogs—three bloodhounds that he had helped train. They were like children to him.

There was a sandy-brown animal with droopy eyelids named Alabama. Hogjaw called him Bama. He was the smallest of the three dogs, but tireless in a chase.

An auburn coat over a tall, skinny frame identified High Rollin' Red—Red for short. Red was the famous lead dog of the trio and was, his handlers bragged, the best tracker in the South. He had served the men of Camp 5 for many years, but now was near the end of his fabled career. Gray hairs adorned his snout. Soon he would be retired in favor of Bama.

Hogjaw's favorite was a muscular hound named Nigger. Although he was Red's son, Nigger hardly resembled his sire. He had a coat of dark brown fur except for his front right leg, which was white from elbow to paw.[37]

Parchman's three bloodhounds were legendary, having participated in the capture of several "rabbits"—fleeing convicts trying to escape the penitentiary.[38]

So trusted were the noses of Hogjaw's three dogs that one of their most famous catches happened because of someone they were unable to locate. In November 1948 Mrs. Idella Thompson was killed with a pair of rose shears in Leland, Mississippi. Mrs. Thompson's daughter, Mrs. Ruth Dickins, claimed that a Negro had done the deed before running into the woods. Red, Bama, and Nigger were brought in and run through the woods for hours. Surprisingly, they could not pick up the trail of the supposed murderer. Authorities decided that if these dogs couldn't find a scent, then a scent wasn't there. As a result, the investigation turned inward, and Mrs. Dickins was eventually convicted of murdering her mother.[39]

Hogjaw Mullen and his animals traveled all over Mississippi providing their services. When someone needed to be found, be it an escaping fugitive or a lost child, local authorities called Parchman. Before long, an official Mississippi Highway Patrol car would be on its way out the front gate with Patrolman Tom Sadler driving, Hogjaw to his right, and a canine trio roaming the backseat.

Manhunts were hugely popular with the public. Wherever Hogjaw and his hounds went, a crowd of admirers watched as he attached extra long leather leashes to the dogs' collars and then led them around until they caught the scent. At that point, the dogs took off like spooked quail, leaving the crowd behind to hear the exciting sound of baying in the distance.

By 1949 the man who had formerly relied on tall tales to enhance his stature had finally achieved a position that matched his stories. As the end of the year approached, Hogjaw awaited the camp's upcoming Christmas get-together, where prisoners and their families feasted outside at long tables topped with heaping porcelain platters of baked ham, turkey, fried chicken, cornbread dressing with giblet gravy, cranberry sauce, turnip greens, black-eyed peas, homemade rolls big as a cats' heads, sweet tater pies, and gallons of sweet tea. And, of course, cauldrons of oil-black coffee for afterward. Prison officials had long ago found that inmates' satisfaction from this single event created less discord during the next year of backbreaking labor.

While the former Clarence Grammer anticipated this up-coming holiday banquet, two brothers from Alabama were making their way south from Cincinnati to spend the yuletide season with their relatives. An unlucky coin toss was about to change their destination and set them on a collision course with the man from Parchman who called himself Hogjaw.

Hogjaw Mullen beside Patrolman
Tom Sadler's Highway Patrol car.

Chapter 6

The Whitt Brothers

Before the Great Depression, hitchhiking was a regular and accepted method of travel for those too poor to own an automobile. During the economic hard times of the 1930s, however, when the land of opportunity turned into a land of desperation, the number of hitchhikers exploded. Highways were awash with scores of downtrodden citizens searching for work or entreating shelter from kindly relatives in faraway destinations.

Hollywood helped legitimize and even glamorize the ambulatory mode of transportation in such movies as *Sullivan's Travels*, *The Grapes of Wrath*, and the 1934 classic *It Happened One Night,* featuring superstar hitchhikers Clark Gable and Claudette Colbert.

Those "hitching a ride" were mostly lone, male travelers. Sometimes two men traveled together, but rarely three, as drivers were wary of groups of three or more men. On occasion, whole families stood by the road.

A less commonplace sight was children hitchhiking alone—like Malcolm and Windol Whitt. In 1936, Malcolm was a scrawny white kid, barely a teenager; Windol was his younger brother by two years. The Whitt boys lived with their father in the northern Alabama city of Huntsville, nestled in a picturesque valley of the Appalachian Mountain foothills fifteen miles below the Tennessee state line. With a population of more than 10,000, Huntsville wasn't a huge town; but it was far larger than Newport, Mississippi, where the boys' mother lived.

Huntsville was 220 miles northeast of Newport, a distance not at all daunting to the Whitt boys. Throughout the 1930s, they hitchhiked several times to visit their mother, Birdie. They did so even though she had abandoned them.

Birdie Bell Edwards was born in 1897 to one of Newport's oldest, largest families.[1] Raised in that isolated community in an era when young girls were expected to be refined and restrained, Birdie bucked the stereotype from the start.

As a teen with mirthful eyes and striking red hair, Birdie was a second-stare beauty.[2] She was active, adventurous, outgoing, and more than a bit wild. She thoroughly enjoyed partying and flirting, smoking and drinking. While most of her cousins and friends were content to spend their lives in comfortably tranquil Newport, she thirsted for the world outside. A fellow from Alabama presented the opportunity to leave when Birdie was seventeen.

The Edwards family occasionally traveled to the Mississippi Delta to visit relatives. During one such trip, Birdie met Buford Whitt from Athens, Alabama, an easygoing young man who was temporarily working in the area. A brick mason, Buford often spent weeks at a time away from Athens on construction projects. He and Birdie hit it off from the moment they met. Following a whirlwind courtship culminating in a marriage proposal, Birdie left the gentle hills of central Mississippi for a new life in northern Alabama.

Over the next nine years, Birdie and Buford Whitt settled in Huntsville and had five children. The youngest were Malcolm, born August 18, 1922, and Windol, born

September 18, 1924.[3] The years were not kind to Birdie. By the time Windol was a toddler, Birdie's winsome attitude had been beaten down by the burdens of being a mother and a wife—a wife in a troubled marriage.

From the time she began having children, Birdie shouldered the vast majority of child-rearing time and responsibilities. While this burden was shared by most of America's women, hers was exacerbated by the lack of any Attala County family to share babysitting duties. Several Whitt family women were nearby, for the Alabama Whitts were a large clan, but she was not particularly close to any of them, nor they to her. She missed having her own blood relatives around. Making matters worse, her husband's work regularly kept him away for extended times.

But Buford wasn't lonely while away; he enjoyed the intimate company of other women on his trips. News of his extramarital activities got back to Birdie. As a result, several years and children into their marriage, the couple temporarily separated. Although they separated and came back together more than once, and had more children together, Buford's wandering habits did not change. Over time, Birdie became despondent and embittered. Her once bright eyes clouded with desperation; her once sexy posture drooped with hopelessness. She grew distant and detached from everyone, including her children.

As their home situation grew increasingly unpleasant, the family began to disintegrate. Birdie's oldest child ran away when he was fourteen.[4]

The situation climaxed one evening as Buford and several children sat down to eat at the kitchen table. Everything seemed normal and calm when, without warning, Birdie approached Buford from behind and slammed a bottle on his head. Pieces of shattered glass flew across the floor as Buford slumped over the table, a deep, bloody gash in his scalp.[5]

Young Malcolm and Windol Whitt listened in horror as their mother began screaming at their father. Wild accusations incubated from years of pain and humiliation spewed from Birdie's mouth in a sobbing, out-of-control rant. Then, the verbal assault stopped—flipped off as if by a switch. After a moment of shocking silence, Birdie turned and ran to her bedroom, where she closed the door to her torment. She packed a suitcase and left.

This time, she didn't come back. Forsaking her husband and children, she retreated to her Mississippi roots.

It was 1934 when Malcolm and Windol's mother went away. They were twelve and ten, respectively. Afterward, these two youngest children in the family began to slide into trouble.

They had always tended to be unruly. Only the daily oversight of their mother had kept their behavior in check. With her now gone, the brakes in the boys' lives were released. Louise, their older sister by four years, attempted to fill the role of mother, but the boys would not yield to her control. Only Buford was able to rein in his sons, but he continued to be absent for lengthy periods. The youngsters' behavior grew wilder, eventually progressing to petty thievery and vandalism.

In their unraveled world, Malcolm and Windol had only themselves. They were inseparable. To Windol, Malcolm was more than a brother—he was quasi parent, role model, and decision maker.

The boys' education had formerly been a no-question-about-it requirement of their mother. With her out of the picture, school was now merely a nuisance. They stopped going after Malcolm's sixth-grade year, Windol's fifth.[6]

Instead of reading and writing, the brothers began learning their father's trade, apprenticing under him, working on projects in Huntsville. Buford did not permit them to travel to his remote jobs, so it was during these idle times that they began hitchhiking to their mother's home in Mississippi.

In years gone by, Birdie had taken her children on summer visits to Attala County. The brothers liked their Mississippi relatives, especially the younger cousins who treated the Alabamans like foreign dignitaries from some exotic place. Also appealing was the adventure of exploring new territory while their mother visited with her people.

Now that Birdie was living in that land of fond memories, the two boys set about to see her. For days they hitchhiked a zigzagging southwesterly route, sleeping in barns, huddling under a bridge during rains, begging for food from strangers, all the way to Newport. Then, after a satisfying stay with their mother, aunts, uncles, grandparents, and cousins, the boys retraced their route home to Huntsville and their father.

As the years passed, Malcolm and Windol became skilled craftsmen under the expert tutelage of their father. They learned the techniques of first-class masonry and demonstrated that they had the touch to do quality work. It was obvious that each would someday acquire the title of master stonemason.

Physically, too, the brothers matured. At five foot ten, Windol stood slightly shorter than his brother. Both were slim with thin, hawklike faces dominated by high, hollow cheekbones and narrow noses under a tangled mat of unruly brown hair. Both had large, round ears that poked excessively outward. Their eyes carried a look of sadness, the sort of look whose entrance to a room brought darkness rather than light.

A revealing display of Malcolm's and Windol's inner character came in their reaction to the December 7, 1941, attack on Pearl Harbor. While scores of America's young men rushed to enlist in the military, Malcolm had no wish to go fight in a foreign land. The willingness to die for his country was not in the nineteen-year-old's makeup. Windol was three months past his seventeenth birthday, legally too young to sign up on his own; but had he chosen to do so, he could have asked for his father's permission or lied about his age. Instead, he merely followed the lead of his older brother and did nothing.

When friends began receiving telegrams drafting them into the military, Malcolm wanted no part in it. Besides, Buford Whitt had a solution to his son's desire to avoid induction.

Located on the western outskirts of Huntsville was a U.S. Army post, the Huntsville Arsenal, which had been selected the previous summer as the site of new chemical and munitions manufacturing facilities. With the United States now thrust into war, construction activities on the gigantic complex increased dramatically, from one to three shifts a day.[7] Recognizing the military's need for workers to build the plant, Buford used his contacts to get jobs with an army construction contractor for his sons. He told them that they were safe from the draft as long as they stayed on this critical project.[8] Without that umbrella of protection, he warned, they were prime draft material.

He proved to be exactly right. In early 1942 Malcolm and Windol began constructing the Redstone Ordnance Plant. With the army in a tremendous hurry to build the weapons facility, all workers put in long, difficult hours. The Whitt brothers experienced the grueling pace of the job, laboring harder and longer than they had ever before done or desired to do. Malcolm began complaining about the slavelike conditions for what he considered too low a pay scale.

Exhausting work can cloud a person's ability to reason. Add youthful impatience, a resistance to being bossed around, and an inflated opinion of one's worth, and the result can be poor decision making. Such occurred with Malcolm when another contractor offered him a higher-paying job. But there was a problem—the work would not be for the military. Bucking his father's advice, Malcolm chose to accept the increased pay. He was gambling against the army. Unfortunately for him, the army owned the casino.

Malcolm was inducted on October 23, 1942.[9]

As always, Windol's life paralleled Malcolm's—all the way through reception of the draft notification telegram. Windol took the army oath of duty one month and ten days past his eighteenth birthday, six days after his brother. Afterward, for the first time in his life, Windol's path headed in a totally different direction from that of his brother.

Meanwhile, during the time that Malcolm and Windol were laying bricks at the Huntsville Arsenal, their mother remarried.

Birdie Bell Whitt's return to friends and family in Newport had been good for her. The old zest for life was back, though tempered somewhat by her mid-forties age. Energy had replaced misery; and excitement, drudgery. In

addition to being mentally restorative, the Newport home-
coming had been physically rejuvenating. Making up for
years of neglect to her appearance, Birdie had recovered a
generous portion of her former beauty. With the addition
of a few pounds of natural padding in the right places and
a clothing selection that accentuated the positive, she now
flaunted a voluptuous look. Her combination of attitude,
looks, and maturity resulted in a sensuousness that could
drive a younger man wild.

And it did. Pat Baldridge, twenty-two years younger
than Birdie, lived and worked on a cotton plantation in the
Mississippi Delta near Five Mile Lake, just east of the community of Louise. His father managed the plantation owned
by Birdie's friend, Oscar Sibley.[10] Birdie sometimes visited the
Sibley family and thereby came to know and become involved
with Pat Baldridge. Their age difference, while providing a
juicy subject of gossip to the small town's social circle, mattered none in their romantic relationship.

Birdie and Pat married on April 10, 1942.[11] Pat moved
to his bride's home just south of Newport and began farming.
The two settled into what would be a long, happy, childless
marriage.[12]

Private Malcolm Whitt could not conform to army life.
The military's strict discipline, mind-numbing bureaucracy,
and demand for unquestioned obedience to orders went
against the grain of his undisciplined, self-directed makeup.
He rebelled against authority and went AWOL more than
once. As a stubborn wild stallion refuses to be broken, he
chose punishment over submission, even if it meant being
thrown in the brig, where he was once locked up for a six-
month stretch.[13] While millions of young American men

willingly fought overseas, the reluctant soldier from Alabama battled within the States to keep from being deployed.

In the end, Malcolm Whitt single-handedly accomplished what the might of Axis Powers could not: he outlasted the United States Army. After two tumultuous years, the government abandoned its efforts to make him into a soldier and instead decided that Malcolm would be more valuable to the war effort as a builder. It agreed to release him from military service on the condition that he resume construction work at Huntsville's army post. On October 27, 1944, Malcolm was released from the army "for the good of the service," that euphemistic gray area between an honorable and a dishonorable discharge.[14]

A civilian once again, he defied the army a last time by working for a builder that had nothing to do with the Huntsville Arsenal or the military. In fact, he never fulfilled his part of the release agreement. This minor detail was lost in the maze of government bureaucracy, however; nothing ever came of it.

Windol Whitt's military career followed a far different route from his brother's. Having spent his youth following Malcolm's directions, adjusting to the army merely meant taking orders from a different leader. Accordingly, his transition to military life was trouble free. After basic, he was shipped across the Atlantic, where he spent the next year and a half fighting in Africa and Sicily.[15]

His ticket home came courtesy of a bullet in the right elbow.[16] After his arm was reassembled and rehabilitated, he was honorably discharged from the service. The date of his release brought his life back in sync with Malcolm's, for, amazingly, just as he had been inducted into the army one week after his brother, so was he discharged a week later, on November 3, 1944.[17]

Windol departed the military with two additions to his persona. He was now a prodigious gum chewer. If he was awake, his mouth was in motion attacking a piece of Wrigley's Spearmint like a hungry squirrel assaulting an unwilling acorn. His thin face and pointed jaw accentuated the movement.

Additionally, he began wearing the faded, olive drab Eisenhower jacket that had been part of his uniform. This waist-high coat was an assured part of his wardrobe during cool weather.

Out of the army and reunited in Huntsville, Alabama, the Whitt brothers resumed working together as bricklayers. When each married and had children, it appeared that life was starting to go their way, that their future held a possibility of normalcy. But the influences of a tumultuous past were not to be so easily overcome by these men of fragile character. Turmoil simmered just below the surface.

It was a problem for their families that Malcolm and Windol spent so much time together. As in the past, each brother spurred on the other's wildness, and no one resented it more than the wives. The women could properly center their man's attention on family concerns when their husbands were at home. But when the brothers were together, this domestic focus became blurry. Making the battle of the hearts even less winnable for the women, Malcolm and Windol were frequently away on out-of-town jobs.

A tug-of-war raged within the two men. While a wife and children promoted maturity and steadiness on the one hand, the closeness of an unchecked brother provided an unhealthy pull on the other. The result was a roller-coaster ride of emotions and allegiances that threatened to upend their precarious balancing act at the brink of stability.

The mortar that held everything together was their father. Although Buford Whitt had seen his sons marry and start families, he recognized that within them still lurked an untamed streak. Frequent contact with his sons through their shared occupation allowed him to play an active role in their lives, more so now than during their youth. It was their father's guidance and influence that served as the strand that held Malcolm and Windol together like a cord—but not for long.

The unraveling began when Buford Whitt died in 1947.[18] Soon afterward, the lives of Malcolm and Windol Whitt turned hard in the wrong direction. Windol was arrested on assault charges in June 1947 and placed in Huntsville's Madison County Jail until released on bond.[19] Forgery charges followed in late 1947 and again in August 1948.[20] Malcolm was arrested for assault in September 1948, but this wasn't his first sign of violence. At home, he was beating his wife.[21]

Both men were free while awaiting court dates in the fall of 1948 when they skipped town. It was not surprising— their legal troubles were getting worse, and at home their wives had grown increasingly contemptuous. Moreover, they had a perfect escape destination: Newport, Mississippi.

Leaving their Huntsville families behind, Malcolm and Windol fled to central Mississippi, arriving just before cotton-picking season. It was fortuitous timing, for growers always needed additional labor to harvest their valuable crop before the rains of late autumn, and the Alabama brothers needed work. Their new stepfather, Pat Baldridge—only five years older than Malcolm—arranged jobs on Oscar Sibley's large plantation near Louise, fifty miles west of Newport, which his father managed.

The two fugitives relocated to the huge farm and picked cotton from sunup to sundown. Despite the hard work, their wages were far less than they had made laying bricks. Malcolm and Windol tried to compensate for this drop in earnings by writing hot checks at local businesses, blatantly abusing their welcome. In laid-back communities such as Louise, where Southern hospitality was an ingrained way of life, members of old, established families were given broad leeway for transgressions; but "visitors" were expected to behave, or else. The unneighborly, slap-in-the-face misdeeds of Malcolm and Windol crossed far over the line of impropriety. Besides causing their employer angst and embarrassment, it also resulted in the local sheriff arresting the brothers on forgery charges. After an investigation uncovered open criminal charges in Alabama, they were escorted back to Huntsville and locked up.[22]

Huntsville's justice system was amazingly accommodating to Malcolm and Windol. By the summer of 1949, the men were once again free on bond.[23] Legal laxity notwithstanding, their family situations were in shambles. Malcolm's three young sons barely knew him, and his long-suffering wife, May, was about ready to give up. Windol's wife, Helen, already had. She had taken their two small daughters and moved back to her hometown of Tanner, Alabama.[24]

By August 1949 the brothers were increasingly restless. Hanging over their heads was a lengthy jail sentence should they go to trial in Huntsville as scheduled near the end of the year. Once more, they decided to skip town. This time, however, they headed north.

Their older sister, Louise, lived in Cincinnati, Ohio, a city large enough to provide ample work opportunities as well as anonymity. It offered another fresh start. Malcolm was twenty-eight and Windol twenty-five when they left their wives and children to seek refuge in the Queen City.

Finding jobs quickly, they laid brick for four months and stayed out of trouble. After finishing a construction project in early December, they decided to take off the rest of the month and go south to visit family for the holidays. Afterward, they would return to a hopeful future in Ohio, possibly even bringing their wives and children.

While their intent for the coming weeks was to spend time in both Huntsville and Newport, Malcolm and Windol disagreed about where to go first. They decided to make the choice during the first leg of their journey aboard a bus heading south.

Malcolm (left) and Windol Whitt

Part 2

Fate is a weaver. With the world her loom and eternity her timetable, she is emotionless in creating the intricate fabric of our lives. Drawing from her lap the colorful threads that are people's flesh and souls, the masterful embroiderer interlaces them into a living tapestry of the human condition—awash with infinitely contrasting shades and qualities. Individual threads may fray with time, but the story told in their warp and weft endures as memory.

After decades of patient preparation, as an otherwise unexceptional winter approached, Fate began weaving the threads of a new creation, a tapestry of select filaments of peace and conflict, joy and sorrow, prosperity and poverty, black and white, skillfully woven. This unique composition was not to be a masterpiece of beauty to evoke cries of admiration and wonder, but a work of tragedy to call forth wails of anguish and sorrow.

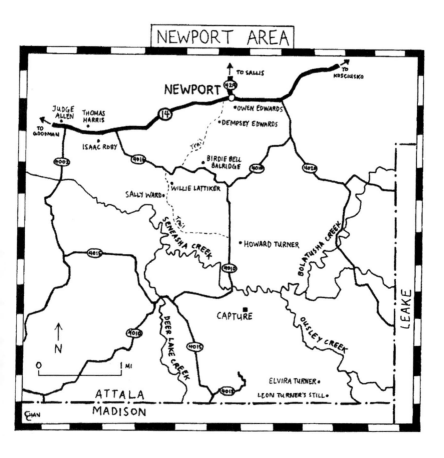

NEWPORT AREA

Chapter 7

Into the Cauldron

D ecember 10, 1949, broke chilly and brilliantly clear in Attala County—a fresh, invigorating Saturday that invited activity. The Turner-Levy family began to stir at dawn, awakened by the rooster's call that served as a natural alarm clock.

Leon Turner threw off the threadbare quilt that barely fit his large frame and rose from the unevenly stuffed mattress that didn't. Three feet away snored his father, Howard Turner. At least the two men had beds to themselves, for each of the other beds in the tiny, run-down shack Leon shared with his father, grandmother, and five half-brothers and -sister held two or more sleepers.

As usual, Leon did not awake in a mood to tolerate the bedlam of morning activity that accompanied the tightly packed household. He dressed quickly and left without a word in his father's pulpwood truck, heading for the solitude of the area's woods and hills. He went for more than just the quiet; the thick forests also offered concealment for his moonshine still located near the crumbling remains of his grandmother's original cabin.

As the rest of the family was waking, Addie Bea "Ape" Levy fired up the wood-burning stove to fix cornbread for breakfast. Ape was relieved that her half-brother left. She wasn't comfortable around Leon. After all, she barely knew him. He had gone to prison when she was seven; and except for a brief period of parole that she slightly remembered, he had been out of her life ever since. Until last year, that is, when she was sixteen. Having completed his lengthy prison sentence, Leon unexpectedly reentered her home and her world. She had understood the circumstances—he was her father's son with apparently nowhere else to go. But that was then. It was now a year later, and he was still here. What she had learned in that time had only increased her unease with the half-brother old enough to be her father.

Ape, who was half-black, knew of Leon's fondness for young Negro girls. And Ape knew that she was attractive. That this large, powerful white man with a violent history and an eye for girls was living in her house frightened her.

Easing her fears somewhat was the presence of her father and grandmother. Howard Turner was a good family man who treated all his children with dignity and fairness. Similarly, his mother, Elvira, was totally committed to her grandchildren. She worked tirelessly on their behalf, though her efforts were now limited by her frailty.

Ape and her siblings were warmly devoted to Howard and Elvira. Leon in particular was strangely fanatical about respecting and obeying the pair. It was Leon's fervent devotion to his father and grandmother that Ape counted on to provide a degree of protection.

Ironically, this loyalty of Leon's would be the cause of her first major confrontation with him.

The incident began when two women made a social call later that same day. Unconventional, free-spirited Rilla Meeks and her great-niece, Martha Harris, walked a long distance to Howard Turner's shack for a friendly visit.[1] Though she enjoyed all of Howard's family, Rilla, a forty-something Negro widow, especially hoped to see Leon, with whom she was having an affair. Upon arriving, Rilla learned that her lover had been gone since dawn. Regardless, she and Martha spent an agreeable time visiting with other members of the family.

Rilla, Howard, and Elvira sat on the front porch discussing the area's happenings. Martha walked around the yard with Ape, chatting with her fellow teenager, schoolmate, and friend. Here and there, Ape's three younger brothers intruded, harassing the two girls as younger brothers do.

At midafternoon, Rilla announced that she and Martha needed to start walking home, for she wanted to be back before dark. Howard then offered to drive them himself. Leon had the only one of Howard's two trucks suitable for more than one person, however, so Howard would have to borrow a car belonging to a neighbor who lived not far away.[2] He volunteered to walk there, get the car, and drive Rilla and Martha home. He told the women to stay put until he returned.

Not everyone appreciated Howard's good intentions. Ape complained that she and Martha didn't want to wait; they would instead walk to Martha's house. Howard again asked her to wait. Ape again objected. At this point, Elvira joined the argument, nagging the girls to wait until Howard came back with the car.

But Ape wasn't going to do it. After her father set off to fetch his neighbor, Ape stated that she and Martha were leaving. While Elvira fussed and Rilla shook her head, the girls walked across the road onto a trail leading north through the woods. Soon, they were out of sight.

Ape and Martha were on one of many paths that cut through the wooded Beat 4. Trampled by decades of foot traffic, the trails provided convenient shortcuts among the scattered houses of the rural community. As the girls walked along, dense woodlands absorbing their gossip and laughter, Howard Turner returned and drove Rilla to her house.

Meanwhile, Leon was on his way home.

Leon Turner drove his father's pulpwood truck along the rugged dirt roads south of Newport like an indestructible man, one who had survived years under the brutal conditions of Parchman Penitentiary. And now he was very inebriated after a day of guzzling moonshine.

The truck skidded to a stop in front of his shack, and Leon stepped clumsily down from the cab, swearing as he stumbled. He shuffled to the porch wearing a scowl that made it plain he didn't want to interact with anybody; he simply wanted to be left alone in the dark places of his own mind.

But it was not to be. Elvira Turner, still sitting in the porch rocking chair, intercepted him. In the manner of old folk who begin discussing a subject at the midpoint as if the listener were intimately familiar with it, she began complaining about Ape and Martha. The girls were young and rude; they didn't have the sense or courtesy to obey Ape's father; they ignored what he asked them to do.

Leon stopped at the porch and listened. Through his alcohol fog, the story of Ape's disobedience to their father sank in. As Elvira continued to talk, a furious pounding filled his ears; a burning heat flushed his face. Any vestige of self-control that Leon owned was overpowered by rage. Ape had to be taught a lesson.

Leon ran behind the house and opened the barbed-wire gate of the small pasture where his horse was kept. He grabbed a bridle draped around a fence post and jammed its bit into the mouth of his scrawny mare. Leaping on the horse bareback, he headed out in search of Ape. Thorny vines and leafless branches grabbed at his clothing as he drove his horse in a full gallop down the half-muddy trail she and Martha had taken minutes before.

Far ahead, the girls leisurely strolled along the pathway. The gentle songs of wrens and sparrows had replaced the din of the large family. Though the air was cool, walking kept them warm. Suddenly, from behind came the sound of swishing branches and thumping. They looked back. A fast-running horse was rushing toward them.

A sliver of fear pierced Ape's heart as she recognized Leon. The sliver became a stake when she looked into his eyes. His stare—wild and hateful—was from a demon in hell. She was in danger.

Everything happened fast. Leon's mouth twisted in a scream of fury. Jerking harshly on the reins, he brought his horse to a halt and slid off the animal's back in one smooth motion. Ape stood frozen as Leon ran at her, cursing and shouting that he was going to kill her. Before she could react, he shoved her roughly to the ground and began punching and slapping her. Blow after blow, he beat her savagely about the body and head. Ape screamed and tried to cover her face with her arms, but it did little good. She was helpless against the out-of-control onslaught by a man with twice her weight and ten times her strength. In the midst of the nightmare, she began crying.

Martha backed away from the violence, overwhelmed by the sounds of Ape's screams, Leon's shouts, and the pounding of hands against body. For a moment she was stunned; then she recovered.

She had to flee!

Martha turned away and bolted in panic down the trail. After what seemed like hours, expecting at any moment to hear Leon approaching from behind, she reached a cluster of shacks. One belonged to Willie Latiker, who Martha knew well. "Miz Willie" was around fifty and a grandmother many times over.[3]

Martha sprinted to Willie's front door and frantically beat on its weather-peeled face until the door jerked opened, revealing a surprised Willie Latiker wearing an apron around her plump waist and a faded red scarf on her graying hair. Before Willie could speak, Martha began babbling. Words tumbled out in broken gasps: "Leon Turner . . . killing my friend . . . ran away . . . need to hide." Willie pulled the child into her home and slammed the door.

Leon thrashed his defenseless sister until she stopped moving. Only then did his rage begin to subside and his senses began to register the towering trees, the smell of crushed grass, Ape's whimpering. Martha! He swiveled his head from side to side looking for the girl, but she was gone. As Ape cowered on the ground, Leon jumped on his horse and headed down the trail, pushing the animal as hard as it could go.

The first house he came to belonged to a black woman named Sally Ward. Children were playing outside her shack. Leon came to a stop and asked if they had seen a girl running. Blank looks and headshakes were the reply. He kicked his horse into a run.

Shortly, he came to Willie Latiker's shack. Willie didn't have a husband, he knew, and her grown sons no longer lived there. She was a damn nosy woman—nothing went on that she didn't know about.

Turner sprang from his horse and stepped onto her porch. Leather heels and a long gait made the intimidating sound of a big man as he strode to the front door. He banged on it solidly four times with a tightly clenched fist, threatening to splinter the wood. Before he could strike again, the door abruptly opened. Willie planted herself with feet wide apart in the middle of the doorway and glared nearly a foot upward into the eyes of the unwelcome intruder.

Leon looked mean and he looked mad. The first words out of his mouth were a demand: "Tell me where the girl is that came through here!"

Anyone who knew Willie Latiker knew that she didn't put up with an attitude from anyone. With clenched jaw and squinting eyes, she ignored the command and fired back, accusing Leon of running around like a king expecting people to do what he wanted.

Turner asked again about Martha, but Willie denied knowing what he was talking about—she'd been cooking supper for her "chillun." But when Leon threatened to come in and look around, she suggested that she *may* have glimpsed someone running a few minutes ago, heading north toward Newport.

Then, in the rudest and most unmistakable of terms, she told Leon to get away from her house and leave her alone.

Leon cursed her.

Willie merely crossed her arms and remained astride the doorway.

Spitting one last curse, Leon turned and walked off the porch. He mounted his horse and took off north along the trail.

Willie breathed deeply as she leaned against the doorframe and watched the white trash leave. She watched until convinced that Leon was not returning. Only then did she bring Martha out of hiding and send her running in the opposite direction of her pursuer.[4]

By the end of an hour, Leon's fury was subsiding. He continued his search, but at a walking pace, asking anyone he passed if they had seen the girl. All gave negative answers; the trail was cold.

Eventually, Leon rode along Highway 14 west of Newport with the setting sun in his face. To his right, beyond a roadside ditch cluttered with broom sage, sat a shack. Gazing at the house, he saw a woman sitting alone on the front porch. There was still enough light to see that it was Mary Ella Harris.

Mary Ella was at the house with her five children. Her husband, Thomas, had been away in Alabama for close to two months making money.

Even though Thomas was a highly capable farmer, being a sharecropper meant he would never earn much from his labor. He brought in a few extra dollars gambling and selling moonshine for Leon Turner, but Mary Ella intensely disliked these activities.

Several months ago, following the birth of their latest child, James, Thomas had heard about road construction jobs in Alabama. They offered steady wages, a workday less than sunup to sundown, and only six working days a week. He and Mary Ella had agreed that he would move to Alabama and work on the roads as soon as the fall's cotton harvest was complete. He would work there until it was time for spring planting. They would then see how much money he made working on the highway and decide whether to keep farming in Newport or move the family to Alabama.

Thomas relocated to Alabama after the cotton crop had been sold. The wages he had since earned allowed him to wire money home during the time of year he previously had to borrow funds for the family to survive. It was regrettable that the job took him away from his wife and children, but he would soon be coming home for Christmas.[5]

Mary Ella was sitting on her porch lost in thought about her husband's return in a few days. The money he had sent home had been a blessing, allowing her to buy school clothing for the children and extra food. The Alabama job seemed to be a good thing.

The daydream ended when movement on the road caught her attention. She saw that it was merely Leon Turner on his horse. From her home's location on the road leading to Holmes County and its bars, Mary Ella was used to seeing Leon come and go. Usually, he passed without paying her any mind; this time, however, he was looking at her.

He shouted something, but she could not understand.

"What you want?" she said in a flat, emotionless voice. Her tone, as well as her body language, reflected irritation.

From his horse, Leon yelled, "I said have you done seen Martha Harris comin' down here."

Mary Ella looked down the road and replied, "No." Just one word; fractious, frigid, and final. Then she stood and went inside.[6]

Leon booted his horse forward with an angry kick. He didn't look back at Mary Ella, but her haughty attitude had gotten to him.

Leon Turner never did find Martha. No matter, for the beating he gave Ape had assuaged part of his anger. What stuck with him now—unfinished business that would gnaw at him as the days counted down until Christmas—was the rude way that certain people had treated him during his search, people like Willie Latiker and Mary Ella Harris.

•   •   •

On the same day that Leon was pummeling Ape and hunting for Martha, Malcolm and Windol Whitt were heading south on a four-hundred-mile bus ride from Cincinnati. They were going to pay a holiday visit to the two widely separated branches of their family. At both destinations, they faced potential for conflict.

Their departures the last time they visited had been under bad circumstances. During their stay in Mississippi a year ago, they had tried to swindle their mother's friends. In Huntsville this past summer, they had jumped bail and headed out of town, leaving behind their wives and children.

But Malcolm and Windol had been in one mess or another since their youth; and relatives in both states, though knowing all about their past transgressions, were still willing to forgive and forget. Malcolm and Windol would be warmly welcomed with hugs and handshakes. Nevertheless, kinfolk would be guarding their wallets until the two rascals left.

The Greyhound Silverside bus rambled southward along U.S. 31 through Louisville and Nashville, soaking its passengers in an atmosphere of diesel exhaust, tobacco smoke, body odor, and a nearly full septic tank. On board, the Whitts had still not decided their first destination. Malcolm wanted to head to his wife and children in Huntsville; Windol wanted to begin with Newport relatives. They tossed the choices back and forth without either brother giving in. Even as their bus crossed from Tennessee into Alabama, the matter had not been settled.

A few miles south of the state line, the bus stopped at the depot in Athens, Alabama, where the passengers got off to stretch their legs. The Athens bus station was at the intersection of two major highways, which meant the time for a decision had arrived. The brothers could get back on the same Greyhound and continue south on U.S. 31—the route leading to Mississippi; or they could switch to a different bus and follow U.S. 72 east to Huntsville.

They stood inside the terminal's small waiting area swigging soft drinks, watching fellow passengers mill about. Windol pulled a crumpled pack of gum from his pants pocket and helped himself to a fresh stick. At the same time, Malcolm pulled a quarter from his pocket. They agreed to let a coin flip decide the destination: heads to Newport, and tails to Huntsville.

Malcolm flipped the coin high into the air. As the brothers watched the silvery piece tumble end over end, they had no idea of the major impact this solo flight of a coin would have on their destinies. The coin dropped to the floor between them, rolled on its edge for a few inches, and fell over motionless. Malcolm and Windol bent over to observe the upward face. Windol smiled—a win was a win no matter how trivial. "Heads," he deadpanned. He had just announced his future.

Minutes later, the Whitts were on the bus headed southwest, and they arrived at the Kosciusko, Mississippi, bus depot the next day. After retrieving their bags, Malcolm and Windol settled into a bench inside the terminal and lit up cigarettes. The day before, at the Athens bus station, they had telegraphed their mother to inform her of today's arrival time. Now they sat down to smoke and wait.

Not thirty minutes later, Birdie Bell Baldridge drove up in a dust-covered Buick and parked in front of the terminal. The Birdie that got out of the car looked much different than the Birdie of past years. Her red hair was now streaked with gray; her face bore the tanned wrinkles of a farmwife; her clothes were simple. And now, a twig used to reposition snuff jutted from her mouth.[7]

Soon Birdie and her two sons were on the road for the short drive to Newport. It was Sunday, December 11, 1949. Malcolm and Windol planned to visit relatives in Newport over the next two weeks. After Christmas, they would retrace their bus route back to Athens, then switch to the bus bound for the Huntsville side of the family.

Their itinerary, however, was about to change. Fate had her own set of plans.

Chapter 8
Drunken Trouble

For eleven days, Malcolm and Windol Whitt lived at their mother's farm and visited relatives. It was a relaxing period spent sitting on porches, in living rooms, or around dinner tables telling about life in Cincinnati.

The brothers returned the hospitality by sometimes helping with chores or repairs. One such opportunity arose when visiting their mother's brother, Owen Edwards. The pump of his water well was housed in an old wooden shed. Edwards wanted to replace it with a concrete block structure, a natural job for Malcolm and Windol. They offered to do the work, figuring it would take little more than a day to demolish the existing structure and build a new one in its place.[1]

A stiff breeze sent low clouds scurrying across the sky as Malcolm and Windol worked at Uncle Owen's house on the morning of Thursday, December 22, 1949. Quickly tearing down the existing woodshed, they laid a square base of concrete blocks surrounding the water pump and put a layer of blocks atop these. Then another, and another. Being an experienced team, they progressed rapidly. By lunchtime, the new pump house was well underway.

The men took a break when their uncle came home for lunch. Sitting on the front porch eating, Owen commented that the clouds looked like rain coming.

Sure enough, after Malcolm and Windol resumed work, the sky darkened. The deep rumble of distant thunder began.

An ominous line of charcoal-gray clouds appeared on the northern horizon, advancing steadily toward Newport. Gusts of strong wind swirled leaves and grit into the air. Soon drops of rain accompanied the wind. All the while, the menacing line of round clouds rolled closer and closer. Seemingly right above the treetops, they churned and roiled angrily, warning of impending havoc to the earth below. The sky behind this harbinger of deluge was a hazy curtain of blue-gray, illuminated sporadically by lightning.

When treetops whipped about violently, the brothers began gathering up their tools. A strong gust brought a blast of cold air. Windol paused to button his Eisenhower jacket.

Then the rain came in a torrent, lashed by the wind into sheets of stinging pinpricks, cold upon the face. Hands full of shovels and trowels, Malcolm dashed for the nearby barn. Windol followed with a wheelbarrow of mortar. Both were cussing and laughing as they reached cover.

Waves of storm-driven rain drenched the surrounding countryside as they waited in the barn. Vapor from their breath turned visible as the temperature plummeted.

But as quickly as the storm had come, it receded, and the downpour reduced to a light trickle. Now free to leave the barn, Malcolm and Windol talked about going somewhere to get warm. Just down Highway 14 was the mercantile store owned by William and Zetha McDaniel. This time of the year, the owners kept a wood stove burning, making the establishment cozy and inviting. The Whitts decided to walk there and have a soft drink while they dried out.

McDaniel's Grocery was a single-story, wood-frame structure with tin signs of various shapes and sizes covering an aging coat of blistered and peeling white paint. Inside was a U-shaped counter atop which sat a hoop cheese box and cutter, an NCR cash register, a set of scales, and two large Tom's cookie bins—one with and one without raisins. Wooden shelves around the store's walls held a small variety of food staples.

The centerpiece of the grocery store was a black potbellied stove. In the spring and summer, it served as a fresh flower rack; in winter, however, the stove always had a fire burning within. A ring of ladder-back chairs surrounding it made the toasty warm spot a popular gathering place.[2]

Two of the chairs were now occupied. Store owner William McDaniel—everybody called him "B"—was in one. As he added another piece of red oak to the fire, B commented that this blue norther might call for some coal tomorrow. Sitting beside him, Leon Turner lazily nodded his head in agreement. Leon had dashed into his cousin McDaniel's store during the rain. His coat lay draped over the chair back above a small puddle of water on the tobacco-stained wood floor.

Picking at dirt under his fingernail, Leon was about to respond to B's comment when the sound of a stretching spring stopped him. He glanced toward the store's entrance and saw the screen door open inward. In stepped two men, younger fellows. They looked alike. He didn't know them.

Windol Whitt pulled the outside door closed and followed Malcolm into the pleasantly warm establishment. He saw Mr. McDaniel and a stranger sitting close to the stove. Considering the numerous visits the Whitt brothers had made to Newport, it was surprising they had never run across Leon Turner. They had heard of him, of course.

Malcolm and Windol took seats opposite the stove from the other men, and the four proceeded to carry on an introductory conversation. Even though it's ordinary for residents of the Deep South to wave, have eye contact with, and talk to total strangers—and enjoy doing so—the first minutes of a meeting are a dance of innuendo and I-know-your-cousin friendliness. For men, it's an opportunity to determine the others' mettle and to find out where they like to hunt and fish. Leon could be a master at country neighborliness. Though this side of his personality had been subdued for years, the old Leon who drew people to him like mosquitoes to a leg lay just below the surface. It simply had to be the right time to bring him out.

And now was right. In only a few minutes, the Whitt brothers and Leon Turner were getting along as if they had grown up together.

McDaniel asked his visitors if they wanted anything to drink. Leon ordered a round of Cokes and flipped the owner a quarter. B moseyed to the back of the store and soon returned with bottles for his customers and a dime in change for Leon. Then he left to attend to business behind the counter.

After the three men took a swallow from their drinks, Leon said, "Let's give 'em a little kick, boys. This'll warm you up good." He pulled a half-pint bottle of moonshine from his coat pocket and poured some into his Coke. He passed the flask to Malcolm and Windol, who copied Leon; and the men drank.

Warmth spread throughout their bodies as they downed swig after swig, swiftly consuming the bottle of 'shine. Leon drew a second half-pint from his coat, and B brought another round of Coca-Colas. Before long, a party was in full swing at McDaniel's Grocery. By the time the second bottle of hooch was drained, loud talking and laughter filled the store. Leon took out a third bottle; and it, too, soon lay on the floor with the other empties.[3] By now, the usually tranquil atmosphere of the country store was history. The men were outrageously, gloriously drunk; but they were also out of whiskey.

"Come on," Leon said. "Let's go get some more." He was just getting started. Saying goodbye to the relieved proprietor, the rowdies staggered outside.

The air was cold and the sky overcast, though it had stopped drizzling. Leon led the way as the group walked an unsteady course to the house of another of Leon's cousins, Billy McDaniel.[4] Billy had some 'shine on hand, and he was more than willing to share it.

Malcolm and Windol had started the day intending to build their uncle's pump house. As the afternoon grew late, their plan had been erased by a large measure of whiskey. Dusk was now pushing the landscape into darkness. Also darkening was the dynamic of the gathering.

Some people become surly when they drink. The rush of pleasure and fun accompanying the first gulps of alcohol are eventually replaced by feelings of irritation and impatience. Such was the case with Leon Turner. In addition to being an angry person by nature, he also tended to take over any situation and do things his way. Alcohol, especially in large quantities, only amplified Leon's undesirable attributes. In a phrase, Leon Turner was a bad drunk.

As the afternoon progressed, Leon gradually transitioned from a good old boy into an angry, controlling tyrant. He became foul-mouthed, brutish, and threatening.

At some point, Leon thought back on his recent chase of Martha and how some women had been disrespectful to him, acting all high and mighty like they thought they were better than him.

"Come on!" urged Leon.

A jug of moonshine being passed around occupied Malcolm's and Windol's attention. By the time Malcolm registered the words and looked over at Leon, the man was already walking off. Malcolm grabbed his brother's arm and pulled him in the direction of their new friend.

There was barely enough light to see by as they hurried down a dirt road and caught up with Leon. Soon the trio entered a trail, the same one that Ape and Martha had walked two weeks before. The men were soused, and they did not attempt to hide it. The ruckus they created easily sliced through the surrounding quiet.

Down the trail, Willie Latiker sat rocking in her house, watching two grandbabies play. She was contentedly humming her favorite gospel song when a noise wafted in from outside. It was the sound of men laughing and shouting. Willie wasn't alarmed—teenage boys lived down the path, and they often talked loudly and cut up as they walked past her house.

But as the commotion drew closer, she could tell that it wasn't the boys she knew. The men she could hear were white. Listening carefully, she realized they had halted right in front of her house. Her skin turned ice-cold as she recognized one of the voices. Willie put her finger to her mouth and tried to shush her grandchildren.

Then, the outside noise disappeared. She strained to hear, but there was nothing. Maybe they went away.

BOOM! BOOM! BOOM! Blows on the front door caused Willie to jump. *BOOM! BOOM!* A voice on the other side of the door shouted, "Miz Willie!" The words were slurred.

Panic gripped her. She stood and looked at her grandchildren, who were oblivious to everything but their wooden spools. Her eyes went back to the door, staring at it in terror.

The pounding began again, but this time it didn't stop. "Let me in, goddamnit!"

Willie Latiker lost it. She bolted to the rear of the house, yanked open the back door, and ran out into the dark.

Simultaneously, Leon Turner kicked the front door open and burst into the house. He held a pistol waist high.[5]

A lantern on a corner dresser and a small fire in the fireplace dimly lit the room. Two toddlers played on a blanket on the floor.

Leon searched through the small house, waving his weapon dangerously as he peered into darkened rooms. No one else was home. Cursing, he strode out the front door and walked past Malcolm and Windol.

To the Whitts, the episode was a mystery. They had stood together in the yard watching their companion kick in the door of a Negro shack and disappear inside. They had no idea who lived there or what Leon was doing.

Leon could care less what the Whitt brothers thought. He was angry with Willie Latiker. The open back door . . . she had obviously run from him.

Willie had not run far—only to the nearby home of Sally Ward.

As the midwife who had delivered most babies of the area, Sally was revered by all the local women.[6] At forty-eight, she was the mother of eleven children by various men. Seven children and grandchildren presently lived in her five-room house.[7]

Willie ran to Sally's door and knocked urgently, the type of knock that at Sally's house usually meant help needed for a birth. The door cracked open, and a young girl peered out. Without saying a word, Willie carefully opened the door wider and hurried into the house. She ran through the main room, uncharacteristically ignoring children who were gathered around a burning fireplace and three beds, and hastened into the kitchen. Dashing to a stove near the corner, she squatted between it and the wall.

Sally Ward rushed in and asked her friend what was wrong, but Latiker was mute. It was a worrisome sight. Willie was a tough woman, not one to be frightened of anything; yet she seemed to be petrified.

Willie's behavior disturbed Sally's sixteen-year-old daughter, Flowery. Although married, Flowery Ward Levy was temporarily living with her mother while her husband looked for a job in St. Louis, Missouri. Recovering from a premature birth five weeks earlier, she spent most of her time resting in a bed next to the fireplace with her infant.[8] But now, after seeing Willie so oddly rush past her, Flowery cradled her baby and joined other family members gawking at the visitor.

All eight inhabitants of the house were gathered in the kitchen either talking to or talking about Willie Latiker. Suddenly, a frightful sound at the front door overcame the voices—pounding, insistent pounding. It was not like Willie's sharp, hurried plea to enter; this was a strong, loud command to enter.

Revived by the battering sound, Willie Latiker blurted, "Leon Turner is coming!" Grunting, she rose to her feet and fled out the back door.[9]

Sally instantly grasped the situation. She knew well of Leon and his explosiveness; if it was *he* who was hammering at the door, there would be trouble. Sally rushed toward the front door, but before she got there, Leon Turner opened it and came inside the house.

The midwife stopped short. "What you doin' in my house?" she demanded.

Leon shoved her aside and came forward. Frightened children drew back as he passed. "I want something to eat," he said, going into the kitchen.

Sally kept her eyes on the intruder, but only for a second. Sensing movement behind her, she spun around and saw two other white men come through the door. Malcolm and Windol Whitt hesitated a moment as they looked about, then walked to the fireplace and turned their backsides to its warmth.

Although she did not know what was going on, Sally knew that the situation was bad. Reaching out, she drew twelve-year-old Mary Katherine to her and whispered into her granddaughter's ear. The girl nodded and slipped quietly into another room. Out of the view of the invaders, she retrieved a tin can from underneath a bed. The can contained a few coins and dollar bills—the family's church money.[10] Clutching the container like it was pure gold, Mary Katherine snuck out the front door.

Leon scrounged for food in the kitchen. He opened the cupboard and shoved aside sundry cans and jars. From a tin on a countertop, he tore off a piece of bread and stuffed it in his mouth.

At that moment, a female voice told him to leave. Pivoting toward the source of this defiance, Leon saw that it was Flowery Levy standing nearby with her baby.

His eyes roamed over the young girl's body. He moved to her and squeezed her upper arm. "Whose baby is this, girl?"

"Mine!" Flowery snapped. Revolted by the touch, she recoiled toward the door. Leon grabbed her shoulders from behind and kissed the back of her neck. Flowery again jerked forward. She hurried a few steps to her bed and sat down, clutching her baby tightly.

Leon followed. He leaned down and touched his lips to hers. Flowery turned her head, but Leon grabbed her chin roughly and forced her mouth toward his. He told her to kiss him.

She did. Leon reeked of moonshine.

Then he put his hands on her.

Chaos erupted. Young children cried; older children shouted. At the fireplace, Malcolm laughed and shouted encouragement to Leon. Windol remained silent.

Flowery began to shake. Finally, unable to bear more, she wailed.

Her reaction infuriated Leon. He stepped back and stood at full height, towering over the small girl. His right hand lashed out and slapped the top of Flowery's head.

No sooner had his fingers registered the sting of the hit than a pair of hands shoved him forcefully toward the fireplace. Leon stumbled, coming close to the flames, but regained his balance. Flushed with anger and primed for assault, he turned to face his attacker. Astonishingly, it was Sally Ward, all 160 pounds of her.[11]

"You leave that girl alone!" Sally shouted. Her fists were clenched and her elbows bent. She was ready to fight.

Turning his full attention to this daring woman, Leon shook his head and chuckled—a sinister sound, like that of a rattlesnake before it strikes. He moved to Sally and pushed her roughly onto the bed next to Flowery.

Sally wore a calf-high dress with cotton tights beneath. Leon knelt down and ran his hands over her thick legs, pinching the tights. He pulled a pocketknife from his pants pocket and unfolded the blade. Sticking the knifepoint into a small hole in Sally's stocking above her right ankle, he started slitting the fabric. Slowly, he brought the blade up her leg.

The room was quiet except for the soft sobs of crying children. By the fireplace, the two Whitt brothers stood transfixed.

Sitting on the bed next to her mother, Flowery Levy watched the stocking being sliced. What initially was shock and fear became anger at her mother's humiliation. Seeing a leather shoe nearby on the floor, Flowery stretched out and grasped it by the toe. Straightening up, she slammed its heel into Leon's head.

The force of the impact was nothing to the sizable drunken man—more like a mosquito bite than a wasp sting. It was primarily the sound that got Leon's attention. Turning away from Sally's leg, he snarled at Flowery, "I'm 'on' whoop your ass."

"You 'n' who else?" she responded.[12]

While Leon was creating bedlam at Sally Ward's house, two escapees from the scene, Willie Latiker and Mary Katherine Ward, were seeking help, albeit each from a different source.

Following her dash from Sally's house, Willie went back to her place, grabbed her coat, and took the grandchildren home. Realizing that she and her neighbors were defenseless against Leon Turner, she then headed to the one person who could stop him, Judge John Allen.

Willie walked rapidly along muddy Highway 14 with head down and crossed arms hugging her body. The biting wind penetrated through her threadbare coat as if it wasn't there. Breathing heavily, she struggled to keep going. Finally, the lights of Judge Allen's house came into view.

When Willie knocked on the judge's front door, Eudora Allen Smithson opened it. At age fifty-one the oldest of his three children and his only daughter, Eudora and her husband, Pat Smithson, lived with her mother and father.[13] Eudora was a happy person who thrived in her environment and adored her father's land and the sharecroppers who lived on it. The names and histories of each family were as familiar to her as the members of her own household. Her love for them was genuine.

And the sharecroppers loved her. They knew that if they needed help in any way, "Miss Eudora" would take care of it. Thus, a sense of comfort swept over Willie Latiker when she was greeted by Miss Eudora's smile.

Likewise, Eudora recognized Willie Latiker. The two women had known each other practically their whole lives. They had played together as children. As she now saw the expression and the sweat on her visitor's face, Eudora's eyebrows furrowed with concern. Something was wrong. Eudora opened the door wide.

Willie gratefully stepped into the cozy warmth of the entryway. The smell of fresh cedar permeated the air; a gaily decorated Christmas tree stood before a window in the living room. A gas floor heater stood along the far wall of the room, its red-glowing ceramic inviting her near to soak in the heat. But there was no time to enjoy the comfortable surroundings or engage in the customary small talk before getting to the subject of the visit. People were in danger.

She launched abruptly into her story, telling Eudora of the surprise visit to her house by Leon Turner, of her flight to Sally Ward's place, and of Turner's subsequent appearance there. Speaking loudly, her voice carried through the house and drew Eudora's parents and husband to the room.

Judge Allen invited Willie to sit at the dining room table. He lit a fresh cigar and sat beside her. As the others took seats opposite them, the judge asked Willie to tell her story. Willie recounted what she had heard about Leon beating his sister. She told of hiding Martha Levy several days ago as Leon looked for her. Then she went again into what happened less than an hour ago at her and Sally Ward's houses.

Thoroughly familiar with Leon's violent temper, Judge Allen knew that Leon was on a dangerous tirade. It was time to get the sheriff.

Newport did not have telephone service. The only way to make a call was to get closer to Kosciusko, from where phone lines were gradually being extended outward. Judge Allen therefore asked Pat Smithson to call Sheriff Roy Braswell from a friend's house in Sallis.[14]

Within minutes, the night was pierced by a lone set of headlights heading north from Newport on Highway 429. Smithson knew it would take fifteen minutes or so to reach Sallis and additional time for the sheriff to respond. No telling what could be happening to those poor people in the hands of Leon Turner. He inched the gas pedal closer to the floorboard.

As Willie Latiker made her way to Judge Allen's house, twelve-year-old Mary Katherine Ward was well ahead of her. Accompanied by the sound of jostling coins in the tin can she held, Mary Katherine had hurried along the trail by her house to County Road 4016, then to Highway 14, where she headed west a short distance. Now nearly a mile from her home, Mary Katherine ran up to the back door of a house and rapped on it loudly. Opening the door, Mrs. Isaac Roby was surprised to see her young neighbor after dark.

"Mamaw said for Ike to come over to our house," Mary Katherine stated.[15] She didn't elaborate—she just did what her grandmother had told her.

At the Roby house was Isaac Roby Jr., or Ike. Also known by "Whiskey," the strapping twenty-three-year-old lived at home with the rest of his family. His mother called him to the back door and told him to go with Mary Katherine to her house. Ike grumbled, but he had nothing better to do. He grabbed his pistol—a normal part of his gear—and headed out the door. Once outside, he reconsidered the gun. Whatever the Wards wanted him to do would not require a weapon, so he went back inside and left it there. Then he and Mary Katherine strolled up the trail toward her house.

Ike surged well ahead of the girl and soon came to Sally Ward's shack. Nothing looked amiss from the outside; Ike had no warning as he stepped onto the porch and casually knocked on the door.

Inside, Leon Turner heard the relaxed tapping. He walked to the front door and yanked it open. Standing before him with a confused look was the young man he knew as Whiskey. Leon reached out and grabbed him by the shirt, ripping off a button in the process, and pulled him into the house.[16]

Ike Roby gave no resistance as he was dragged inside. The next thing he knew, he was standing by the fireplace alongside Sally Ward's family and two unfamiliar white men.

Leon was in absolute control of the situation, free to do as he pleased. He took his time searching the place, looking for money or anything else that struck his fancy. As the home invasion drew out, the Whitt brothers also made themselves at home. The three intruders even forced Sally Ward to cook supper for them.[17]

Later that evening, another young black appeared. Tommy C. "Bo" Roby had gone first to Ike's house to hang out with his cousin. He had been redirected to Sally Ward's and, as a result, ended up subdued by Leon Turner, standing helplessly by the fireplace with Ike.

After well over two hours, Leon finally grew bored. He had found no money or liquor, and the hostages were totally cowed. Some of the children were even asleep on the floor.

But Leon was not ready to quit. He wanted another drink, and he wanted more action, the kind driven by his tendency to get amorous when drunk.

His thoughts turned to good-looking Mary Ella Harris and her daughter Verlene. Leon had heard that Mary Ella's husband was back in town, but that was of little concern—he had always dominated Thomas. Thomas might even have some moonshine on hand.

Unconcerned about the youngsters nearby, Leon talked freely and crudely of his desires. He told Windol and Malcolm that he knew a place where they could have some women and get more whiskey.

At last, Leon was ready to move on, but he had a problem. If released, the two young black men who had wandered into his clutches would undoubtedly go get other men, a scenario that Leon did not want to face. Leon pulled his pistol and pointed it toward Whiskey and Bo Roby. "You boys are comin' with us."

Into the December night walked five men. They formed an odd assemblage: two white brothers from Alabama, visitors to the area; two young black men, uncertain and subdued; and a shock-haired, cruel-eyed white man, hardened by life and desensitized by years in the state pen.

They were headed to another black household—the third of the night. Only the grim mind of Leon Turner foresaw what lay in store once they arrived.

The pump house started by Malcolm and Windol Whitt as it is today. It was eventually completed after the brothers' arrests left it unfinished.

Chapter 9
The Ordeal

Thomas and Mary Ella Harris and their five children lived in an unpainted four-room shack two miles west of Newport. Both rooms at the front of the shack had a window looking south at Highway 14 and a door leading out onto a porch. The room on the left, as seen from the front yard, was the main bedroom, containing two beds, a table and chair, and a chifforobe. The right room served as a living room, with three cushioned chairs and a small table, and a bedroom, with two beds and a dresser.

A lean-to at the rear of the house contained the kitchen and another room they called the "back room". Its only furnishing was a bale of cotton sitting in the middle of the floor that served as an indoor toy for the children. Each of the rear rooms had a door leading to the backyard.[1]

The entire structure sat on a slight downhill slope, requiring the house front to be raised off the ground on unsure columns of bricks and concrete blocks. Three wobbly steps led down from the center of the front porch to a featureless yard.

Though the Harris cabin was similar in size and appearance to those of the other sharecroppers living on Judge Allen's property, it alone had electricity.[2] Electric wiring to the area was strung high on wooden poles standing like creosote stalagmites along Highway 14. A lone cable sagging from this main line to Mary Ella and Thomas's house presented visible evidence of one-upmanship for which the family took pride.

Because the Harris's had little money to buy modern conveniences, the utility was used for only two functions. A radio in the living room provided entertainment, and a naked seventy-five-watt lightbulb hanging from the main bedroom ceiling provided light.[3] A long cotton pull-string, stained brown from countless oily hands, turned the light on or off.

A stone fireplace in the middle of the main bedroom's west wall made this the warmest room of the house. Accordingly, the women and little children slept here. Mary Ella, Nell, and baby James shared a bed beneath the front window; Verlene and May C.'s bed was four feet away. The adjacent living/bed room, darker and colder than the main bedroom, was the men's area where Thomas and Frankie each had their own bed.

On December 22, 1949, just after 10:00 p.m., Mary Ella was in bed with her two youngest children. She didn't mind their wiggling—she found their closeness satisfying and comforting. Providing an extra measure of contentment tonight was the knowledge that her husband slept in the next room.

Thomas had come home from Alabama two days before. He had even brought Christmas presents for the children and Mary Ella.[4] The children had been unbelievably excited to see the gifts; they had never before known such bounty. The gaily wrapped presents now lay under the family's modest but beloved Christmas tree in the living room.

Mary Ella had been impressed by her husband's thoughtfulness. When he later told her that he had missed her, Mary Ella had been thrilled. At last, her man seemed to be settling down. She allowed herself to feel hope and happiness—emotions repressed since her youth.

In the next room, Thomas lay awake in bed, contemplating the future. His road construction job was going well; if it continued, he would stop farming altogether. Quitting would be difficult—he loved nurturing tiny seeds into a bountiful harvest using his bare hands. But farming was so unpredictable; too many variables were beyond his control.

As Thomas and Mary Ella drifted off to sleep, the house was peaceful and quiet. Only the occasional sizzle and crackle of burning logs in the fireplace and the ticking of a clock on the dresser disturbed the stillness.

And then came knocking. Mary Ella and Thomas both stirred in their beds and waited.

The knocks came again, longer and louder, from the main bedroom door.

Thomas spoke into the darkness. "Who's knockin'?"

"Dammit. You know who I is," came a voice from outside.[5]

Indeed, Thomas knew. Leon Turner. What was *he* doing here? Sometimes Leon came by during the day, dealing with moonshine or money; but the last time had been months ago. And he had never shown up *this* late.

Thomas threw off the covers and pulled on his pants. The floor felt cold as he walked barefoot into the adjacent room. In the flickering light from the fire, the string dangling from the middle of the ceiling was barely visible. He grabbed it and gently yanked downward. Light flooded the room.

Squinting in the sudden brightness, Thomas glanced left and saw Mary Ella watching him. In the other bed, Verlene pulled a quilt over her head. Thomas shuffled to the front door, flipped up a hook latch, and opened the door.

A pistol was pointing at his stomach. Holding it was Leon Turner. Leon kept his firearm leveled at Thomas and stepped through the door.

A gust of cold air fluttered the window curtains above Mary Ella's head as she watched Leon come through the doorway. Instinctively, she pulled Nell and James to her.

Ike and Bo Roby followed Leon into the house with heads hung low. This surprised Mary Ella; she had no idea these boys were involved with Turner. Perhaps their presence was good, for if trouble arose, they would surely help. It would be Bo, Ike, and Thomas against Leon. But then Malcolm and Windol Whitt walked in and her glimmer of hope was extinguished. Mary Ella had no idea who these two white men were.

The small room was crowded. Thomas, Leon, Ike, Bo, Windol, and Malcolm stood facing the fireplace, with two beds of people behind them.

In one bed, eight-year-old May C. had her arms around her big sister's waist. Verlene was trying to be brave for her sibling, but actually she was scared to death. She knew that Leon wanted her, and he was standing only a few feet away. Verlene clutched the covers concealing her nightgown tightly against her neck.

Leon Turner stuck the pistol in his waistband and turned his back to the fire. Before him, lying vulnerable in their beds, were two women that had long been objects of his desire. He was in total control, able to do anything he wanted. His loins responded to the thought.

But there were other needs to satisfy first. Miles of walking along wet, muddy roads had soaked his shoes and socks. He told Thomas to add more wood to the fire. Thomas fetched several pieces of split pine from a stack on the porch and soon had the blaze roaring.

Thomas also gathered chairs for the six men, and all sat facing the blazing fire. Malcolm was closest to the front door, then Thomas. Leon sat closest to the flames with his legs stretched out, ankles crossed, vapor rising from his shoes. Next to him were Windol, then Ike and Bo Roby.[6] Leon pulled out a crumpled pack of Camels from his shirt pocket and tapped out a cigarette. After lighting it and flicking the match into the fireplace, he leaned back and slowly exhaled a lungful of smoke into the air.

Cocking his head toward Thomas, he asked, "You got some whiskey?"

Thomas paused. "Sho' do."

"My friends here wanna buy some."

"Two dollars," Thomas quoted his standard price for a half-pint.

Windol fished a worn leather wallet from his back pocket, pulled out a couple of one-dollar bills, and handed them to Thomas.[7]

Thomas stuffed the bills into his pants pocket as he stood. He walked into his bedroom and retrieved a pair of tar-covered work boots from under his bed. While wrestling them on, he glanced anxiously at his family. Then he walked out the back door.

With liquor on the way, Leon turned his attention to Verlene. She lay in bed with eyes closed; pretty, young, dark-skinned—irresistible.

The silence was broken by the sliding of Leon's chair, then heavy footsteps. In a moment, Leon stood at Verlene's bedside, staring down at her. Her head was even with his thighs.

Verlene opened her eyes and saw Leon directly in front of her. She pulled the blanket over her face. Leon grabbed the covering and drew it off of her head and shoulders. Verlene buried her face in the pillow.

Leon leaned forward until his knees nudged the mattress, inches from her head. Verlene could hear his deep and rapid breathing.

"You know what to do," he said in a low voice.[8]

Verlene only forced her face deeper into the pillow.

Slowly and sensually, Leon began to rock back and forth against the mattress. The girl's neck and shoulders were exposed to his lustful gaze. He reached out and touched the top of her shoulder, caressing her skin. His fingertips slid from her shoulder to her neck, moving lightly along her skin. One finger glided across her cheek toward her hidden lips. In a raspy whisper, he repeated, "You know what to do."

Twenty miles away, Sheriff Roy Braswell rolled over in bed and reached for the ringing phone on the bedside stand. Pat Smithson was on the line. The sheriff knew Smithson well and considered him to be a reliable and trustworthy straight shooter. Pat launched directly into the matter, summarizing the story told by Willie Latiker at the judge's house. He concluded by saying that it looked like Leon Turner was on a rampage, and this could mean big trouble. He asked Braswell to come down.

Smithson was the kind of man who normally handled trouble himself. That he was asking for help indicated a serious problem. Roy agreed to meet him at Judge Allen's house.

Sheriff Braswell dressed, strapped on his holster and gun, and put on a warm coat with two cigars in its pocket. After kissing Inez goodbye, he stepped out into a blustery wind.

It was after 10:30 p.m. when he drove through the deserted streets of Kosciusko, headed toward Newport.

Thomas Harris found the stash of whiskey he kept hidden in the woods behind the shack and was soon headed back with a jug of moonshine and an empty half-pint bottle. He reentered the house through the back room door and continued into his own bedroom, where Frankie lay sound asleep in his bed despite all the commotion.

Leon was waiting next to Verlene's bed when Thomas came into the room. Seeing the jug, Leon turned away from the girl and returned to his chair in front of the fire.

Saying nothing of Turner's movement, Thomas followed Leon and sat down next to him. He removed the cork from the jug and began pouring its contents into the empty bottle. It was a sloppy operation; several drops spilled onto the floor. When the bottle was full, Thomas handed it to Windol, who drank down a big gulp and passed the bottle to his brother, who took an even bigger swallow. Leon simply yanked the jug out of Thomas's hands and took a pull.

For several minutes, Leon and the Whitt brothers drank and shot the breeze in front of the warm fire. Occasionally, they passed the bottle or the jug to Thomas, Ike, and Bo. The three black men drank sparingly.

Eventually, Leon stepped out the front door to piss. He stood at the edge of the porch relieving himself, a cigarette in his free hand.

Inside, Verlene lay covered up to her chin. She had watched Leon walk outside and had then kept her gaze loosely on the front door. Unfortunately, the warmth of her bed caused her to lapse into a mindless state. When Leon stepped back inside, she wasn't paying attention; but the movement brought her eyes into focus. Leon was looking her way. Their eyes met for an instant. Horrified, Verlene snapped her eyelids closed.

Leon stared at the covers draped along the curves of Verlene's body. He pushed the door shut and moved toward her.

Sensing his approach, Verlene rolled over to face away from the door. Leon grabbed the blanket, his powerful fingers digging into the soft flesh of Verlene's arm, and tugged the covers violently toward the foot of the bed.

As the cold air hit her bare arms and legs, Verlene jumped to the floor and charged past Leon. She ran to her traditional place of refuge when frightened as a little girl—her mother's bed; crawling over Mary Ella, Nell, and James, she scampered to the spot of the mattress at the room's corner. Turning around, she hugged her knees tightly with her back against the walls and a blanket over her legs.

Responding to the assault on his stepdaughter, Thomas jumped from his seat and rushed toward Turner. Leon turned toward the sudden sound and, before Thomas could strike, reached out his right hand and halted him. Wrapping two fingers around Thomas's belt, Leon pulled the smaller man until inches separated their faces.

"How much money you got?" Leon questioned.

Thomas felt the hot breath. "I got two dollar."

"That's two dollars more 'n you need." Leon yanked savagely, tearing the leather belt in two.[9]

The tug pulled Thomas forward into Leon, but Leon was ready. He pushed Thomas back, crashing him into Ike's chair. But Thomas quickly regained his balance and again faced his opponent. Leon glared at the younger man and drew the pistol from his waistband, aiming it from point-blank range at Thomas's heart.

Sweat glistened on Thomas's forehead. He didn't move; he didn't speak.

Malcolm Whitt sat holding the jug as he watched the drama. He made no move to intervene; he was merely a spectator waiting for Leon's next move.

Then Malcolm sensed a change in Leon. The big man's lips curled into a cold smile and his pistol slowly lowered to his side. As though Leon had realized that this confrontation wasn't a fair fight—it was plain that Thomas was powerless against him—Leon relaxed.

"Gimme that jug," he ordered.

The muddy condition of Highway 14 caused Sheriff Braswell to drive slower than he would have liked; but despite the late hour, lights were on at Judge Allen's house as Braswell parked in the gravel driveway.

Coming out to greet him, Pat Smithson stated that Willie Latiker was still inside. The two men went into the kitchen where Eudora Smithson, Judge Allen, and Latiker sat at a small table drinking hot tea.

For the next few minutes, Willie Latiker went over the night's frightful events for Sheriff Braswell. She was obviously fearful for her friend, Sally Ward; for all she knew, Leon Turner could still be there.

Moments later, Braswell accelerated his car east on Highway 14. Pat Smithson was on his right holding a pistol and his whip. In the backseat, Willie Latiker gazed at the dark landscape as she expanded her story for the sheriff. Braswell quizzed her extensively about Leon beating his sister. It was difficult to make a connection between that and tonight's events, but Roy was scratching for any explanation as to why Turner would be harassing harmless women like Latiker and Ward.

The piece of the story that the sheriff wasn't told—Willie Latiker didn't know—was the presence of the Whitt brothers. Braswell and Smithson thought they were going to deal with only Leon Turner, but they would in fact be outnumbered.

After a short drive, Sheriff Braswell parked at the head of the trail leading to Latiker's house. He grabbed the flashlight from the glove compartment, and all three exited into the dark, cold night.

With his gun in one hand and the flashlight in the other, Roy started down the trail, listening carefully for any unusual sound. Willie stayed two steps behind, crouched over slightly, expecting Leon Turner to jump out at her. Pat covered the rear.

Within minutes they reached the front door of Willie's shack. Braswell slowly pushed it open and went inside. He moved bit by bit through the small house, shining his light into each room. At last, he gave the all clear.

Before going inside, Willie pointed out the house of Sally Ward, which could barely be seen in the darkness. There was no sign of activity, no light. Sheriff Braswell and Pat Smithson began walking toward it.

The inside of Sally Ward's house was as quiet as the outside. After Leon Turner's departure, the family had stayed up discussing their traumatic episode; but now the lanterns and candles were extinguished and the family was finally in bed.[10] Sally lay awake—although exhausted, she was too keyed up to fall asleep.

They had been so near tragedy.

A rapping at the front door shattered the quiet. Sally's first reaction was panic—He's back! But she calmed when the sound repeated. This wasn't Leon's pounding; this was different, normal. She got up and trudged to the door, noticing a faint white light beneath it.

"Who's there?" Her tone was strained. She had been through enough surprises tonight.

"Sheriff Roy Braswell," responded a hushed voice from outside. "Is everything all right?"

Relieved, Sally opened the door, and there stood Roy Braswell gripping a downward-pointing pistol. Several feet away, someone shined a flashlight at her face.

Gazing over Sally's shoulder into the house, Braswell again asked if everything was okay. She told him that everything was fine—now; Leon Turner had been there earlier tonight, but he was gone.

Roy asked to look inside. Although Sally did not like the thought of another man with a gun at her house tonight, this was different. When he told her that Pat Smithson was with him, she pulled the door open and stepped aside.

Holding his gun at the ready, the sheriff cautiously went inside, followed closely by Smithson. They glanced from side to side with the sweeping flashlight, noticing two occupied beds. Everything seemed to be in order, and Sally gave no indication of duress. Satisfied, Sheriff Braswell holstered his weapon and asked Sally to go over what had happened.

Flickers of light and shadow darted about the room as Sally Ward, Roy Braswell, and Pat Smithson stood by the fire, speaking quietly. Sally described the evening's events in detail, beginning with Leon's pounding on her door. Why he had come to her house she didn't know. She also didn't know who the other two white men were. Roy was alarmed to learn of more men.

Sally took her time. There was much to tell; and she wanted to tell everything, for this was an opportunity to have Leon sent away again. Only as she neared the end of her narrative did she remember what Leon had said about Mary Ella Harris. She recounted his harsh talk and sexual innuendo, the implied danger. While she had previously narrated her story slowly and emotionally, she now spoke rapidly, describing what Leon threatened to do at the Harris house.

Concerned by this new information, Braswell quickly wrapped up his questioning. He and Smithson left Sally Ward's house in a run. They dashed down the trail to Roy's car and jumped inside. Pat knew the location of the Harris house; it was only a couple of minutes away.

Mary Ella could barely fit on her bed. With three children on the mattress, she struggled to keep from falling off the edge. She glanced at the wind-up clock on top of the corner dresser. The intruders had been inside her house for over an hour, but she had not left the bed.[11] Her only way to protect the children was by staying put.

She had been pleased by Thomas standing up to Leon when Verlene was threatened. Her husband could have easily been killed, but he showed bravery, nonetheless. Turner had backed off and left Verlene alone.

Leon's attention had swung back to drinking. He now stood behind his chair, draping his left hand over its back, grasping the jug with his right. Conversation had slacked off, allowing Leon's train of thought to turn inward. Unfortunately, he remembered why he had come.

Mary Ella was an attractive woman whom he had pursued for a long time. But she had always rejected him. Even two weeks ago, when he had called to her from the highway while hunting Martha, she had turned her back on him.

And now, she was at his mercy.

Leon stepped toward Mary Ella, who lay covered from the neck down at the very edge of her bed. He noticed her high cheekbone—a feature that had always allured him.

Mary Ella looked up at him. Her face showed contempt, not fear.

Leon held out the jug of moonshine to her with his eyebrows raised invitingly.

Mary Ella coldly rejected it. "I don't drink."[12] She could smell filthy clothes, unwashed body, cigarette smoke, whiskey—a scent uniquely Leon.

A hardness came into Leon's eyes, a look that warned of immediate, profound danger. Mary Ella thought about running; but before she could act, he pounced.

With the quickness of a cougar, Leon thrust his right hand down the neck of Mary Ella's nightgown and groped her left breast. There was no attempt at gentleness. His rough, calloused hand scraped her skin like sandpaper.

Mary Ella was shocked by the suddenness of the assault. Panicked, she grabbed Leon's forearm and yanked it away from her body. Her nightgown ripped as his hand pulled free.[13]

Leon heard the fabric tearing and felt fingernails digging into his arm. While her strength surprised him, she was no match for his brawn. Leon lashed back. He grasped the covers, trying to pull them away. She held them tightly, tugging against him. He tore at her clothing. She screamed in his face. He grabbed. She clawed.

BOOM BOOM BOOM—from the front door a few feet away.

Leon froze for an instant, then backed away from Mary Ella and drew his gun.

BOOM BOOM BOOM BOOM.

Turner positioned himself behind the closed door, raised his pistol, cocked the hammer, and placed his finger on the trigger. Then he grasped the door with his free hand and jerked it open.

He was staring directly into the barrel of a .38. Holding it with outstretched arms was Sheriff Roy Braswell.

"Drop it, Leon," ordered the sheriff.

Leon hesitated.

"Drop your gun, now!"

Slowly, Leon brought his arm down and dropped his pistol onto the floor. He raised both hands.

Keeping his weapon pointed at Leon's head, Braswell slowly advanced past the doorway, forcing Leon backward. With a sideways kick, he pushed Turner's gun onto the porch. Inside was a crowd of men sitting to his left. The sheriff maneuvered right until he stood between the two beds, all the while facing Turner. Pat Smithson came through the door with pistol drawn.

Sheriff Braswell scanned the men by the fireplace and counted three whites and three blacks. Roy gazed at each carefully, looking for any sign of a threat, be it a weapon or a look. He saw none. Even Leon appeared to be composed. In a calm, steady voice, Braswell asked Leon to sit down in the empty chair.

Roy kept his .38 trained on the group as Pat Smithson searched each man for weapons. There was nothing but pocketknives.

Over the next several minutes, Braswell questioned the room's occupants, and the events of the evening unfolded. Leon and the Whitt brothers had barged in uninvited. Ike and Bo had been forced to accompany them. Thomas had sold them whiskey. Leon was molesting Mary Ella when the sheriff arrived.[14]

In the end, Roy released Ike and Bo Roby and confiscated Thomas's moonshine. He arrested Leon Turner, Malcolm Whitt, and Windol Whitt.

It was past midnight when the sheriff's car left the judge's house after taking Pat Smithson home. Leon, Malcolm, and Windol sat handcuffed in the back.

Braswell had earned the people's pay tonight, and now he was anxious to get the men locked up in jail and get back to bed. Roy was relieved that no one had been injured this night. It could have been bad; Leon and his friends had caused a lot of trouble. Only one thing bothered the sheriff at the moment, one thing he couldn't get out of his mind: Leon's final words.

Although Turner had given up peacefully, his mood had soured once Braswell put handcuffs on him. As the sheriff ushered him out of the house, Leon had turned to Thomas and Mary Ella and declared, "I'll be back."15

The Harris shack off of Highway 14.

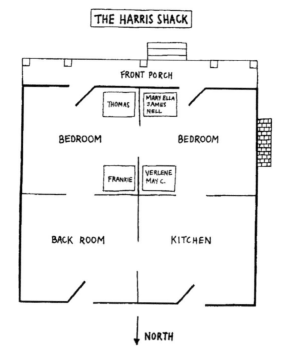

Chapter 10
Confined

Life as an inmate at the Attala County Jail is a dreary proposition, no matter what the time of year. At Christmas, however, it is most terrible. Few things are worse than being locked up during the holiday of peace and goodwill toward man. But there they were, the jail's three newest residents, behind bars on December 25, 1949.

Acceptance of the incarceration varied among the trio. For Leon Turner, the yuletide lockup wasn't particularly unsettling. After all, he had forcibly entered the Harrises' house and tried to molest two women. He could accept the justice of being jailed.

The Whitt brothers, on the other hand, believed that they had committed no crime.[1] Though they had accompanied Turner to the houses of several black families, they had been mere bystanders. Leon had caused the trouble, and even that had been minor—no one had been hurt.

The three were in a filthy, smelly cell known as "the Cage," a highly observable room with walls of iron bars located in the center of the white men's cellblock. Like an identical cell on the black men's floor below, it was where men arrested for crimes of violence were placed. Confinement in the Cage offered the foulest conditions and the least privacy on the floor. A barely functional lavatory and a leaking commode made sanitation practically nonexistent. It was here that Leon, Windol, and Malcolm spent a miserable Christmas Sunday, although they were let out for brief visits by family.

The following day, the men were moved into one of the floor's "regular" cells. Located along the outside wall of the building, these larger rooms had two barred windows with a radiator on the floor between them, four cots with grungy mattresses and no sheets, one commode, and one lavatory, whose single cold water faucet was used in lieu of shower facilities.[2] Solid metal panels made up the floor, ceiling, and end walls. The exterior wall was covered with a thin layer of dirty white plaster decorated with colorful writings and crude, anatomically correct drawings. In places, large sheets of the plaster were missing, exposing the building's red brick exterior.

The normal pace of governmental business in Attala County is slow. During the week between Christmas and New Year, however, it is near catatonic. But it was different during the final week of 1949, when the county's legal system would experience its busiest week in years.

Monday, December 26. Sheriff Roy Braswell drove to Newport to meet separately with Sally Ward and Thomas Harris about the harrowing events of the previous week. Braswell explained that they could press charges against the intruders, though doing so may require testifying at any result-ing trial.[3] Both victims decided to file formal complaints.

That same afternoon, Attala County District Attorney Henry L. Rodgers held his first jailhouse interview with each of the accused men.[4]

Tuesday, December 27. Leon, Malcolm, and Windol ap-peared that morning in Justice of the Peace Court for ar-raignment. Revealing that officials considered the Whitts' involvement in the episode to be minor, the State of Mississippi only charged them with housebreaking and possession of whiskey.[5]

Not so for Leon Turner, who was viewed as far more culpable. He was accused of these same offenses plus the weightier allegations of carrying a concealed weapon and attempted rape.[6] There seemed to be little doubt that he would be returned to Parchman Penitentiary when his case came up for trial—a fact not lost on Leon.

Accordingly, he returned to jail with a belligerent attitude. As soon as the cell door clanged shut, Leon exploded: shouting, cursing, kicking the toilet, throwing his mattress.

Overlooking that their detention was certain to be short, the Whitt brothers joined Leon in the commotion. Sounds of the small-scale revolt reverberated throughout the building.

But not for long. Before any real damage could be done, the rabble-rousers were thrown back into the Cage.

Thomas Harris came to the courthouse office of the sheriff later that day and signed an affidavit against his family's tormentors.[7] Sally Ward's formal complaint accompanied Thomas's in the case file.

Wednesday, December 28. Malcolm, Windol, and Leon sat quietly on their bunks in the Cage when a man arrested for public intoxication was placed into a regular cell across the aisle. Turner and the Whitts could easily observe him. The drunk, not at all happy to be locked up, chose to register his displeasure by defacing the building. Using a metal spoon as his instrument of destruction and a bare area of brick as his target, he dug into the mortar between the bricks. Slowly the old cement fell away as he meticulously scraped back and forth.[8] For several hours, even after the cellblock lights were extinguished, the scratching noise could be heard in the Cage. Finally, it was replaced by snoring.

<u>Thursday, December 29</u>. The drunk prisoner, now sober, was released at midmorning, his night's work unnoticed by the jailer. Leon, Malcolm, and Windol were transferred to his former cell later that day.

Despite the slightly improved accommodations, their present conditions were barely tolerable. Making matters worse, their stomachs were nearly empty. Meals that were neither good nor plentiful came only twice a day.

But even the food, the filth, and the smell were not the worst attributes of being behind bars. Arguably the toughest aspect of confinement is psychological: the loss of freedom. Penal incarceration, by definition, removes a man's God-given right to simply dust himself off and walk away from a disagreeable situation. It not only goes against an American's sense of liberty and self-determination; freedom lost can foster an overpowering urge to regain it that dominates a person's thinking. Rather than wait out their time in jail while the legal system runs its ponderous course, some inmates seek to regain their freedom as soon as the opportunity arises. For the cellmates in Attala County Jail, it arose that night.

Following supper, Leon, Malcolm, and Windol discussed the groove carved in the brick mortar the previous night. The amount of damage inflicted by a jailhouse spoon tellingly revealed that the strong and imposing-looking jail had, in reality, been ravaged by age. Unknown to them, several past Attala County grand juries had reached the same conclusion, criticizing the old building as too vulnerable to escape.

An editorial in the Kosciusko newspaper even quipped that "prisoners are confined in the structure merely by the power of suggestion."[9]

During the evening, the three men decided to finish what the drunk had started and try for a jailbreak. A fourth man who had been put in the cell with them refused to be part of the conspiracy. Leon Turner threatened to kill him if he ratted on the others.[10]

Work began after lights-out. Two tools were available for the task: the spoon used the previous night and a beer can opener that Leon probably acquired during a visit by Parvee Rutherford.[11] Though simple and small, the two implements proved perfect for scratching out brick mortar.

Friday, December 30. Shortly after midnight, the trio paused to examine their work. They were making steady progress. Chiseled deeply into the brick wall was the outline of a hole just large enough to allow passage of broadshouldered Leon Turner.

Work resumed, with the prisoners laboring two at a time while the third rested his cramped and blistered fingers. The trench slowly deepened, and a layer of fine gray powder thickened on the floor. The deadline was 2:00 a.m., when the jailer would make his nightly rounds.[12] He would surely notice the smell of mortar dust hanging thick in the air. The men had to be out by then.

It was well after 1:00 a.m. when Malcolm estimated that the mortar should be sufficiently weakened. Leon wrapped a blanket around his shoe to muffle any noise and kicked hard at the brick with his heel. The wall reverberated with a dull thud, and a puff of dust shook loose; but nothing yielded. Mustering all his strength, Leon again slammed his foot against the bricks; but, again, the mortar failed to budge. Leon cursed and began kicking the brick with savage lunges that would have sent a man flying, but the wall remained intact. His face grew wet from the effort.

Windol and Malcolm also took turns striking the brick; but they, too, could not break through. After several futile minutes, with time closing in on the jailer's visit, Malcolm rethought the strategy.

Sticking out of the nearby radiator was a one-inch lead pipe, a long segment of which ran along the wall just above the floor until passing through a hole in the wall shared with the next cell. The three men pulled, twisted, and bent the pipe until they broke loose a straight portion several feet long.

Using the pipe as a battering ram, Malcolm punched at the bricks in the upper corner of the opening. Bits of brick and mortar chipped away with every blow. At last, a hit at the right spot knocked a brick askew. Two more thrusts and it fell away backward. Sticking his hand through the resulting hole, Malcolm glanced back at his comrades with a triumphant smile.

After that initial breakthrough, it was quick work to enlarge the breach. Chunks of mortar and a dozen or more bricks soon littered the ground along the outside wall. It was past 1:30 a.m.

Cold air drifted through the jagged opening as Leon, Malcolm, and Windol knotted blankets together into a rope. Tying one end to the cell bars opposite the breach, they threw the other end outside. Grasping the blankets tightly, Leon crawled backward out the hole and down the brick wall. The Whitts quickly followed.[13]

All three men stood on the dew-covered grass outside the Attala County Jail, looking about for any indication that they had been seen. There was none—they had not been noticed. A dog barking in the distance sounded the only alarm as the three former prisoners sprinted away. Within seconds, they were swallowed by the inky darkness that is deepest while communities sleep.

Freedom.

Fifty-five-year-old Howard Turner was sound asleep in his bed when something grasped his shoulder and shook him awake. In the predawn darkness, Howard could barely discern a shadowy figure next to the bed. He was confused for a moment, then came recognition; it was his oldest son.

Howard came to full wakefulness when Leon whispered that he had broken out of jail. Two other men—the brothers who had been arrested with him last week—had escaped with him. They were hiding in the woods out back.

Complaining that they had barely eaten in jail, Leon asked if there was any food in the house. Considering that he and his companions would spend today hiding out from the law, they wouldn't have much chance to find food. Howard had an idea. It involved someone sleeping on the floor nearby.

Although Howard's shack was small and crowded with family members, it was not unusual for a boarder to be staying there. If any man who worked for Howard needed a temporary place to live, he could room at his employer's house for a few days or weeks.[14] The arrangement was advantageous to both the worker, who got free room and board, and Howard, who could be loose about paying his helper.

Boarding at the time was a young Negro named Roosevelt Whitcomb.[15] Roosevelt, whom everyone called Whit, was quite a character, even in this land of characters. Twenty-two, single, carefree, and wild, Whit's favorite recreational activity was drinking whiskey, be it local moonshine or commercial stuff bought from the "whiskey store" in Holmes County.[16] On Saturday nights, he could usually be found at the Blue Flame juke joint in Goodman wearing faded jeans with patches patching patches at the knees, dirty old boots, and a short-billed denim cap atop center-parted hair. Everybody felt kindly toward Whit, the same way you feel toward a friendly stray dog that wanders your way. His good looks and good-time personality made him especially popular with the ladies.

Rising groggily out of bed, Howard hobbled to the corner of the room where Whit lay. He nudged the young man hard with his stocking feet and told him to go earn his keep by cooking up a bunch of flapjacks.

While Whit fired up kindling in the kitchen stove and began making batter, Howard dressed and followed Leon into the woods behind the house. He stood in the cold talking with the newly freed trio for fifteen minutes before hearing Whit yell, "Mizza Howa', Mizza Howa'." Howard went back to his house and returned with a heaping stack of pancakes.[17] A hint of light was just touching the eastern sky as he watched the escapees wolf down every last crumb.

With stomachs full for the first time in days, the fugitives left Howard Turner's house. Leon led the way south, staying out of sight of the early-rising populace, as ground fog swirled about them. The sun's first light was on the uppermost tree branches when they arrived at a broken down structure, the rotting remains of Elvira Turner's old cabin where Leon had been raised.

The men could now lay low until the trouble blew over. It was just a matter of time.

The jailer discovered the breakout during his 2:00 a.m. late-night rounds. In a short time, several Kosciusko policemen, Sheriff Braswell, and a deputy were on the scene. The escapees' former cellmate was more than happy to provide details of the breakout. It appeared that Turner and the Whitts were armed with nothing more dangerous than a beer can opener.

For the remainder of the night, Attala County lawmen searched in and around Kosciusko. As the hours passed into day, the manhunt extended southwest to Newport. The extra geographic coverage only stretched thinner the anemic manpower that Attala County expended on the hunt. No law enforcement personnel from surrounding counties were called; no citizen posses were formed. Frankly, no one wanted to waste much effort on the search, for nobody expected to find Leon Turner in his home territory. Furthermore, all he had allegedly done was terrorize some Negroes. In this day of an active Ku Klux Klan, such an occurrence was not uncommon. To many lawmen, the worst crime Leon and his partners had committed was breaking out of jail.

Sheriff Braswell devoted more effort to the hunt than anyone. He talked to Howard and Elvira Turner, Parvee Rutherford, and assorted members of the Turner and Rutherford clans. Not surprisingly, they all denied seeing Leon or knowing of his whereabouts. Likewise, Roy had no luck with Birdie Bell and Pat Baldridge, or any other of Malcolm and Windol's relatives.

Of all the citizens of Newport, the family of most concern to Sheriff Braswell was the Harrises. Leon's aggression against them had been the worst of that frightful evening, and his last words while being led off in handcuffs now took on a new, sinister significance.

The morning after the escape, Braswell drove to the Harrises' house. Thomas and Mary Ella had already heard. They accepted the news matter-of-factly; it was just another dose of bad luck in their long struggle for survival.

Thomas took it to heart when the sheriff advised him to keep a gun handy. Since he didn't own a weapon, he went to Judge Allen's house seeking help. Realizing the potential danger facing the sharecropper and his family, Pat Smithson loaned him a shotgun and a box of buckshot shells.[18] Thomas took the weapon to his house and kept it leaning against the wall next to the back door in the kitchen, fully loaded.[19]

Around Newport, word of the getaway spread like a grass fire in a pasture. Everyone figured that Leon was hiding out in the nearby woods. Now and then, someone reported seeing him. Rumors spread throughout the skittish community that Leon supposedly made threats against Judge Allen, Sally Ward, and Thomas Harris. Black neighbors offered to keep watch on their houses. Judge Allen, for one, accepted.

The judge's daughter, Eudora Smithson, and her husband had a son in college, Pat Smithson Jr. Known as "Little Pat," the lanky youngster was back home in his grandfather's house between semesters at Ole Miss. After being out one night, he arrived home late to discover a sizable black fellow sitting on an upside-down bucket in the judge's carport. The man was dozing with arms draped loosely over a shotgun lying crossways in his lap. Little Pat knew him well—it was Percy Mac Harmon. The two had grown up together.

Hearing the crunching sound of Little Pat's shoes on the driveway gravel, Percy Mac opened his eyes and smiled in recognition. Little Pat asked what he was doing. "I'm a bodyguard," Percy Mac replied.

"You're not much of a bodyguard. You were asleep when I drove up," Little Pat kidded.

From somewhere nearby, an unseen man spoke, "You don't have to worry about it. Ain't nobody gonna bother none of your family." Little Pat recognized the familiar voice of Leon Turner.[20] Percy Mac nearly fainted.

Among those men volunteering to protect Mary Ella was her second cousin who had served time in Parchman for killing a man in the 1930s. He suggested to Mary Ella that she and the children move into his house while he stayed with Thomas until the threat lessened; but as was her way, Mary Ella silently ignored the suggestion. She merely hoped the situation would work itself out.[21]

While the people of Newport fretted over the whereabouts and intentions of Leon, Malcolm, and Windol, the men lived in the wilderness area surrounding the remains of Elvira's house. There was no doubt that they would continue to elude capture, but their quality of life was lacking.

Elvira's old cabin gave protection from the elements only a little better than no shelter at all. The men slept on damp, scratchy beds of straw populated with tiny insects. They had little money—as Sheriff Braswell reported, "They did not have over $2" among them when they escaped—and most of this was depleted by their having paid a Negro boy to bring them canned goods, dried beans, and flour.[22]

Water from spring-fed creeks crisscrossing the land was plentiful. And one other resource was in abundance: liquor. Leon's still was not far-off, and he had stashed a cache of moonshine in a nearby dirt cave.[23] With little else to do, the escapees stayed drunk to pass the time.

Leon decided to cook a new batch of moonshine. Alongside the still was a steel drum containing an old batch of slop, as previously used mash is called. Leon recharged it by adding water, sugar, and cornmeal. After sitting during a few days of fermentation, the concoction would be ready for the next step.

Although alcohol was plentiful, there was never enough food. The woods held an abundance of squirrels and rabbits, but the men had no way of killing them. Accordingly, they set about to get guns.

A black man with whom Leon arranged to bring them supplies involuntarily supplied the first firearm. Joe Willie Wilson carried a .38 caliber pistol in his belt the day he toted a half-sack of groceries to a hillside meeting with the escapees. In his characteristic what's-yours-is-mine attitude, Leon told Joe Willie to give him the pistol. Joe Willie refused to hand it over, so Leon forcibly wrested it away.[24] He also confiscated the few extra bullets Joe Willie was carrying.

Malcolm Whitt stole a .22 rifle and a couple of boxes of cartridges from his mother's home.[25] Windol obtained his gun from Parvee Rutherford, who stopped by to visit the fugitives while hunting with a .12-gauge pump shotgun. After drinking one fruit jar full of 'shine at the hideout and getting another to go, Parvee loaned the shotgun and several No. 1 buckshot shells to Windol.[26]

Leon Turner frequently wandered off by himself to hunt and to get a feel for how actively the law was searching for him. He also met with allies like his father or Parvee. There was one additional person with whom he had contact, and their meetings had nothing to do with alcohol, guns, or food. He rendezvoused with Rilla Meeks. Whether in the woods or at her home or in a barn, their passionate but risky trysts defied the stereotypes of the period and the logical actions of the circumstances.

Through Rilla, Leon learned of the complaints filed against him by Thomas Harris and Sally Ward. He was furious that these two had trampled the unwritten rule of the South that blacks would meekly endure bullying by whites and keep their mouths shut about it. It was an insult that his victims had taken the matter to the law. Leon gave his lover a warning to pass on to her nephew Thomas: drop the charges—or else.

Monday, January 2, was Ruby Nell Harris's fourth birthday. Her mother planned a small celebration and invited Nell's grandmother, Big Momma, to the house for dinner. To Mary Ella's surprise, Big Momma brought her sister, Rilla Meeks, to the party. Rilla and Mary Ella didn't particularly get along.

When the two women arrived, Mary Ella was in the midst of preparing Nell's special birthday meal. She had caught a plump hen, wrung its neck, plucked and gutted it. Now she was cooking the bird along with dressing and collard greens. Completing the feast would be Nell's favorite, coconut cake.[27] As Mary Ella flitted about the kitchen, chatting socially with Big Momma and Rilla, she wasn't sure where Thomas was. But Rilla knew; twice she stepped outside to talk to him without telling Mary Ella.[28]

The discussions concerned Thomas's complaint against Leon and the Whitt brothers. Worried that Leon may retaliate, she tried to convince Thomas to drop his suit.[29] But Thomas would not budge. Leon Turner had harassed his family too much to reconsider withdrawing the charges. Nothing Rilla could say would change his mind.

Thursday, January 5. Six days after the jailbreak, the weekly issue of the *Kosciusko Star-Herald* hit the streets carrying front-page news of the escape.[30] In the story, Sheriff Braswell reported that "he did not have a trace of the escapees" and that they "might be in the woods around here." Concerning the long-term plans of Malcolm and Windol, he opined, "I think the Whitt brothers may go to Huntsville, Ala."[31]

In fact, all three outlaws continued to lay low in Beat 4, avoiding the main roads during daylight. That evening, Malcolm and Windol met with their mother at a pond near her house. Birdie Bell Baldridge had exciting news: She had inquired at the sheriff's office about what it would take to get her boys out of trouble. Paying a fine of "eighteen or twenty dollars" had been the surprising answer.[32] At this encouraging news, the brothers determined to somehow get the money and head back to Cincinnati with the whole mess behind them.

Friday, January 6, marked one week since the escape. Until Thursday night, it had seemed that many identical weeks would follow. But the news about paying a fine to get out of trouble had given the Whitt brothers hope. They had a real prospect of being cleared. Although Leon's situation was murkier, given the additional charges he faced, his relatives had not yet inquired about paying a fine to clear him. There was always a chance.

One important obstacle to freedom yet remained—money to pay off the fine. The best answer to that problem was Leon's still.

Reduced bubbling in the still's recharged slop indicated that the mixture needed one more day of fermentation before being ready to brew another batch of moonshine. The trio decided to make a production run tomorrow night. After that, they would sell the hooch and use the proceeds to pay their fine.

Having plenty of time to kill, they talked about other things, including how they had gotten into this lousy situation. Rehashing the night of their capture, they found it odd that Sheriff Braswell had showed up to arrest them. How had he known that they were at the Harrises'? Only Thomas Harris had left the shack that night when he went outside to get whiskey. Somehow, he must have alerted the law.

This made two unpardonable acts of disrespect against Leon that Thomas had committed. Not being the kind of man to forgive acts of treachery or let them go unpunished, Leon swore to get revenge.

Saturday, January 7. The weather was blustery, with rain coming and going all day. The only thing Leon, Malcolm, and Windol could do was to sit around their wet hideout and get drunk. They drank heavily, no longer concerned to conserve their last supply of hooch, for Leon had checked earlier and found that his mash was ready to be cooked.

After sunset, the inebriated men trudged through the woods to the still. The Whitts started a fire while Leon configured the hardware. Their final step was to pour the mash into an iron kettle positioned over the flames. Laughter erupted when a clear liquid began dripping into a ten-gallon keg they used as a collector.[33]

Once enough liquid had accumulated, taste testing began. The plan was to cook and to sample their product all night long.

Chapter 11
Mistaken Revenge

Sunday, January 8. It was a sight oddly out of place in the virgin thicket: three men sleeping on beds of straw in a small clearing beside a stream. More passed out than asleep, their unwonted snoring clashed with the gentle sounds of nature. A trace of white smoke wafted upward from a pile of smoldering ashes, gently scenting the otherwise pure air. Seven half-gallon fruit jars full of clear, colorless moonshine sat against the base of a towering tree.

The sun, hidden behind gray clouds, was hours past rising when the scraggly-looking jail escapees finally awoke, suffering from bear-sized hangovers. They had stayed up most of the night making and sampling moonshine. Talk was minimal as they carried the jars of hooch to their hideout of two weeks.

As Leon, Malcolm, and Windol heated beans for breakfast in the remains of Miz Elvira's old house, they decided to wait until nightfall before going out to peddle the moonshine. Then to cure their hangovers, they resorted to a tried-and-true method employed by drinkers throughout the ages: hair of the dog.[1] That they were downing potential profits did not concern them a bit.

Leon also used the time to roll cigarettes. The strong and harsh smokes were Leon's favorite. Store-bought, filtered sticks were for women and dandies.

Late that afternoon, when it was sufficiently dark to leave the hideaway, a curious procession of three bedraggled white men trudged along the sloppy back roads, headed toward

Newport. Each carried two fruit jars, and they drank from a seventh. Malcolm and Windol toted rifles; Leon's pistol handle stuck out of his waistband.

Several miles away, twelve-year-old Frankie Thurman hurried to get home before dark, afraid of his mother's fussing should he be late. But even if he didn't make it, she had no call to be angry; after all, she had insisted he get a haircut.

The barbershop was Edward Roundtree's front porch, where clumps of black, brown, red, gray, white, curly, kinky, and straight hair coated the boards like a furry carpet. Roundtree charged a dollar a cut and had both black and white clientele, including Leon Turner.[2]

Frankie hated getting a haircut—an inconvenient intrusion on his playtime. To show his displeasure, his Army Air Corps cap was pulled down tightly over the newly trimmed hair.

Souring his mood even further were his cold, cramped feet. The old shoes he wore were a size and a half too small, and they leaked worse than the school roof. Frustratingly, a brand-new, perfectly fitting pair—a welcome Christmas present—lay beneath his bed at home. He had tried to wear them for this muddy outing, but his mother wouldn't allow it. They were only for school and church, she had ordained.[3]

It turned out that Frankie's fretting about his mother's complaints was unnecessary; for when he arrived home near dark, she didn't say a word. Mary Ella's mind was on her husband. He had gone to a neighbor's house that afternoon and still hadn't returned.

Thomas was down the road at the Roby shack, spending time and having a few drinks with brothers Ike and Buck

Roby. Thomas stayed there a long while. He ate supper with the Robys and even took a nap afterward.[4]

Mary Ella wasn't the only woman in the house upset about Thomas's location. Verlene, too, was peeved; the time her stepfather was spending with Buck was time she coveted. Since the romantic relationship with her eleven-year-older cousin was a secret, the couple had snuck together whenever they could, and today, Thomas was preventing it.

All in all, the state of affairs at the Harris home this night reflected a typical family: a preteen boy worried about his mother's wrath; a wife angry with her husband, as was her teenage daughter; two sisters, ages eight and four, playing with baby brother under foot as their mother cooked the evening meal.

That same night found Leon, Malcolm, and Windol walking on a trail to the house of another of the Whitt brothers' uncles, Dempsey Edwards. Windol wanted to get Uncle Dempsey to go see the sheriff the next day to pay off his and Malcolm's fine. They would pay him back with money they were about to make from the new batch of moonshine. Near Dempsey's house, the three men hid the guns and all but one jar of moonshine alongside the trail. They were staggering from a day of nonstop drinking.

After kidding his nephews about their inebriated condition, Dempsey Edwards invited them and Leon to stay for supper. The half-starved fugitives shoveled down the food eagerly and loudly. Afterward, the men retired to the porch to smoke, shoot the breeze, and drink more moonshine. It wasn't until after 8:00 p.m. that the three men finally left.

By now, they were so drunk that they couldn't find their way back to the trail. Malcolm shined a flashlight all around, but they wandered far off track, ending up at a pond on a neighboring farm. It became funny that they couldn't find the way, particularly in light of Leon's self-proclaimed mastery of all Beat 4 territory. Naturally, some good-natured ribbing followed, culminating with rambunctious horsing around. Their whooping and hollering was most unusual for a Sunday night.

Dempsey Edwards heard the ruckus from his house and went to check on it. He was alarmed to see that it was his fugitive nephews making so much noise. "Did you boys get off the path?" he asked.

"Yes, sir," replied Malcolm, breathing hard.

"Come on. I'll go on a piece with you and show you the way."

The older man guided the three drunks back to the trail opening and then left them. He sensed something ominous afoot. He knew well that Leon Turner was trouble's best friend.

Even though now on the trail, Leon, Malcolm, and Windol still couldn't find their guns and moonshine. They looked unsuccessfully for several minutes, and the frustratingly slow search began to try Leon's patience. Finally unable to take any more, he yanked the flashlight out of Malcolm's hand and soon located their stash.

Turner moved down the trail, his flashlight aimed at the soggy pathway ahead. Scurrying to keep up, Windol asked Leon where they would sell their whiskey. Leon told him that he knew a fellow who would buy all of it; they were going there now. Leon had a name in mind, a man whose name had not been far from his thoughts since before Christmas, but he didn't say who it was.

Stars peeked through thinning clouds as the three headed north a short distance to Highway 14, and then turned west.

They kept out of sight, leaving the road whenever a car passed. Only a couple of miles to go, Leon knew. It was time to teach 'em a lesson; time to get revenge. It was payback time.

Mary Ella Harris was irritated when her husband got home long after his family had eaten, but Thomas didn't care. He was returning to his Alabama job soon; he deserved a little fun beforehand.

And on the inside, Mary Ella understood. She knew Thomas needed to get in his final moments with friends before he left for another two or three months. Her anger did not last long.

Also acting to dissipate her aggravation was the fact it was Sunday, which was always a special evening at the Harrises'. Although 10:00 p.m. was their usual bedtime on school nights, the family stayed up until 10:30 on Sundays. During this extra thirty minutes, they listened to a Nashville radio station's broadcast of a music program that "all the colored people liked."[5]

Everyone went to bed after the popular program ended. For a few minutes, conversation bounced back and forth between the two bedrooms as the family discussed the radio program. Finally, Mary Ella shushed the talking and all became quiet.

It was eleven o'clock as Turner and the Whitts neared their destination. Up one last hill on Highway 14 they trudged. Arriving at the summit, they could see moonlight shining in the distance through breaks in the cloud cover, illuminating parts of the land like dim spotlights. Highlighted by one of the weak moonbeams, Thomas Harris's shack stood a quarter of a mile away.

"We better leave this whiskey here until we see who all is down there," Leon stated as he moved off the road.

Only now did Malcolm realize where they were going; but he had no chance to question the situation, for Leon placed his jars of moonshine behind some bushes and started down the hill. The Whitts quickly stashed their whiskey and caught up. All the men carried were guns.

Minutes later, they crossed into the Harrises' front yard. Malcolm whispered to Leon, "What are we doin' here?"

Leon finally announced his intentions. "We're goin' up there in that house and fuck those women." It was a statement, not a suggestion.

"Naw. Let's get out of here," Malcolm appealed.

Leon merely glared at the younger man. This night had been in his mind for two weeks; and now the moment was here. The matter was not up for discussion.

The three men walked toward the shack in silence, with Windol and his .12-gauge shotgun in the rear. Approaching the front porch, Leon told him, "Git on to the back of the house. Don't let none of 'em git out that way." Windol disappeared around the corner.

Malcolm followed Leon up the steps onto the porch and stopped at the top while Leon went to the front door. Leon pushed on the door, but an inside latch held it closed. He knocked and waited. Nothing. No movement, no sound, no anything.

At this point, he stepped to the west end of the porch and urinated. Malcolm joined him. As they stood peeing into the yard, Malcolm quietly repeated, "C'mon, let's get out of here."

Staring into the distance, Leon mumbled, "I'm goin' in there and fuck those women or kill the whole damn pile of 'em." When they were finished, Leon told Malcolm to go to the front yard and not let anyone in the house come outside.

Malcolm went down the steps and walked to the middle of the yard. Facing the shack, he stood with his .22 rifle cradled in both arms. The moonlight colored everything within sight a shade of gray, including the dark shadow of Leon Turner moving on the porch.

Leon switched on a flashlight.

Verlene lay awake, a million thoughts and emotions that accompanied being fourteen and female racing through her mind. It seemed that every time she was about to drift off, May C. wiggled.

She heard something—footsteps on the porch.

Now someone knocked at the door. Verlene did not move.

In the room's other bed, Mary Ella also heard the footsteps. When the knocking followed, her mind jumped to high speed, but her body stayed still.

In the next room, Thomas and Frankie remained asleep.

Both Mary Ella and Verlene heard the person move away from the door, and within seconds, a different sound of footsteps. My God! It was someone else.

Then came the low, muffled tones of men talking, a pause of several seconds, and footsteps again approaching the door.

Tiny flickers of light leaking through gaps in the front wall caught Verlene's attention. But as quickly as they began, they stopped, replaced by a circle of light moving across the window curtain by her mother's bed. Soon, this, too, vanished, and the room became dark and silent.

Standing next to a six-panel window, Leon pointed his flashlight through the window, but a dingy curtain blocked his view inside. He turned off the light and set it down at his feet. Then he pulled the pistol from his waist and touched its barrel against the lower left windowpane. He drew it back a foot and then immediately thrust it forward.

The pane exploded, spraying shards of glass on the blanket covering Mary Ella's feet. Reacting instantly, she threw off her covers, swung both feet out of bed, shook Nell awake, gathered a blanket about James, and snatched him up in one arm. With her free hand, she grabbed Nell's wrist and yanked the four-year-old to her feet.

Glowing embers in the fireplace provided a weak orange glow as Mary Ella ran with the children through the kitchen to the back door. Letting go of Nell, she jerked it open.

Seeing her mother scramble out of the bedroom, Verlene jumped up from bed and followed her into the kitchen.

Mary Ella stood in the doorway holding James, cold air on her face. She seized Nell's hand and took one step outside.

"Get back in there!"

Someone was in the backyard! Surprised, Mary Ella looked out and saw a man standing not twenty feet away. He held something—it looked like a rifle.

"Get in there!" the trespasser yelled louder.

Mary Ella jumped backward into the kitchen and slammed into Nell. The child tripped sideways and stumbled over her father's borrowed shotgun leaning against the wall. The gun fell over with a loud crash. Nell landed on top of it and began crying. Her mother stooped to help.

Thomas awoke when the window glass shattered. Hearing the flurry of activity as Mary Ella and Verlene fled into the kitchen, he hustled out of bed and into the back room. Avoiding the cotton bale in the middle of the room, he ran to the back door and pulled it open.

From the backyard, someone yelled, "Y'all get back in the house or I'll have to shoot ya."

Thomas didn't look for the shouter. Instead, he turned and hurried toward the kitchen, leaving the door ajar.

After Verlene saw Nell fall, she ran into the back room and bumped into Thomas with a bone-jarring lurch. In too much of a rush to fall, she sidestepped to the open back door and squeezed through.

Windol Whitt stood only a few yards away. Seeing Verlene, he swung his shotgun toward her and screamed, "Get on back in there or I'll shoot ya." All these people coming out the doors had him frazzled. He pointed the .12-gauge into the air and pulled the trigger.

BOOM!

Verlene ran back inside.

Windol fired again.

BOOM!

In unison with the second blast, the door slammed shut behind Verlene.

After breaking the window glass, Leon Turner had reached through the opening, flipped up the front door latch, and rushed inside, leaving his flashlight on the porch. Now he stepped slowly, pistol in hand, feeling his way around Mary Ella's bedroom, the front entrance open wide behind him.

His free hand stretched into midair, groping for the string hanging from the electric light.

Unfazed by his collision with Verlene, Thomas pressed in darkness toward the kitchen. Again, he was sideswiped, this time by his unseen wife moving in the opposite direction.

He continued onward, driving to get to Pat Smithson's shotgun leaning next to the back door. He touched his way past the kitchen table to the door, but when he felt for the weapon, it wasn't there! Frantically, his hands swept back and forth along the wall, groping for the one item that may save his life. Where was it? How could it not be here? He could not see it lying on the floor at his feet, accidentally nudged against the wall by Nell.

After her collision with Thomas, Mary Ella hugged James more securely and tightened her hold on Nell's hand. Both children were crying.

Amidst the crowded confusion and howling children, Mary Ella ran into the back room in time to see Verlene rush out the back door. A bright flash accompanied by an appallingly loud blast from outside caused Mary Ella to veer right toward the living room.

The string brushed against Leon's hand. He grabbed it and yanked downward. Light filled the room.

He looked into the kitchen and saw Thomas standing at the back door. Thomas didn't notice Leon, however, for his gaze was on the floor, on the now visible shotgun. Just as Thomas bent over with outstretched arms, Leon spotted it too.

"Hold on!" Leon warned. "Don't touch that gun or I'll shoot yo' ass."

Thomas froze. The weapon was so close, inches from his fingertips. To go for it, though, risked death. Slowly, Thomas stood and faced his adversary. Leon's pistol was aimed at his chest.

Eight-year-old May C. was awakened by the sudden bright light above her bed. She grimaced and pulled the covers over her head.

The light came on just as Mary Ella rushed into the living room. Blinded by the brightness, she crashed hard into Frankie's bed and fell forward. Only by letting go of Nell and using her hand to brace herself on Frankie's mattress was she able to keep her balance.

When she looked up, she saw Leon Turner standing frightfully close in the next room. She could see the swollen veins of his forehead, the bulging eyes. The sight of the madman caused her to panic. Leon was shouting into the kitchen, not seeing her. Behind him, the front door was wide open. It promised a chance for escape, for life.

There was no time to think, only to react. Mary Ella lunged forward.

Frankie awoke when his mother collided with his bed. He saw her standing next to him, holding James with a wide-eyed look on her face. Nell stood crying at the foot of the bed. Before Frankie could utter a word of surprise, his mother bolted out of the room.

Verlene's ears rang from the staggering shotgun blasts as she flung the back door shut. She darted into the living room, only to face an overpowering scene. Her mother was bent over Frankie's bed holding a screaming James; behind her, Nell cried uncontrollably; and Leon Turner stood in the next room holding a gun. As Verlene struggled to grasp the bizarre spectacle, her mother sprinted toward Turner.

Mary Ella wrapped both arms tightly about James and ran. Filled with the courage of desperation, she passed mere inches behind Leon's back. An instant later, she was through the front door and onto the porch. Heart racing, she bounded down the three steps, girding herself for the bullet that would surely strike her from behind. But it never came.

She reached the ground and rushed into the darkness.

As Leon trained his gun on Thomas, a blur passed behind him. He twisted around, only to see Mary Ella's backside dashing away. Before he could spring after her, a blood-chilling shriek erupted beside him. May C. had flung the blanket off her head and found, to her shock, a ten-foot-tall, wild-eyed white monster at the foot of her bed. She screamed.

In the moment of surprise, Leon hesitated—oh so briefly— but just long enough for Mary Ella to disappear out the door with James. Leon roared in contempt at the still screeching child and then shifted his gaze back to the kitchen.

Frankie grasped the situation after seeing his mother run out of the house. Following her lead, he jumped out of bed, grabbed his cap off a nail on the wall, and shot toward the front door. But this time, Leon was ready. As Frankie passed by, the big man stuck out his right arm and wrapped it around the boy's waist. Frankie felt the gun dig into his side as his forward motion stopped. His next feeling was a flying sensation as Leon flung him onto May C.'s bed. Frankie's feet hit the mattress as his head slammed against the back wall. The boy collapsed heavily onto his sister's legs.

In all the pandemonium, little Nell had been forgotten as her mother dashed out of the house. Now, the four-year-old ran into the room toward her brother and sister, wailing loudly. Leon grabbed her wrist and threw her by one arm onto the bed with May C. and Frankie.

Verlene stood alone in the adjoining bedroom, backed against the wall by Frankie's bed and out of Leon's sight. She had watched helplessly as Turner captured first Frankie and then Nell. The thought of being in Leon's hands knotted her stomach. She crept toward the door directly in front of her until Leon was barely in view. When she spotted him looking away, she darted to the front wall, using her hands against it to brake to a stop. Opening the front door, she quickly slipped outside and pulled the door shut.

Now, where to hide?

She scampered left to the end of the porch and jumped, a leap of about two feet. Upon hitting the ground, she bent low and scrambled beneath the porch. Barefoot and dressed only in a cotton nightgown, she sat on the cold ground. Then she wept.

With no more action out the back doors, Windol decided to return to the front yard. He stepped around the rear corner of the house as Verlene was ducking beneath the front porch. One second more and he would have missed her.

Mary Ella stood motionless in the middle of the front yard, her escape attempt over. Seconds after running from her house, she had come upon a man. In the dim moonlight, she recognized that it was one of the Whitt brothers, the taller one. He had a rifle pointed at her.

Malcolm Whitt spoke, his voice quiet and calm, "You gotta get back in the house. You cain't come out here."

The barrel of his .22 was so close that Mary Ella reached out and grabbed it with her right hand. Malcolm moved forward, gently poking the muzzle into her stomach; she backed up holding on to the cold steel.

Tears of despair filled her eyes from the cruel turn of events—she thought she had made it.

Inside the house, Leon stared Thomas in the eye and shouted, "Get in here, now!" Thomas moved in his direction.

The children were screaming and crying. Leon looked at them—clumped together on one bed—and barked, "Shut up your crying!" He added, "Go stand over there next to the fireplace." When they didn't budge, he swatted at Frankie with the pistol and yelled, "Now, goddamnit!"

Frankie and May C. got out of the bed and moved in front of a window next to the fireplace. Nell nearly fell scurrying down from the mattress. She ran to May C. and buried her head in her big sister's nightclothes, sobbing in terror. May C., too, was crying. Frankie stood in front of his sisters.

Thomas stood at the opening between the kitchen and bedroom with his arms folded, waiting. Leon smirked as he savored the control. These people were powerless against his desires, and they were frightened. It was a shame that Mary Ella had gotten away; he would take care of her another time.

Then he remembered Verlene.

"Where's Verlene?" he asked Thomas. The teen's stepfather only shrugged his shoulders.

Leon shouted for her, "Verlene! Verlene! Come here, girl!"[6] But, of course, she didn't.

He threatened Thomas. "You'd better find her and bring her to me if you want to live."[7]

Thomas did not flinch. Instead, he asked Leon why he was doing this to the family.

A stream of cursing and screaming followed as Leon accused Thomas of getting the sheriff and having him thrown in jail. Thomas denied it, but Leon ignored him, yelling, "You've been telling damn lies on me, you son of a bitch. I'll kill you."[8]

Thomas again refuted doing anything bad to Leon. Taking the offensive, he accused Leon of messing with his wife and children.

Leon spat at the backtalk. He ordered Thomas to turn around and walk into the back room. Harris did as he was told, but only after glancing at his children. Frankie, May C., and Nell returned his gaze, and then watched the man they called "daddy" walk away.

Leon followed Thomas, keeping the gun trained on his back. He halted in the middle of the kitchen while Thomas continued walking into the back room. Leon's temper was at the boiling point. Thomas had pushed him too far; it was just too much to stand; only Thomas could be blamed for the consequences.

Leon squeezed the trigger.

POW!

The impact pushed Thomas forward onto the cotton bale.[9] The slug had nicked his spine and exited his right chest, but he was alive.

After watching Thomas crumple, Leon stepped toward the children.

The tip of the rifle barrel pushed uncomfortably into Mary Ella's stomach, prodding her toward the house. She took small, backward steps, her right hand grasping the cold steel, her left holding the baby. Malcolm continued to talk to her in a soft voice: "You gotta get back in the house. You ain't allowed to come out. Get on back in there and I won't shoot you."[10]

Mary Ella let go of the rifle when she heard pistol fire from inside the house. Disoriented and confused, she kept moving backward toward the house. The hopelessness of the situation struck when she reached the porch steps. She would go back inside the house and face Leon Turner and whatever cruel tricks fate had in store for her.

Turning to go up the steps, Mary Ella glimpsed through the open door and saw Frankie standing next to the mantel, shaking his head. His left hand was extended palm outward as if trying to stop something; his cap was in his right hand.

POW!

Mary Ella heard Frankie holler, "Oh!" and saw him fall backward against the wall. She tore her eyes away from the horror and looked outward into the night. No longer did she care about anyone blocking her path—she had to get away! Grabbing the .22 barrel with her free hand, she shoved it aside roughly and bolted away from the house.

As she ran, she heard the sounds of more gunfire.

Instinct took over, James's survival its only objective. Mary Ella sprinted wildly across the yard, praying that her bare feet wouldn't slip in the mud, praying that the man with the rifle wouldn't shoot.

Malcolm was momentarily stunned by the sound of gunfire. In a daze, he felt the rifle wrench in his hands; he realized that the woman was running away from him. He brought his weapon up and aimed at her retreating back. It was an easy shot, but he didn't take it.

To May C. and Nell, the staccato report sounded like a loud firecracker, but when their brother slammed backward into the wall, the girls screamed. May C. looked at Leon Turner and saw him pointing a pistol their way. A second shot went off. She darted toward her bed and jumped, landing on the mattress in a controlled crash. She heard a third ghastly gunshot while struggling to cover herself with a quilt.

Nearby, Nell scrambled to her own bed, squealing. It was too high for her to jump into; she began to climb up its side.

Smoke drifted from the barrel of Leon's pistol. He had fired three times into the group of kids. Two slugs had ripped into Frankie—one passing through the boy's chest; one through his left arm, breaking the windowpane behind him. The third bullet slammed into the wall, missing the falling boy by a fraction of an inch.

Leon had become an executioner, giving no thought to what he was doing—simply doing it. He stepped backward, moving further from the fireplace as May C. rushed to hide beneath the covers. The young girl looked up and saw Leon watching her. His expression was a bottomless pit; rather than a look of hate or pity or excitement or regret, there was nothing—no emotion, no feeling, no humanity. "Please, Mr. Leon, don't shoot me," she begged.[11]

He fired from the waist.
POW!

Nell clawed at the covers, her tiny legs flailing in mid-air as her torso inched forward onto the mattress. She was halfway up. The little girl didn't see Leon towering over her, gazing down vacantly from point-blank range.
POW!

Thomas Harris lay conscious in the back room, his chest on fire. His girls were screaming. He tried to get up, but his legs wouldn't respond. In the cruelest of circumstances, Thomas remained awake, hearing everything but unable to act as the shooting continued. With every shot, the screaming lessened. Finally, there was silence. Mercifully, Thomas blacked out.

Underneath the porch, Verlene hugged her knees tightly and shivered from the cold. She had heard Leon Turner calling for her, then Leon and Thomas arguing, then a single gunshot. As she struggled to remain in control of her fear, someone spoke to her.
"Get back in the house. If you don't, you'll get shot." Windol Whitt was down on one knee, calling into the blackness below the house. More gun blasts sounded, but Windol did not notice them. "Come on, come on out now. If you don't get out, I'll shoot you."
Verlene had no choice. Slowly, she crawled on her hands and knees toward the voice. Windol was only a few feet away when she emerged from beneath the porch. They both stood, facing each other. Windol's shotgun was loosely pointed toward the girl.

"Go on," he commanded, motioning the barrel toward the porch. "Get on back in the house."

Leon scanned the carnage as a haze of gunsmoke spread through the air. The bloody figures of three black children, unmoving and silent, surrounded him. The killer stepped to the stone mantel and unhurriedly pulled the few spare bullets out of his pocket and reloaded—primarily to get their weight out of his pants rather than needing any more. He laid his pistol atop the stone, and with a steady hand, pulled a cigarette and a small matchbox out of his shirt pocket. Lighting the rolled tobacco, he inhaled deeply and blew a lungful of smoke toward Frankie's lifeless body.

There was nothing more for him here. It was finished. He retrieved his gun and walked out the front door.

Verlene grabbed the corner post and struggled to pull herself onto the end of the porch, but the encouragement of Windol's shotgun gave her strength. Once on the deck, she took two steps. Then she saw Leon emerge from the door at the opposite end. Verlene spun left, preparing to jump to the ground.

Under normal circumstances, Leon's reflexes were fast; in his present state of adrenalin-filled alertness, they were extraordinary. Perceiving movement to his left, he brought up his pistol and fired.

POW!

The bullet ripped into Verlene's right elbow and lodged in her forearm.

POW!

A second slug passed through her right breast and exited below her left breast. She collapsed onto the porch.

Leon walked to the fallen girl and stood over her. He took a drag from his cigarette and flicked its ashes onto her white nightgown.

Verlene was barely conscious, peering through half-open eyelids. She saw the feet of her attacker and shifted her vision up his body until she saw his face. The eyes returning her gaze were cold and heartless.

"I'll kill every one of you," she heard as she slipped into unconsciousness.

Having witnessed the drama on the porch, Malcolm and Windol saw Leon hovering over the motionless form of Verlene. They moved to him.

"I shot the whole damn bunch," Turner spoke softly.

Windol exchanged a concerned look with his brother. "Come on, let's get on out of here," he said.

Leon didn't respond.

Malcolm tried: "Leon, let's go."

The murderer stepped down from the porch to his companions. Early in the morning of Monday, January 9, 1950, Leon Turner, Malcolm Whitt, and Windol Whitt left the Harris cabin for the last time.

When they reached Highway 14, the men ran. With guns in hand, they jogged up the hill and found the moonshine they had left an eternity ago. Retrieving only two jars, they headed east on Highway 14 toward Newport.

Chapter 12

Survival and Death

Mary Ella fled from the continuing massacre of her family in sheer terror, the sound of each gunshot like a red-hot iron branding her mind. Cutting through the watery ditch alongside Highway 14, her bare feet sank ankle-deep in mud, but her balance stayed true despite the extra weight of baby James. She ran a short distance down the road and crossed into the yard of her nearest neighbors, the Robys. There was no visible activity at their house, but she knew they were home for Thomas had returned from there only hours ago.

The shack was indeed occupied. Buck and Ike Roby, twenty-five and twenty-three, were home with their mother and five younger sisters.[1] Despite the late hour, everyone was awake.

The Robys had been asleep earlier, but sounds of shooting nearby had them soon looking out windows toward the Harrises' house. They could see their neighbors' light on; someone even swore they could see flashes of gunfire. Along with everyone else in Newport, the family knew of the recent trouble between the Harrises and Leon Turner; and they knew that the dangerous white man was on the loose. It took no crystal ball to predict what was happening.

At one point, Buck Roby had grabbed his pistol and started to run outside to help; but his mother physically held him back. Buck struggled to escape her grip, but the determined woman would not let go. Exasperated, Buck drew back his gun, preparing to strike. Before he could swing, however, Ike grabbed his arm.

"You better not hit my mother," Ike warned. The sobering words sank in, and Buck held back.[2]

As a result, no one from the Roby house went to help. Nor did any of the other neighbors who may have heard the tempest at the Harris home.

The last gunshot had been fired by the time Mary Ella arrived at the Robys. She banged on their front door in a frantic plea for help.

Inside the house, the loud pounding caused alarm. It could be the attackers—finished with the Harrises and coming to wreak havoc on another family.

Mary Ella knocked again, harder. The emphatic knocking sounded threatening to Ike, who stood ready with an ax just inside the entryway. His younger sister, Helen, who was Verlene's age, stayed close to him.

Panicked that no one was letting her in, Mary Ella pushed on the door, but it was latched shut. A second, stronger shove also failed to budge it. Now Mary Ella was frantic; she had to get inside to safety. From many visits to the home, she knew that the back door was left cracked open so the Robys' dog could freely come and go. Clutching James, she ran around to the back.

As Mary Ella had guessed, the door was slightly ajar, but the gap was narrow—barely enough for a skinny mongrel to pass through. When she nudged the door with her right hand, the opening widened two inches before the door hit something inside with a solid *clunk*. A trunk was directly behind the door, she recalled, keeping it from opening any wider. Moving the obstruction would take a hefty push. She cinched James against her body with her left arm, shouldered the door with her right, and shoved with all her strength. The gap increased slightly; one more heave would do it.[3]

Ike was ready for the intruder's entry. The bumping noise at the rear of the house had caused him to rush to the kitchen, where he now guarded the back door with ax raised and heart pounding. Helen remained near, and Buck stood a few feet back with his gun.

Mary Ella again pushed the door inward. It opened a bit wider, enough for her to fit through sideways. Sticking her right foot into the opening, she carefully squeezed her baby through headfirst.

All that could be seen from inside the dark kitchen was a shadowy form coming through the door. Ike Roby elbowed his sister rearward and cocked the ax high over his shoulder, ready for the swing.

Mary Ella twisted slightly so that James's head wouldn't hit the doorframe. When she did so, moonlight hit the baby's shiny scalp at just the right angle, causing a tiny glint. Helen Roby saw the flicker of light and focused on its source. Only then did she see the outline of a head—a baby's head! She grabbed the handle of Ike's ax and whispered urgently, "Uh-uh. Don't hit 'em! It ain't him!"[4]

The insistent tone of his sister's voice caused Ike to check his swing. A moment later, the identifiable profile of Mary Ella Harris holding a baby came into the room.

At last, Mary Ella was inside, safe from the demons of the evening. After an hour of unimaginable fear and stress, she could release her emotions. The dam burst, and her feelings gushed forth in a wave of tears and moaning. The Roby family gathered close as, between sobs, their distraught neighbor told of the night's horror.

Her story was truly shocking and hideous, but it was far from complete. Mercifully, Mary Ella Harris had witnessed only a portion of the tragedy in her home; she could not know the additional death and suffering experienced by her family. She could not know that, even now, the drama continued.

A mere fifty yards away, three men ran eastward along Highway 14. Jogging in silence, they drew abreast of the Robys' shack. Its dark, uninviting exterior revealed no hint of the activity inside. Luckily, its ordinariness provided nothing to attract attention.

Had the three runners become aware of a particular woman inside the house—a woman who was, even now, re-gurgitating their deeds—the evening may have suffered even more calamity. Unaware of Mary Ella's presence, they continued down the road, disappearing into the night.

Verlene awoke shivering. The uncontrollable trembling racked her body, wrenching her into a dreamlike conscious-ness. Awareness slowly gained a foothold and she noticed the silence; shortly before, it seemed, there had been noise and confusion. More memories surfaced—recollections of panic, desperation, running, hiding, gunfire, and pain. Through closed eyes, Verlene saw Leon Turner standing over her, gloating. She awaited death. Only when it failed to come did she realize that Leon wasn't there. She was alone, but where? Something was hard and cool against her body. Finally came the realization that she was outside on the porch, laying on her back. Her chest felt as though someone were sitting on it.

Turning her head a fraction, Verlene looked about. It was dark except for a light at the other end of the porch. She remembered Leon standing in that light, a cigarette in his lips, coldness in his stare.

A noise interrupted the silence, a barely audible whimper. Inside the house.

Verlene rolled to her left side, trying to get up, but a hot spear of pain froze her. Something was horribly wrong with her right arm. Only by pressing it motionless against her body could she bear to move. Slowly, she stood and wrapped her left arm around a post for support. After a pause, she began shuffling the length of the porch, stooped over in pain. Seconds seemed like hours, but finally she arrived at the open bedroom door and looked inside.

It was the stuff of nightmares: Frankie slumped with his back against the wall next to the fireplace, eyes open but unseeing, patches of bright red staining his long johns; May C. in her bed, doubled over atop a crumpled blanket, face buried in the cover, as still as death.

A moaning sound came from Verlene's right. She glanced to her mother's bed and saw Nell laying facedown on the mattress, head and torso on top, legs and feet hanging over the side. The back of her nightgown was dark and wet.

And then Nell moved, ever so slightly, but a sign of life. Verlene nearly cried out. She knelt and softly cradled the back of Nell's head with her left hand, stroking her sister's hair tenderly.

"Nell?"

The little girl opened her eyes; they showed pain and confusion. "That man hit me in the stomach," she whispered.

For the first time this evening, Verlene cried. She longed to cradle her baby sister, to make things all right, but she could do nothing. Even when Verlene attempted to lift Nell and lay her more comfortably on the bed, a dagger of pain twisting through her breasts prevented it.

A wave of dizziness struck, and Verlene realized she had to seek help urgently before she passed out. Grasping the metal frame at the foot of Nell's bed, she labored to her feet and looked about the room one last time. A twinge of guilt struck at the thought of abandoning her siblings; it was her responsibility to look after them. But to seek help, she must go. With a final look at her brother and sisters, Verlene left.

The few steps to the porch were agony. Forced to lean against the post at the top of the steps, she gasped as deeply as the fire in her chest allowed. Making it all the way to the nearest neighbor seemed an impossibility, but there was no choice. She let go of the post and staggered down the steps into the yard.

Weakened by the loss of blood and numbed by the cold, she nearly fell several times. Somehow, though, she kept going. A trail of blood recorded the progress as Verlene staggered across seemingly endless ground. The moon over distant treetops gave her comfort. At a time when she needed resolve, its never-failing presence gave her the light and strength to press forward.

At last she came to Highway 14. Only a little farther to the Roby house. Buck was inside. If only she could get to him, the bad dream would end.

Onward she struggled, a phantom in a bloodstained white gown.

Buck paced the floor, beads of sweat dotting his forehead. It had been several minutes since the last gunfire. He had no way of knowing if Verlene lay dead, but it was clear that

Leon Turner had come—and against him, Verlene stood no chance.

As his anguish sank deeper toward despair, a weak rapping noise came from the front door; a hesitant, irregular knocking that did not seem that of a deranged killer. But Buck wasn't going to take any chances. Approaching the entryway, he cocked his pistol while Ike followed with the ax. The rest stayed back, watching from dark corners of the room as Buck unlatched the door and cracked it open. He saw someone leaning against the doorframe not four feet away. Verlene!

Buck threw open the door and rushed forward. Dark splotches streaked Verlene's nightgown as she looked briefly into the eyes of her lover and then collapsed into his arms.

Thomas opened his eyes and didn't know where he was. The room was dark, but somewhere there was a light. Breathing was difficult; he couldn't get enough air. For a moment, he didn't understand what was happening, and then memory came. Leon, the argument, the threats, the gun. Finally, being shot.

As the mental fog lifted, Thomas perceived that he was facedown on the cotton bale in the back room. He tried to get up, but strangely his legs would not respond; there was no feeling below his waist. He strained to push up with his hands, but gained only an exhausting coughing spasm from the effort. As the seizure subsided, Thomas grasped that he could barely move, much less stand. He closed his eyes and surrendered.

Then a tiny voice called, "Mommy, Mommy."

He spoke into the room, hoping, "Ruby Nell, honey, are you all right?"

"That man hit me in the stomach," Nell sobbed.

He could barely hear her. Where was she? "It's all right, baby child. Daddy's right here."

"I'm thirsty. I want some water."

"Baby, I cain't get none for you right now. Get some for yo'self."

"My tummy hurts. I'm thirsty. Get me some water."

"Nell, Daddy cain't get you no water. Just stay put, honey, it'll be all right."

The minutes became an eternity as Thomas's unseen little girl whimpered and begged for water. Tears wet the cotton where his face lay. Physically, only a small distance separated parent and child; practically, the span may just as well have been the Mississippi River.

Thomas drifted in and out of consciousness as Nell's crying grew less and less, her voice weaker and weaker. Finally, she was silent.[5]

Verlene lay on a mattress, strips of clean sheeting binding her wounds. The Robys were gathered around, listening in stunned silence as the stricken girl told her tale. Her normally strong and defiant voice now weak and subdued, she told of running through the house, hiding below the porch, being found by one of the Whitt brothers, and being shot by Leon Turner.

Throughout her daughter's narrative, Mary Ella sat silently in a nearby chair, struggling to cope with what had happened to her family. Quiet tears flowed down her cheeks as Verlene described finding Frankie, May C., and Nell.

Minutes later, a raccoon scampered away from the sound of approaching footsteps. Buck was running down Highway

14. With the violence apparently over and Verlene resting safely back at his house, Buck's strong legs bore him briskly toward Judge Allen's house.

Soon, the judge and Pat Smithson stood on the front door stoop, listening somberly as Buck Roby told of gunshots at the Harris house, of Mary Ella's story of terror, and of wounded and bloody Verlene. They knew this meant the worst had happened: Leon Turner had gone berserk.

After sending Buck home with an admonition to protect his mamma and sisters, Pat Smithson dressed warmly and set out to call the sheriff. First, though, he would drive to Thomas Harris's house to see for himself what had happened. Fearing that Leon could still be around, Pat solicited help from neighbor Willie B. McCrory.[6] Together, they rode to the Harrises'.

As Smithson's car slowed to a stop, no movement was evident at the shack; but the front door was wide open and a light was on. The two men got out of the car and cautiously approached the house, keeping a watchful eye for any threat. They quietly climbed up onto the porch, walked toward the doorway, and gazed inside.

Carnage greeted them. The two lifelong hunters had seen a lot of death in their day, but nothing matched the scene they now witnessed. Splattered blood covered the floor, beds, and walls. Sprawled about the room were three children, parts of their clothing soaked in dark red. After taking a moment to absorb the grim sight, the men went inside and checked the youngsters. A boy and a girl lay dead, but another girl—a delicate little child not much bigger than a toddler—still clung to life. Going through the other rooms of the house, they also found Thomas Harris alive.

Obviously, the house had just experienced a violent event of heinous proportions. Just as obvious, there was nothing here that Smithson and McCrory could do to help. They needed to get an ambulance; they needed to get the law. And they needed to hurry.

Twenty minutes later, Attala County Sheriff Roy Braswell was awakened by the call that he had been halfway expecting but fully dreading since Leon's jailbreak. When Turner had escaped, Braswell feared that a time bomb had been set. With this phone call, he was to learn that time had run out.

On the line was Pat Smithson, calling from Sallis. As he had two weeks ago, Pat launched right into the disturbing subject of the call. He told of Buck's story of violence and his own visit to the Harris house, vividly detailing the arena of death. Normally staid and controlled, Pat's voice cracked with emotion as he disclosed that even a little girl had been shot. She now lay seriously wounded, along with her father. Both needed an ambulance immediately.

Sheriff Braswell listened to Smithson's description of the butchery with half his brain, for the other half was already formulating his next move. He realized the magnitude of the crime called for major action. This was going to be a long night.

Braswell ended the call by telling Smithson that he and an ambulance would be right there.

As soon as he hung up, Roy lifted the handset and called the hospital, telling the nurse who answered that he needed a Negro ambulance at the Harris's house. He gave directions from memory.

Normally, Roy would have driven to the crime scene to check it out himself before taking drastic measures, but this situation was different. He trusted Smithson's description of the site—he could almost picture the dead children in his mind. There was no time to gather more facts. The area needed to be cordoned off. He had to catch the killers in a noose, but the noose would be too big for his tiny staff to handle. They needed reinforcements.

Roy dressed, put on his gun, and drove the five minutes to the square. The hurried sound of his leather-soled shoes on the courthouse tile echoed off the empty building's marble walls as he rushed into his office. On the corner of his desk was a sheet of statewide phone numbers.

Braswell knew that Leon Turner—possibly aided by the Whitt brothers—had committed the murders. They would not be easily found. After all, he and his men had not been able to locate them following their jailbreak, even though it was almost certain they were hiding in Beat 4. How much harder they would be to find now that the three were running from a multiple homicide.

Child killers! The crime was so much more abhorrent than the typical murder that a rural sheriff had to handle: a man killing another in a liquor-fueled argument or a life bought too cheaply over the few dollars in someone's wallet. No, this one was different. The massacre of innocent children in their own home was way over any line one might conceive. Only an animal could have done such a thing—an animal that had to be caught or killed using all the resources the State of Mississippi could muster.

His call to District Headquarters of the Mississippi Highway Patrol in Greenwood went through quickly.[7] Roy explained the situation and requested that an all-out manhunt be initiated right away. He needed manpower to cordon off the southwest corner of Attala County. Again he emphasized speed—much precious time had already passed.

Braswell's third call was to Parchman Prison, location of the state's tracking bloodhounds.[8] He had utilized the dogs to hunt people on previous occasions and knew that the fresher the trail, the higher their likelihood of success. Roy requested that hounds be brought to Newport as soon as possible.

The sheriff's last call summoned his counterpart in the adjoining county to the north, Sheriff Dewitt Tyler of Montgomery County. Tyler was a good friend; Roy suspected that he was going to need the help of many such friends.

No one else was in sight on the Kosciusko Square as the diminutive sheriff slid behind the wheel of his car, slapped an emergency rotating light on the dashboard, and checked that his revolver was fully loaded. Then he backed out of his parking space and sped toward Newport.

It was 2:30 a.m. Monday morning when Sheriff Braswell stopped in front of the Harris house. Several cars were already there; an ambulance was not one of them. Pat Smithson, Willie McCrory, and Attala County Constable Hugh Bailey stood in front of the porch with hands in their coat pockets. When Braswell exited his car and walked to the group, Bailey removed a cigarette from his mouth and launched into a description of the carnage inside the house, shaking his head in disbelief. He further explained that a quick look around the property had found no one outside.

Braswell walked up the steps onto the porch, and Bailey pointed out two .38 caliber bullet casings lying on the floor. Then Roy entered the house.

Although he had been warned what to expect, the cruel sight stunned him. Strewn about the room were three children. The sickeningly sweet smell of their blood permeated the air. Braswell stepped to the boy slumped against the wall, a blank stare announcing his death. Squatting next to Frankie,

Braswell saw what appeared to be bullet wounds through the middle part of his body and left arm.

This kid would never play again.

Behind Braswell, Deputy Q. Q. Harris stood next to a tiny girl facedown on a bed. The back of her nightgown was stained by an ugly circle of blood. Harris informed his boss that the child was still alive, but just barely. The sheriff moved to her; putting his fingers on her wrist, he detected a very slight pulse.

Grimly, Braswell looked over to the bed holding May C. A crimson pool on the covers below her chest glistened in the light.

"She's dead," someone said.

Roy bowed his head and remembered the last time he was here. It had been only two weeks ago, right before Christmas. At that time, he had thought—actually, it was more of a hope—that the family's dealings with Leon Turner were ended. Violence had been averted and Leon was in handcuffs, soon to be headed back to prison. How wrong he had been; how clueless his foreshadowing of the future had proven. Roy had known Leon Turner's propensity for violence and disregard of society's rules, his volatile unpredictability. But who could have ever anticipated that he would be capable of something like this—the cold-blooded murder of small, defenseless children?

A noise caused him to look up. Another deputy stepped out of the kitchen and, gesturing rearward with his thumb, stated that there was a casualty in the back of the house. Roy followed him, expecting to find the body of Mary Ella Harris or her older daughter. He was surprised to see that it was Thomas Harris, alive.

The sheriff kneeled next to Thomas and called his name. Harris's eyes fluttered and cracked open.

Roy put his mouth inches from the wounded man's ear and asked Thomas who had shot him.

Struggling to breathe, Harris replied in a whisper. He spat out one word: "Leon."

Several minutes later, the ambulance still had not arrived. Roy and his deputies used the waiting time to inspect the house. Five .38 cartridge cases were scattered throughout the bedroom; one was in the kitchen. These and the shells outside the front door appeared to have come from the same pistol. On the porch, they discovered an area of smeared blood on the planks by the other door. Blood drops trailed from there into the bedroom where the children lay. More drops led from the doorway to the steps.

Around 3:15 a.m., Ruby Nell Harris died. Roy was shaken that this small child had been so senselessly cut down. His mood was sour as he milled about the front yard, alone in the crisp air.

He was pacing near the road when the ambulance arrived. As soon as driver John Wiley Brown, from the Century Burial Association—Kosciusko's black ambulance and funeral business—exited the vehicle, Sheriff Braswell ordered him to load up Thomas Harris and get him to the hospital, then come back and collect the bodies. At the mention of "bodies," Brown raised his eyebrows in surprise. He raised them again upon entering the house.

The search for evidence continued after the ambulance left. In the backyard, a deputy found two freshly fired shotgun shells and wadding. Here was the first indication that more than one gun had been involved. Braswell realized that Leon was not alone. The Whitt brothers didn't go back to Alabama after all. Roy now knew that he had to concentrate on hunting three men—three armed, dangerous, and probably desperate men.

Action picked up dramatically after 4:00 a.m. Greenwood-based Mississippi Highway Patrol cars came down Highway 14 from the west along with lawmen from Goodman, Pickens, and Durant. Patrolmen from the Starkville district, as well as police from Sallis, McAdams, and Kosciusko came from the east. Winona's Sheriff Tyler brought support from the north; units from the Jackson and Meridian Highway Patrol districts arrived from the south.[9] Roadblocks were set up on roads to the surrounding towns of Sallis, Pickens, Goodman, Thomastown, and Carthage. Officers were stationed for protection at Judge Allen's house.[10]

In the midst of the activity, a Highway Patrol car from Parchman Prison arrived. Driving was Patrolman Tom Sadler; sitting unshackled to his right was prison trusty and convicted murderer Hogjaw Mullen, Mississippi's Main Mos' Dog Boy. Moving about on the backseat were his three top bloodhounds: 'Bama, Red, and Nigger.

The dogs' tails wagged furiously as Hogjaw opened the rear door and attached tracking leashes to their brass collars.[11] At their trainer's signal, they bounded out of the car to the ground with snouts down and sniffing.

Sheriff Braswell briefed Sadler and Hogjaw on the situation, explaining that, as best he could figure, the dogs would be searching for three men. He then led the trackers into the house.

The bodies of Frankie, May C., and Nell lay where they had died as Hogjaw Mullen led his charges through the house under the admiring eyes of Mississippi lawmen scrambling to keep out of the way. Hogjaw next took his hounds outside, well away from the cabin and its multiple, confusing smells.

A hundred yards distant, he began circling the house, waiting for his animals to pick up a human scent.

Early morning was the ideal time for hounds to search, before the sun had a chance to burn off the scent and before the morning breeze blew it away for good. Unfortunately, Hogjaw's quarry had fled down Highway 14, whose bare dirt and clay surface was poor for retaining scents. Additionally, the recent vehicular traffic had totally obliterated the trail. As a result, the animals were unable to locate the killers' track despite hunting until well past dawn.[12]

Daylight colored the sky, illuminating a beehive of activity expanding from the shack that once housed the Harris family. The obscurity the family had known in life was about to be erased by death. Because of their tragedy, dozens of police, deputies, and highway patrolmen now scoured the countryside of Beat 4. Highway 14 bustled with official cars speeding to and fro, activity that caught the attention of locals doing their early morning chores. Newly married Bailey Hutchinson was in a barn milking cows with a crippled old helper named Sel Chester. Noticing the heavy law enforcement vehicle traffic on the highway, Bailey and Sel figured something was up. After leaving the gathered milk next to the road to be picked up by a milk truck, they scrambled down the highway to the Harrises', where a lawman explained that there had been a shooting in the house. While Sel chose to stay outside, Bailey walked through the door unchallenged. The sight of the dead children would forever remain etched in his memory.[13]

Sheriff Braswell and his men began interviewing the Harrises' neighbors. Naturally, they started at the closest house.

Mrs. Roby and everyone in her home were asleep when the sheriff knocked. The exhausted woman trudged warily to her front window and peeked around tattered curtains. She then opened her door for Roy Braswell with a smile of relief.

Verlene was soon in a police car on her way to the hospital. Mary Ella spent the next hour going over the events of the night with the sheriff. Following the interrogation, she and her baby left to stay several days with her sister.

Sheriff Braswell now had a clear picture of the incident. He knew exactly who and what he was up against.

Word of the crime spread rapidly. The sheer brutality of these incomprehensible murders touched the hearts of all who heard about them.

The grim news greeted Mississippi's leaders as they came to work Monday morning. Each recoiled in disgust at the atrocity committed against God-fearing people. It did not matter that the killers were white and the victims were black—responses to the crime transcended the racial boundary. It could not be tolerated. Orders were issued at all levels of state government to support the efforts to apprehend the murderers. One of the most intensive manhunts in the state's history began.

Unfortunately, several critical hours had passed since the slayings. The circumstances had given Leon Turner and the Whitt brothers a sizable head start, and they had not been idle.

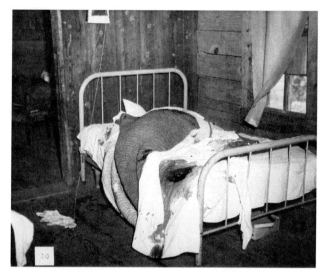

Nell's blood stains on her bed. Wind whipping through the broken
window pane blows the curtain and light string.

The survivors. Mary Ella holding James
with a wounded Verlene.

Chapter 13
Escape from Attala

Minutes after the shootings, the killers jogged along Highway 14, engulfed by a darkness that described both the depth of the night and the cruelty of their deed. All three carried guns, two carried fruit jars of sloshing moonshine, and one carried the burden of innocent blood, although he didn't seem to be bothered with it.

In fact, Leon Turner was pumped with adrenaline from the murderous frenzy. More than once he gushed, "Goddamn, I killed the whole damn bunch of 'em!" Spoken not as an admission of guilt or remorse, the words were more a surprised proclamation of accomplishment. Leon sounded proud of himself.

Contrary to their companion's excitement, Malcolm and Windol Whitt were subdued. The dizzying events of the last hour had left them confused about what had just happened. They had heard the yelling and screaming and gunfire within the Harrises' cabin, but they hadn't known what was really happening. The only violence they witnessed was Verlene's shooting. Now they found themselves running alongside Leon, with him bragging about killing everyone.

After a short time on the highway, where not a single car appeared from either direction, the men turned south onto less traveled County Road 4016. Their gait slowed to a walk.

Trudging along the muddy road, they discussed their next move, though Leon did most of the talking. The bodies would be discovered after sunup, he supposed, and a search for them would begin. Before that ensued, they needed to get away from Attala County.

Being on the run would require money. A quick pocket check revealed that, combined, they had barely more than a dollar. Turner knew where they could get more.

In a repeat of ten nights before, Howard Turner was shaken out of a deep sleep by his oldest son. Howard dragged himself out of bed, draped a blanket about his shoulders, and went with his son to talk on the front porch.

Leon explained what he and his cohorts had done at the Harris house. "I killed the whole damn bunch," he said matter-of-factly. Of course, he lay the blame squarely on Thomas Harris, who had snitched to the sheriff and gotten Leon and his friends thrown in jail when they had done nothing more than have a little fun. And then Thomas had had the gumption to press charges. He deserved to die. It was just bad luck that the others got killed. The whole family was no account, anyway; wouldn't nobody miss 'em.

Throughout the telling, Malcolm stood silently on the porch with his head down, listening to Leon's story and excuses with growing apprehension. Had that damn idiot actually killed the family? Hearing Leon so straightforwardly tell his father made the madness sink in. It must be true.

And Malcolm wanted nothing to do with it. His unease boiled over when Leon told his father that the three of them were going away.

"Me and Windol ain't goin' nowhere," Malcolm interrupted. "We ain't killed nobody and got nothin' to run from."

Insolence was not something that Leon tolerated, especially when caught by surprise. "Yes you will too!" he flared, shattering the quiet like the first clap of thunder. He stepped to Malcolm, the weak moonlight providing just enough light for the two to stare face to face. After a brief moment, Malcolm broke eye contact and nodded his head in mute compliance.

With that brief rebellion quelled, Leon asked his father for some money. Howard went inside and came back with a ten-dollar bill. Handing it to his boy, the two shook hands and said goodbye. Then Leon led his companions away.

As the jailbreakers-turned-killers walked back to the road, Malcolm and Windol talked of going to see their mother; but Leon said they couldn't risk it—they had to get out of the area fast.

They needed a car. Leon had eyed the pulpwood truck back at his father's place, but the old clunker couldn't be counted on to travel very far. Heading back toward Newport, the men checked out automobiles at houses they passed. Since all the homes belonged to dirt-poor farmers, the cars and trucks were few in number and poor in condition. Well away from Howard's house, however, they spotted an interesting vehicle. A gray Studebaker pickup parked in front of a nondescript old shack looked to be in decent shape. It even had red wheels.

Leon walked to the door of the darkened house and knocked. After a few moments, a Negro woman dressed in a tattered robe appeared. Leon recognized her but didn't know her name.

"Who does that truck out yonder belong to?" Leon asked nonchalantly, as if it were a perfectly normal question to ask any stranger awakened in the middle of the night.

Mrs. Ezra Burns had no doubt who Leon was. Straining to steady her voice so the fear wasn't obvious, the woman answered truthfully, "Caesar Young."[1]

Leon knew Caesar, a bootlegger who had gotten in trouble with the sheriff a few months back.[2] He would be no problem; he wanted to avoid the law as much as Leon.

"Go git 'im," Leon ordered.

Mrs. Burns backed into the dark interior of her home and tried to close the door, but Leon blocked it with his foot. The woman turned and walked away. Soon, a sleepy-looking Caesar Young peered out from behind the door with only his head and bare shoulders visible.

Malcolm and Windol stood in the yard next to the truck. They could see Leon talking to someone; and judging from his animated gestures, the discussion was heated. A minute later, they saw Leon turn away. A flash of yellowish light illuminated his scraggly face as Leon lit a cigarette and waited by the door. Eventually, Caesar Young came out fully dressed. The two strode together to Caesar's truck.

Taking a jar of moonshine from Windol, Leon handed it to Young and told him to drink up. The four men stood at the front of the pickup passing around the moonshine for a minute, and then Leon told the Whitt brothers that Caesar was taking them for a ride.

The pickup was crowded. Caesar Young sat behind the wheel. Next to him on the bench seat was Malcolm Whitt, holding his .22 rifle and a jar of hooch. Windol was to his brother's right, next to the door, with Leon Turner sitting in his lap. Leon had a pistol in his pants' waist and Windol's shotgun, along with the second jar of moonshine, in his hands. Under Leon's instructions, Caesar drove to Highway 14 and headed west.

Traveling at a decent speed in a well-running vehicle allowed the murderers to breathe easier. They drank moonshine to celebrate their escape. They drank a lot, as did Caesar Young. Attala County became history halfway over the Big Black River. After two miles, the gray pickup crossed over a set of railroad tracks in Goodman and turned south onto Highway 51. They passed several honky-tonks, the usually packed parking lots now empty, the gaudy lights dark. It being Sunday night, the establishments were getting their only respite of the week.

Ten miles later, as residents of Pickens slept peacefully in their beds, a hijacked truck carrying three dangerous criminals and their kidnapped driver passed through the town. South of Pickens, the truck turned onto County Road 432 heading toward the Mississippi River.[3] Overhanging nude hardwood trees lined the narrow road forming a tunnel of sticks in the truck's dust-covered headlights.

The travelers were soused by the time they reached Yazoo City. A closed service station outside of town provided a place to stop and piss. During the pause, Windol told Leon about the trouble he and Malcolm had gotten into while working on a well-off farmer's plantation about fifteen miles away. Turner could care less about the past problems of his companions, but he perked up at the mention of a rich man. The fugitives needed money. So long as they were in the vicinity of a wealthy planter, why not take advantage of it?

Having once worked on Oscar Sibley's plantation, the Whitts knew the area well enough to guide Caesar Young to Louise, and then to Sibley's home near Five Mile Lake. They arrived at 4:40 a.m.

Leon took a swig of 'shine before he and Malcolm got out of the truck. As the pair walked toward Sibley's house, two

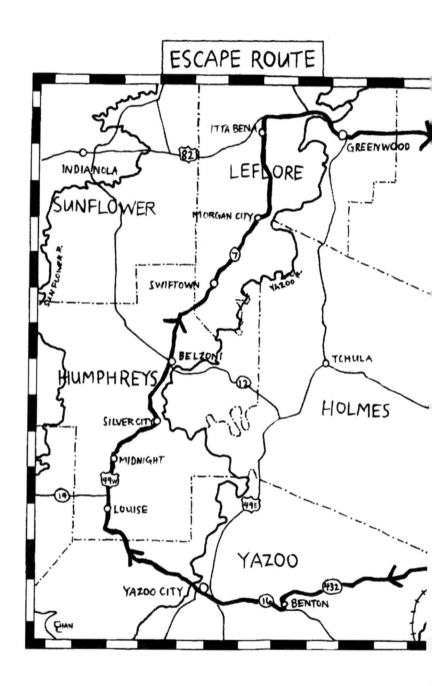

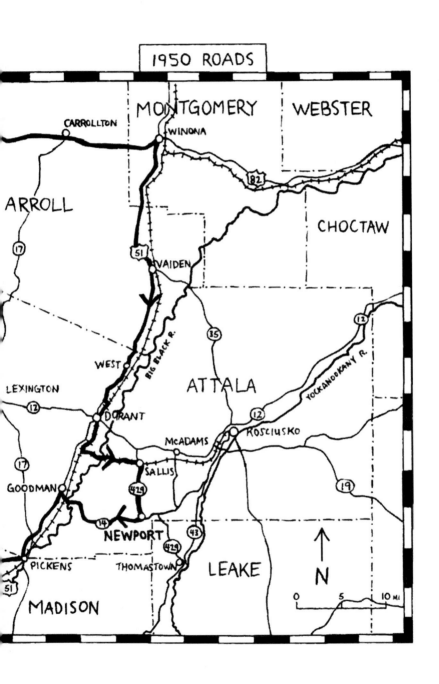

1950 ROADS

dogs came running, barking furiously. Unfazed, Leon merely stooped toward the animals and snarled as he continued walking. He didn't worry about the racket they were making; he planned to wake up the residents anyway.

Malcolm knocked on Sibley's door as Leon hid to his side. The porch light came on, the door opened, and there stood Oscar Sibley. Suspicion registered on the farmer's face as he recognized Malcolm. Sibley had suffered a lot of trouble two autumns before because of the misadventures of Malcolm and his brother. Things had eventually returned to normal, but only after a Herculean effort by the respected planter to smooth the feathers ruffled by his former employees.

Sibley eyed Malcolm from head to foot and warily asked the younger man what he wanted. Before Whitt could respond, Leon Turner stepped into view aiming a pistol at the homeowner. Sibley froze and Malcolm backed away as Leon came closer.

No one was going to get hurt, Leon explained; he just wanted money. All Sibley had to do was fork over his wallet, and the visitors would be on their way.

Sibley calmly said he would comply, but he needed to first fetch his wallet.

Leon stepped into the entryway and told Sibley to hurry. The homeowner glanced angrily at Malcolm before walking out of the room. He came back a few seconds later carrying his wallet. Leon grabbed it out of his hands and pulled out the contents: six one-dollar bills.[4]

Satisfied with the easy money, Turner backed out of the door and strode toward the pickup truck with Malcolm following.

Caesar Young was so drunk and sleepy he could barely drive. His pickup drifted off the right side of the dirt road more than once as it sped northward out of Louise.

The journey continued through Midnight and Silver City. Later, with the gas gauge reading low, the truck pulled into an all-night service station in the town of Belzoni.

Gulf station attendant Lloyd Turner admired the red wheels on the ton-and-a-half pickup waiting at his pump.[5] Coming closer, Lloyd noted a rather unusual sight: a Negro man driving and three white men in the cab with him, one holding a shotgun. Strange goings-on were an occupational hazard of the late-night shift, the attendant knew from experience, but this circumstance had the potential of being extremely dangerous. He wanted these guys gone.

The noticeably large man holding the shotgun said, "Put in two dollars' worth." It was all the instruction Lloyd Turner needed. He hustled to the gas cap.

While the gas was pumping, Windol got out briefly to stretch legs tortured from Leon's weight. When he got back in, they traded places and he sat on Leon's lap.

When everything was done, Leon paid the relieved worker, and the truck pulled back onto the road.

Monday's daybreak saw the men driving northward on State Highway 7, surrounded by Mississippi Delta land flatter than felt on a dance hall pool table. They passed through Morgan City and Itta Bena, where two or three early-morning visitors arranging flowers or praying at the city cemetery were oblivious to the crowded pickup speeding by. Five minutes north of Itta Bena, Highway 7 intersected U.S. Highway 82, a major east–west road. Rather than steer left toward Arkansas fifty miles away, Leon directed Caesar Young to turn right.

"Welcome to Greenwood, Cotton Capital of the World" read a sign on the outskirts of this moderately sized town. As they approached a country store on the right, Leon told

Caesar to pull in. When the truck came to a stop, Leon swung open his door and announced, "This is where we get out at."

Maybe not. The ride from Belzoni with little conversation had given Malcolm time to contemplate the trouble he and his brother were in. Their situation was grim, and all because of that crazy son of a bitch Leon Turner. They had to get away from him.

And now, the opportunity was here. Malcolm made a quick decision. "We're not getting out," he challenged.

Leon took the pistol from his waist and pulled back the hammer with an ominous *click.* "Yes, by God, you are."

"No, by God, we ain't," Malcolm said. It was time for the showdown. Going with Leon meant being on the run or being in jail for the rest of his life. The only possibility of freedom was to stand up to him now. It risked getting shot, but he had to take the chance.

Leon cursed and threatened Malcolm, calling him a goddamned coward. Malcolm screamed back, blasting Turner as a lunatic who was going to get them all killed. The look on Turner's face warned of danger; he was perilously close to exploding. But before he did, Windol intervened.

"Let him go. I'll keep goin' with you," Windol shouted amid the storm. His exclamation produced a moment of silence. "Two can get by better than three anyhow," he continued, proposing to let Malcolm and Caesar take off. Two separate groups would be harder to track.

It made sense to Leon. Two groups on the run would cause any lawmen that were chasing them to have to split up. He decided to let Malcolm and Caesar go. After more discussion, Leon became convinced that the law would be on the lookout for their pickup truck. He would be better off without it.

And so it happened that, shortly after seven o'clock Monday morning, January 9, 1950, Leon Turner and Windol Whitt stood outside a Greenwood store as Caesar Young's pickup pulled away. Caesar was driving, Malcolm to his right. On the floorboard lay Malcolm's .22 and Windol's shotgun.

At this same time, a morning mist was yielding to the sun as Sheriff Braswell and his deputies began calling on the relatives and associates of the three fugitives. First on their list was Howard Turner.

The lawmen were understandably anxious as they parked in front of Turner's shanty. Should Leon be there, cornered and desperate, he would likely put up a fight.

The tension was thicker than cold sorghum molasses as deputies approached the home. Quietly and slowly, two men snuck around the house to cover the back. Suddenly, a figure bolted from the rear of the cabin. A deputy shouted in alarm; Sheriff Braswell jumped behind a tree, one man crawled beneath a patrol car, while others hit the dirt. But no shots rang out; no bullets came whizzing by. The panic evaporated once the runner reached the nearby woods and turned around. It was Roosevelt Whitcomb.[6]

After an unproductive search of the house and grounds, Sheriff Braswell stood on the porch with Leon's father and grandmother, telling of the mayhem that had occurred at the Harris home. Out of respect to the old woman, he did not outright accuse Elvira's grandson of murder, but he heavily implied that Leon was the prime suspect. Howard denied any knowledge of his son's whereabouts, saying he had not seen Leon since the boy had broken out of jail. Elvira dabbed the sores on her face and declared steadfastly that Leon could not have committed such a terrible act.

Malcolm and Windol's mother and stepfather similarly claimed no awareness of the pair's location.

All morning long, Braswell or his men visited anyone connected to the fugitives. Friends and neighbors, shopkeepers and customers, moonshiners and bootleggers—all denied having any recent contact.

Rumors abounded that Leon and the Whitt brothers had committed the murders, and Beat 4 citizens believed them. Upon first learning of the atrocity, people became angry. Condemnation of the crime and loathing of the criminals were unanimous reactions. Man or woman, poor or wealthy, black or white—no one excused or forgave the killers.

And then came fear. Everyone assumed that Leon and the Whitts were still in the area. Now that they had killed, they might do anything to avoid capture. Folks were plain scared.

Caesar zigzagged erratically through the southern part of Greenwood after leaving Leon and Windol. Fearing that the truck's weaving would attract police attention, Malcolm had him stop at a store for cigarettes and a Coke. As they drove away, Malcolm was at the wheel. The truck had gone barely a block before Caesar was leaning against his door, sound asleep.

Malcolm, too, was extremely tired, but he had a goal to keep him going. The only way to clear his and Windol's names would be to explain their innocence to the authorities. He was heading back to Newport.

Driving eastward on Highway 82, Malcolm picked up a youngster hitchhiking and let him ride in the truck bed. He dropped off the youth several miles later in Winona and then turned right onto Highway 51.

Caesar Young awoke briefly as they cruised through the small town of Vaiden. Malcolm told him that they were on their way back home; and for the first time since his adventure began, the truck owner smiled. Then he dozed off again.

Ground fog along the swampy marshlands of the Big Black River slickened the roadway as Malcolm continued southward. He made Caesar slide to the middle when he picked up another hitchhiker, an old man in faded overalls, who was traveling to Durant. Climbing into the cab, the farmer didn't flinch at the sight of two rifles on the floorboard. Malcolm chatted with him all the way to Durant. That the rider did not mention the previous night's murders was a hopeful sign to Malcolm.

After discharging his passenger in Durant, Whitt steered onto Highway 12 for the eastward run to Sallis. He would not pick up any more hitchhikers—his mother's home was only a few minutes away, and he was anxious to get there.

Only ten miles remained when Malcolm turned right onto County Road 429 at Sallis. Speeding to get home, he caught up with a Mississippi Highway Patrol car going the same direction. He slowed and nervously trailed the patrolman by a healthy distance.

Nearing Newport, Malcolm spotted a roadblock ahead. He could not avoid it—turning around would be a dead giveaway. Malcolm slid the guns underneath the seat with his feet and steeled himself for the inevitable. Approaching the barricade, he slowed down and lowered the window; but to his surprise, a patrolman guarding the road casually waved the truck on without a second glance. Officers were looking for fugitives traveling north. Anyone going south was passed through unimpeded.

Although he had not been detected, much less captured, Malcolm found the experience unnerving. Now he knew without a doubt he was being hunted. To make matters worse, the presence of highway patrolmen signified he was being pursued by the entire state of Mississippi.

Thankfully, no lawmen were in sight when he pulled into his mother's driveway. It was midmorning, not twelve hours since the surreal events that had precipitated the long circuitous odyssey. As Malcolm killed the engine, a quiet settled in, and with it, the harsh realization that he had come home without his little brother. Windol was still out there somewhere, still in the company of the madman who had brought this tragedy crashing down on their lives.

Wearily, Malcolm got out and closed the truck door, leaving behind the weapons and the sleeping black man. He wanted nothing more to do with them. He had taken only a few steps when his mother came tearing out of the house. Birdie Bell ran to her son, threw her arms around him, and burst into tears. No words were uttered as they remained locked in a hug of desperation. At last, Birdie Bell grabbed Malcolm's hand and pulled him into the safety of her home.

She had been choked with worry since Sheriff Braswell had appeared at her home earlier that morning. Her boys could not have been a part of what the sheriff described. While far from perfect angels, they were not murderers. What reason would they have to kill someone? Other than relatives, they barely knew anyone around here.

Malcolm collapsed on his mother's couch and laid his head on the back cushions, eyes closed tight. Birdie Bell stood beside her son, gazing at his exhausted face, filled with worry for him and Windol. She didn't speak; she merely waited. Her husband, Pat Baldridge, came into the room and quietly put his arm around her waist.

Eventually, Malcolm covered his face with his hands and began to talk. The events of the previous evening spilled from his lips in a narrative of the macabre. Birdie Bell wept as Malcolm told of hearing gunshots and children's screams. He did not know what had actually happened, but he repeated Leon Turner's brags of killing the family. Next came stealing the truck and escaping the county. While omitting the part about robbing Oscar Sibley, Malcolm went into detail about Windol's staying with Leon so Malcolm could go free.

The chronicle was anguishing for Malcolm's mother, but she believed every word. She wanted—she desperately needed—to believe every word. Her sons were innocent.

Malcolm next told her of his decision to surrender to the authorities. She totally agreed. It was the only way to convince the law of his and Windol's innocence. Surely, Sheriff Braswell would believe them. He knew that the brothers' Attala County relatives were decent people. The boys were from good stock.

With the whole story laid out, the next action was clear. Birdie Bell asked Pat to go get the sheriff.

By now, news of the murders and the ensuing manhunt had made it to the state's press. At the *Kosciusko Star-Herald*, which rarely had more to print in its weekly editions than the mundane happenings of a rural county, reports of the crime created a stir of excitement. Quick to rush out the door with his camera bag was the newspaper's staff photographer.

Thirty-five-year-old Billy McMillan was a talented, wavy-haired workaholic who seized any opportunity to use his photographic skills.[7] He had hardly ever used a camera before marrying the daughter of the *Star-Herald*'s owner and publisher. But once recruited by his father-in-law to work at the newspaper, McMillan had taken to photography with a passion. His camera of choice was an Anniversary Speed Graphic 4 x 5 using Ansco Triple S film.

After gaining unrestricted access to the Harris cabin, McMillan took several photos of the murder scene. Though the bodies had been removed, the bloody remnants of the slaughter provided ample subjects for his lens.

When finished, McMillan walked outside as newly arrived Pat Baldridge was telling a surprised Sheriff Braswell and his men about Malcolm Whitt's intention to turn himself in. Upon seeing McMillan, the sheriff—never one to avoid publicity when the opportunity arose—invited the local press representative to witness the hunt and inevitable capture of the killers.

Parked in front of the Baldridge residence when Braswell arrived had been a gray pickup truck with a sleeping Negro and two guns inside. Caesar Young was promptly yanked out of the cab and placed under arrest. He now sat handcuffed in the back of a patrol car.

A dozen lawmen surrounded the house, taking cover behind automobiles, trees, farm equipment, and a barn. Each man held a gun. Should things get ugly, a massive volley of firepower was ready to be loosed.

A safe distance away, a group of bystanders looked on. Alerted by a highly efficient word-of-mouth network, the locals had been drawn to the action like birds to a tomato patch. Standing among them was Billy McMillan.

Once his men were in position, Roy Braswell yelled for Malcolm Whitt to give himself up peacefully and come out with his hands up.

An eerie silence crept over the scene in anticipation of the next move. Witnesses to the drama heard no sound of birds, no swish of leaves fluttering in the breeze, no nervous heartbeats thumping in their ears. Only that house existed. All eyes were locked on it in a hypnotic, open-mouthed stare.

At last, the front door budged. Slowly it opened halfway. There was an excruciating pause, then out walked Birdie Bell Baldridge. She took three steps, nervously flattened her skirt, and took a deep breath. Then she announced that her son was in the house and wanted to surrender. Hesitating slightly, Birdie Bell moved to the door and pulled it fully open. From the shadows slouched Malcolm Whitt with a cigarette between his lips and both hands up. After advancing several feet from the house, he stopped and gazed vacantly at the weapons pointed his way.

Roy Braswell holstered his weapon and coolly walked up to Malcolm. Whitt lowered his arms to straight in front of him with wrists together, ready to be handcuffed.

As the sheriff began putting on the restraints, Malcolm began talking. He denied any wrongdoing, pinning all the guilt on Leon Turner. When Roy asked where Leon was, Malcolm told of leaving his brother and Leon in Greenwood a few hours ago.

Malcolm continued to proclaim his innocence even as Deputy Q. Q. Harris escorted him to a squad car. Photographer Billy McMillan walked backward in front of the two, capturing the scene that would be featured in many of the nation's newspapers the following day.

It was shortly after noon when Sheriff Braswell left the scene.[8] Roy now knew that the killers had fled to the western part of Mississippi. He hurried to relay this information to state officials. The search needed to concentrate on the Delta.

Events happened quickly after Braswell sent notice of the killers' last known whereabouts. By that afternoon, over one hundred highway patrolmen, sheriffs, deputies, and constables were involved in the manhunt.[9] Joining them were small groups of armed white men enraged by the act of killing children, no matter what their color. These citizens wanted Turner dead, and should they see him, they intended to take the first shot. Spoke one shotgun-wielding volunteer, "I don't reckon he'd give a man much of a chance. A man who'd kill children . . . well, he ain't been preaching lately."[10]

Based on Malcolm's information, the primary focus of the search shifted westward. Reports of sightings in that area confirmed his story. Someone claimed that two men had been let out of a pickup truck Monday morning in Yazoo City. Oscar Sibley told of being robbed by Malcolm and another man early that morning at Five Mile Lake.

The posse thought they had their quarry when information was received about men hiding in a cabin next to Wolf Lake, near Louise. Dozens of lawmen surrounded the cabin and an officer called for the men to come out. Receiving no response, the posse invaded the cabin en masse, inflicting impressively heavy damage to the structure and its contents. But no one was inside.[11]

Another rumor had the fugitives either at Greenville or Indianola catching a freight train to Memphis. This report sent segments of the posse scampering in different directions in a fruitless check of rail yards all over the Delta.[12]

Back in Attala County, Sheriff Braswell operated on the assumption that Leon Turner might return to Newport like

Malcolm Whitt. Roy worked to prevent anyone from helping Leon should that occur. He also wanted to pressure—as
well as punish—those people who had already provided assistance. He had learned a hard lesson from his lackadaisical
response following the December jailbreak. Because he had
not forced the escapees' friends and relatives to tell of their
whereabouts, several children were dead. That mistake would
not be repeated.

Monday afternoon, the sheriff rounded up several Beat 4
residents and put them in the Attala County Jail on charges
connected with the jailbreak and subsequent hideout. Parvee
Rutherford was arrested for providing a gun. Birdie Bell and
Pat Baldridge, despite their earlier cooperation, were jailed
for aiding an escaped fugitive. Two unidentified men were
taken into custody for helping to operate a still.[13]

The harshest treatment was imposed on Leon's immediate family. While sparing Elvira Turner from incarceration, Roy locked up every other person who lived in the
Turners' shack. Howard Turner was placed in the Attala
County Jail on a charge of aiding an escaped fugitive. Five
of his children—ranging in age from Bug, nineteen, to Rat,
ten, were crammed into the backseat of a Highway Patrol
car and taken to jail in Durant. The hardnosed highway
patrolman who drove them was rough and abusive to the
children.[14]

The Durant jail was a dreary facility badly in need of
repair—for the youngsters, who had never before even visited
a jailhouse, it was an especially frightening, terrible place.
Its interior smelled of unwashed bodies, urine, and filth.
Rainwater leaked from the ceiling. The children were herded
into a cold cell with water covering the floor. They huddled
near the far wall, the young ones crying as the jailer slammed
shut the cell door.

A single cot with a disgustingly stained mattress was the cell's only furniture. Bug and Ape put the younger kids on the bed and then sat in the water with their backs against the walls.[15]

News of Malcolm's seizure did not relieve the fears of Beat 4 residents, for two killers were still on the loose. That Malcolm had been caught at his mother's home reinforced suspicions that the murderers may still be in the area.

As Monday afternoon faded, bearing no sign of an impending capture, many Newport families fled to relatives' homes elsewhere in the county. Those who didn't leave grouped together for mutual protection and prayer. Menfolk kept an armed vigil through the night. In homes with no inside plumbing, children weren't allowed to venture outside to the outhouse. They used buckets instead.[16]

Everyone was scared. All felt vulnerable. Even those who got along with Leon were frightened, for they knew well of his unpredictability. Sheriff Braswell advised Newport residents to take up arms. He even provided extra ammunition to those who needed it.

For a brief time following the murders, these concerns were groundless. Leon was escaping away from his neighbors, traveling into northwestern Mississippi on his way to parts unknown.

But things changed. Even as the citizens of Newport tried to sleep that Monday night, tossing and turning with worry about a cold-blooded maniac on the loose, Leon Turner had turned around and was heading home.

Malcolm Whitt (in handcuffs) being led away by Q. Q. Harris.

Chapter 14

On the Lam

The clerk shook his head as he parked in front of the Greenwood store when coming to work early Monday morning. Two scraggly-looking white men were loitering outside—hobos, probably. The smaller man wore an Eisenhower jacket. Though the strangers stopped conversing when the worker got out of his car, their proper enough "Hey" and "How do" gave no impression of troublesome intent. Still, the clerk eyed them warily as he unlocked the store and slipped inside.

Once the shopkeeper was out of earshot, Leon Turner and Windol Whitt resumed discussing where to go. They would be able to travel quicker and with less decision-making hassle now that Malcolm Whitt and Caesar Young were out of the picture. Or so it would seem. In fact, the determination of their next destination was far from settled.

Leon wanted to head to Memphis. Odds were, the crime hadn't been reported yet, and he wanted to be well away from Attala County when things heated up. Windol had other ideas. Like Malcolm, his goal was to return to Newport. The trick was convincing Leon.

Since Leon was physically larger than Windol, thirteen years older, and the one who generally called the shots, there would presumably be no doubt as to where the pair would go. Something about Windol, however, caused Leon to listen to him; and if there was ever a right moment for Windol to influence Leon, it was now. Windol cast out his lure, hoping Leon would go for it.

Heading off into the unknown didn't feel right, he opined. Being in unfamiliar territory would put them at a disadvantage if lawmen came searching. Windol expressed admiration for Leon's abilities to survive and thrive in the woods around Newport. He firmly believed that Leon could stay hidden in Attala County forever.

Having laid the foundation, Windol now finished his case. Back home, he reasoned, the two of them stood a good chance of escaping the law; plus, their time on the lam would be more comfortable than if they were in some unknown, unfriendly place. He concluded by saying they ought to head back to Newport.

Society will never fully explain the mental processes of a psychopath like Leon Turner—in this situation, why the child murderer would so willingly accept Windol's arguments. But he did. Despite his quick and successful escape from Attala County, Leon changed his mind. Instead of relying on his own expert sense of survival, instead of continuing in a direction away from the scene of the crime, Leon Turner decided to return home.

The fugitives began walking along Highway 82, right hands up, thumbs pointed eastward, cigarettes dangling from their lips. Someone picked them up and took them a few miles into Greenwood. Another ride dropped them off on the other side of town. In such fits and starts, Leon and Windol hitchhiked twenty-five miles to Winona.

Winona was a busy little town at the intersection of two major roads: U.S. Highway 82, connecting communities across the width of Mississippi from Arkansas to Alabama; and U.S. Highway 51, which traversed the state lengthwise on its run from Memphis to New Orleans. Located at their junction was the Tri-State Trailways Bus Terminal & Café.

One of the busiest bus stations in the state, Tri-State hosted thirty-two scheduled buses daily.[1] It was here that Leon and Windol's last lift dropped them off shortly after 10:00 a.m.

Yellowed linoleum floors dulled by countless leather soles greeted the two travelers as they entered the bustling terminal. Leon went directly to the ticket counter and inquired about the next bus heading south. He was told that a bus to Jackson would leave at noon.

The other end of the station contained the Trailways Café.[2] Its delicious smells wafted throughout the terminal, proving irresistible to Leon and Windol. Despite the danger of lingering in such a crowded spot, they were soon seated in a booth near the back corner, hunched forward, devouring lunch. Whitt had a hamburger, and Turner an egg sandwich.

When they finished eating, more than an hour remained until departure of the Jackson-bound bus. The terminal was crowded with strangers, including an occasional Winona policeman. Although no one gave him a second glance, the teeming conditions were too much for Leon. "Let's get out on the highway and thumb until time for the bus," he told Windol. "We can stop it on the highway if we don't catch a ride."

The pair walked out of the bus terminal and strolled south along Highway 51, thumbs skyward.

They were not the only ones heading south from the Winona depot.

It was traveling day for members of the Mississippi legislature. With the Christmas break ending, solons were making their way toward Jackson for the spring legislative session. They came from each of the state's eighty-two counties, traveling by train, car, or bus. Among the riders of the latter mode of transportation was a representative from Winona, John Aldridge of Montgomery County.

Representative Aldridge was on the Jackson-bound Trailways that left Winona at noon. Sitting next to him was eleven-year-old John Jr. Jack, as the boy was called, was excited. For the next several months, he would be a legislative page, working for his dad and staying with him in a fancy downtown Jackson hotel.

Jack was a smart lad, particularly adept at capturing details. He considered it great fun to perform legal research for his lawyer father. His mind was always searching for the new and unusual, and he remembered those things that interested him.[3]

He and his father had been on the bus only a few minutes when it stopped just south of Winona. Two men climbed on board and sat several rows forward of Jack. One, a notably rough-looking character, especially captured the boy's attention. Big, unshaven, and dirty, with a crumpled gray hat, he carried no bag, no luggage, no sack lunch. But the oddest thing was the paranoid way he acted. Before sitting down, the stranger looked about the bus, suspiciously scanning each passenger. Only at the very last second did Jack withdraw his stare to avoid the man's unfriendly eyes. Frightened by the close call, the youngster looked at his father and noticed that he, too, was watching the men.

The bus again rolled on, making brief stops along the way to offload and pick up passengers. While his father was absorbed in work papers, Jack gazed at the passing countryside. Winter's drab forests and bare fields surrounded them. Only fleeting glimpses of the Illinois Central railroad tracks, running parallel to the highway, broke the visual monotony. Jack was bored.

An hour later, they came to a swampy area a few miles north of Durant. Fed by the nearby Big Black River, dark and murky water clung to the bases of trees as far back in the woods as Jack could see. It was an uninviting place, where a boy's imagination spotted alligators and snakes under every fallen log or clump of bush. Suddenly, the engine sound changed and the bus began slowing. A few seconds later, in the middle of this watery nowhere, it stopped.

It was ordinary for a commercial bus to pull over and disembark a passenger who signaled, but the stopping place was typically in a community or near a farmhouse or country store. Nothing of the kind was now in sight; only water. Jack thought the bus was having mechanical difficulty. He wondered how long his trip to Jackson would be delayed.

The answer came immediately. Rising from seats ahead of him were the two men who had boarded outside of Winona. Jack watched the pair hurry to the front of the bus and get off. As mysteriously as the peculiar riders had appeared, they vanished.[4] The door closed and the bus began to accelerate. "Daddy, why are they getting off here?" Jack asked.[5]

John Aldridge put down his work and gazed at the sodden landscape. He honestly had no idea why anyone would get off at such an odd place.[6]

A few miles later, the bus pulled into the Durant terminal. Jack's attention now shifted to the loading passengers with their interesting new looks and behaviors. The bus resumed its journey and arrived in Jackson on schedule later that afternoon.

Being on the bus surrounded by strangers had been difficult for Leon Turner. After failing to catch a ride hitchhiking,
he and Windol had flagged it down. Leon had fidgeted the
entire ride, nervously glancing about, fully expecting someone to call out his name. Finally coming to a location that
he recognized north of Durant, he had signaled the driver to
stop the bus and rushed off with Windol following.

As the Trailways bus faded out of sight in a blurry wake
of diesel exhaust, Leon and Windol walked along Highway
51 toward Durant. At the first bit of dry land, they left the
road and plodded east a short distance to the raised bed of the
railway. They scrambled up the berm to the tracks, and then
headed southward. For several miles the pair walked, leaving the rails only to bypass downtown Durant to avoid being
sighted. Once south of town, they again took to the tracks.

Overcast skies made the late afternoon even darker as,
three miles south of Durant, they reached the Aberdeen
Junction, where a branch off the main north–south rail line
turned eastward. Cold and weary from two days without sleep,
Leon and Windol followed the tracks in a sweeping curve to
their left until the setting sun was behind them. They pressed
onward; only fifteen or so miles remained.

Progress was difficult and slow. Uneven railroad ties
covered with years of grime made for treacherous footing.
A pewter sky brought cool, damp air, which thickened into
a fog that engulfed the men as they crossed a trestle over
the Big Black River. Midway across the span, they reentered
Attala County.

Monday became Tuesday as the fugitives stumbled their
way in darkness to Sallis. Just south of town, where the tracks
crossed County Road 429, Leon and Windol left the railway
and headed along the muddy road toward Newport. It was

the heart of night, a hushed, lonely time. Two mud-splattered men wandered in a black world, slogging down a barely visible road, struggling to keep from falling down. Leon swore as he stepped into a water-filled rut. Behind him, Windol Whitt—exhausted, bone-cold, and miserable—cursed the day he had met Leon Turner.

Headlights appeared from a bend in the road ahead. Leon and Windol scrambled into the soaked woods and watched as a car passed. Leon recognized it as a Mississippi Highway Patrol cruiser, a chrome-covered siren mounted atop the roof like a backward-facing bullet. Only after the red taillights had disappeared from view did the desperados continue their trek.

An hour later, more lights pierced the distance. They appeared to be unmoving sets of headlights. Once Leon and Windol got closer, they took to the woods and slowly sneaked forward until they could tell the lights belonged to two patrol cars forming a roadblock. Red-glowing embers evidenced the cigarettes of people inside. Turner and Whitt ducked farther into the trees and continued warily onward. The bored lawmen remained totally unaware of their target slipping past them.

At last, Leon was back in his native territory; only a few miles more and he would be home. But Windol's mother's house was closest. They would go there first.

No lights were on in Birdie's home when they arrived, but it was early morning—everyone would be asleep. Leon dropped heavily into a chair on the front porch as his companion entered through the unlocked front door. Feeling his way past the furniture, Windol advanced slowly to his mother's bedroom. The wood flooring squeaked with each step as he tiptoed to her bedside and reached out to gently awaken her. Unexpectedly, he felt only bedcovers. Moving his arms about, Windol discovered that the covers lay unruffled over the made-up bed.

Puzzled, Windol roamed through the house and found that no one was home. He had no inkling that his mother and her husband were locked in the Attala County Jail.

Nor did Leon, but neither did he dwell on the mystery. With no use staying, he abruptly rose from the chair and strode away.

The sky brightened as the two men walked to Leon's shack. Upon arriving, they received another surprise. Elvira was sitting on the front porch, alone and in a surly mood.

The old woman's only reaction upon seeing Leon was to launch into a tirade about no one being left to take care of her. Leon asked what happened, and Elvira described how Roy Braswell—an uppity young fellow who wasn't old enough to be the High Sheriff—had come to the house yesterday talking about some murders. Leon was a suspect, he said, but she didn't believe him. The sheriff's men returned later and took Howard and the children to jail.

Surprised by Elvira's story, Leon and Windol decided to get going before the law came again. They snatched a couple of quilts off beds inside and left. It was past sunup.

The exhausted pair decided to head to Leon's still and sleep. Traveling deep into the countryside near the southern border of Attala County, they trudged in plain view along the primitive roads. They passed an abandoned farmhouse that had been boarded shut; locals knew it as the old Albin place.[7] Two wooden sheds were on the property. The men discussed stopping there to sleep but decided to continue.

Leon's still wasn't much farther. It seemed a lifetime since they had last been there—in fact, it had been three lifetimes—but the place remained as they had left it Sunday. Within minutes, Leon Turner and Windol Whitt were wrapped up in their quilts on the ground, asleep.

That same morning, citizens across America sat at their breakfast tables reading a tragic newspaper story about three Negro children shot and killed in Mississippi by a gang of jail escapees. The motive was reported as "mistaken revenge," because "the jail breakers evidently believed [Thomas] Harris had tipped officers they were in his house when they were hunted last month."[8]

The news also made national radio, where one famous broadcast personality had trouble pronouncing the county's unusual name. Local residents were amazed to hear the story mentioned by popular commentator Gabriel Heater but were shocked to hear him butcher the pronunciation. In clear, precise syllables, with millions of devoted listeners tuned in, Heater said "Ăt' ah lah" instead of "Ah tă' lah."[9] To Attala citizens, who had never before heard their quiet, secluded locale mentioned on such a prominent national stage, the error was appalling.

Statewide radio carried lurid details of the murders along with exaggerated reports of Malcolm Whitt's capture—a daring and dangerous effort miraculously accomplished without the loss of a single life due to the courageous efforts of Sheriff Roy Braswell and his highly trained men. With grave Shakespearean voices, newscasters cautioned listeners to be on the lookout for two armed and dangerous murderers on the loose. Children dressing for school were captivated by the narration. In a downtown Jackson hotel room, one boy preparing to accompany his father to work listened with particular interest. Jack Aldridge of Winona remembered the suspicious men on the Trailways bus the previous day.

Kosciusko's radio station, WKOZ, AM 1340, broadcast hourly updates on the search for the killers to the county's skittish residents.[10] Regrettably, there was little progress to report.

Citizens were openly angry at the murderers, and it was common knowledge that one of the killers was housed in the Attala County Jail. Fearing that a mob might attempt to take justice into its own hands, Sheriff Braswell moved Malcolm Whitt to the Holmes County Jail in Lexington, Mississippi.[11] The incarceration site was withheld from the press; news reports referred to Malcolm being taken to an "unannounced jail."[12]

Unfortunately for Caesar Young, his hard luck continued. Suspected of being some sort of accomplice, the hapless pickup truck owner was also relocated to Lexington.

In its hunt for the fugitives, the huge posse seemed to be jinxed. Thus far, the only leads received were Monday's false ones. Not even bogus sightings had been reported Tuesday. Authorities were clueless as to their quarry's location. Orders were issued splitting the manhunt in two: half the group stayed to search around the swampy Yazoo River bottoms of west-central Mississippi; the other half shifted back to the woodlands of Attala County. But the results remained negative.

The searchers' morale plummeted, due in large part to exhaustion. Because Mississippi's anemic coffers could not afford an abundance of law enforcement officers, the state could not reinforce a large-scale manhunt. Most of the possemen had been going nonstop since the previous day and had not slept.

Deteriorating weather added to the gloom. Periods of heavy showers began Tuesday afternoon. Combined with the winter chill, search conditions were miserable.

Sheriff Braswell was among those feeling discouraged. Leon Turner had now twice escaped his grasp. Admittedly, Braswell's search attempt after the jailbreak had been half-hearted; few men had been involved, and the scope of their search had been minimal. This time, even with the resources of the entire state mobilized to assist, the results appeared to be again headed toward futility. Despite Braswell's best effort, it seemed that his nemesis might, once again, get away.

A block from where Roy Braswell sat in his courthouse office lamenting the sorry state of the search, a small crowd stood in front of the Star-Herald Building on Madison Street. Several pictures dealing with the Harris murder were taped inside the business's plate-glass windows. High-quality 8 x 10, black-and-white glossies taken by Billy McMillan the previous day displayed dramatic views of the crime scene, the sheriff's posse, and the capture of Malcolm Whitt. The *Star-Herald* posted them in the window as the best "live coverage" the newspaper could accommodate.[13]

A cold rain Tuesday afternoon awakened Leon Turner and Windol Whitt. Their blankets were soaked, and sleep had become impossible. Remembering a potentially dry site they had passed that morning, the men rose and hustled to the abandoned Albin farm, where two small wooden sheds stood side by side. The larger of the two, a nine-by-nine-foot structure once used as the farm's blacksmith shop, was in poor condition.[14] Gaps in its termite-eaten walls and a large opening in the front let wind-blown rain soak the interior.

Next to this unappealing building, the smaller shelter was about the size of two doghouses put together.[15] Its plank siding and wood shingle roof were in fairly sound condition. This was a potato shed, a place for the winter storage of raw vegetables, jars of canned fruit, and the like. The half-buried shed's roof stood four feet above the ground, and its dug-out floor was two feet below ground level. Filling the evacuated earth was a thick layer of hay and cornhusks into which food-stuffs were buried to keep from freezing during the moder-ately cold Mississippi winters. Although the shed was open in front, a low overhanging roof kept out most of the rain.

Seeing that the potato shed looked dry inside, Leon and Windol threw in their blankets, crouched down, and moved through the low opening onto the thick layer of straw. Removing the pistol from his waistband, Turner pushed it into the hay. Then he and Windol rearranged their blankets and, once again, dozed off.

By late Tuesday afternoon, it appeared certain to Sheriff Braswell that the objects of his search had left the state. Arkansas police had just notified him that two men matching Turner's and Whitt's descriptions had been seen in Greenville crossing the Mississippi River Bridge into Arkansas.[16] Braswell also knew that Whitt had relatives in Memphis.[17] With little doubt that the two were presently in Arkansas or Tennessee, and with nightfall approaching, Braswell de-cided not to waste any more time or effort. He called off the manhunt.

The posse was disbanded. Roadblocks were removed. Surrounding states were officially notified to be on the look-out for two highly dangerous criminals. The center of the investigation was moved to the Delta town of Moorehead, sixty miles northwest of Kosciusko.[18] The search transitioned from an active hunt to detective work.

Roy Braswell was angry and disgusted. Three children had been brutally murdered in his county; and now, with the whole nation watching, he would have to admit failure in bringing their slayers to justice. Worst of all, the madmen were still on the loose, free to kill again. And based on the cold-hearted nature of their crime, they probably would.

It would take a miracle to stop them.

Thankfully, even in a world so filled with cruelty, struggles, and heartache, miracles *do* sometimes intervene in the destiny of man.[19] Sometimes they come in the form of an attentive eleven-year-old boy.

Befitting its stature as Mississippi's largest city, Jackson had two major daily newspapers. In addition to having different owners and different styles, the Jackson papers were published at different times. The *Clarion-Ledger* was printed for early morning delivery, and the *Daily News* was the late-afternoon paper.

During the day on Tuesday, Parchman Penitentiary authorities as a matter of course distributed prison mug shots of Leon Turner to the press. The release occurred too late to be included in the *Clarion-Ledger*'s edition. Thus, residents of the city got their first view of the alleged killer that afternoon when the *Daily News* hit the street.

One of the last duties that young Jack Aldridge performed every day as a page in the Mississippi House of Representatives was to stop by the Capitol Building's mail distribution center, pick up a bundle containing the afternoon mail and editions of major newspapers, and deliver the bunch to his father's office. This particular afternoon, as Jack exited the mailroom carrying the bundle in his arms, his eyes scanned the newspaper on top of the stack, the *Jackson Daily News*. To his astonishment, displayed clearly on the first page were the front and profile photographs of the man he had seen yesterday on the Trailways bus.[20] Above the photos was the caption "DESPERADO HUNTED IN ATTALA SLAYINGS."[21]

Representative John Aldridge Sr. was seated behind the desk of his capitol office when his son burst in, a heap of papers in his hands, a wide-eyed Look-what-I-have! expression on his face. Jack ran to his father's desk and plopped down the copy of the *Jackson Daily News*. Jabbing his finger repeatedly at the front-page picture, he breathlessly exclaimed that this was who they had seen on the bus.

"Dad, that's the man that did the killing!"[22]

Representative Aldridge stilled his son's thrusting hand and gazed at the pictures. It was true. He vividly remembered the two men who had gotten off the bus from Winona in the middle of a swamp. And, unbelievably, there was one of them. The man being sought for murder had ridden with him and his son.

Internally as excited as his son, but externally striving to remain calm, Aldridge picked up the phone and called his friend and colleague Henry Lee Rodgers, the district attorney whose jurisdiction covered both Winona and Kosciusko.

Rodgers sat at his desk with ear glued to the black telephone receiver, listening in amazement to John Aldridge's astonishing story about spotting Leon Turner on a bus. Aldridge also spoke of the other man with Leon. The other murderer, perhaps? Representative Aldridge did not understand why

Turner would be heading toward Attala County if he had just killed someone there, but District Attorney Rodgers told him that Malcolm Whitt had similarly returned home after a short period on the run.

Sheriff Braswell was nowhere to be found when the district attorney called his office. It took a deputy nearly an hour to locate him and relay the urgent message to contact Henry Lee Rodgers.

When Braswell called Rodgers, he sounded subdued. He obviously needed good news, and Rodgers was delighted to supply it by repeating the details of John Aldridge's bus ride story.

Law enforcement officials readily admit that solving a crime often requires luck. They long for it, they count on it, and they use it. As Sheriff Braswell spoke with the DA, he realized this could be his break. His spirits and energy perked up appreciably. By the time he hung up the phone, the frustration and exhaustion of the past two days were gone. It was time to get back to work.

The rain slacked off that evening. Where there had been a steady rumble of a downpour on the potato shed's roof, now there was silence. The change in sound roused Leon Turner. He nudged Windol awake. It was dark, and both men were famished. Leon decided they would check his daddy's house again to see if the family had been released.

The road was a slippery slew of dirt and clay mud that coated shoes and pants legs as they sloshed to Howard Turner's shack. To their disappointment, the house was completely empty—even Elvira was gone. The trip wasn't a total waste, however, for the kitchen had a few scraps of food. Moments later, the pair headed out the back door; and while nothing to eat was left behind, muddy shoeprints ranging throughout the shack were.

Birdie Bell's house was also unoccupied. Fortunately for Turner and Whitt, the food pickings were better.

It was late Tuesday night by the time Leon and Windol walked out. They talked of going to some of their relatives' houses but concluded that everyone would be asleep. They decided instead to head back to the potato shed.

The air was dead still as Leon and Windol once again wrapped in their blankets and lay down on the natural cushion inside the shed. Leon stuffed his gun in the straw, and for the third time that day, the hunted men slept.

Chapter 15

The Circle Tightens

Newspapers would later report that it began with a "hot tip" from an "unnamed source."[1] To be sure, the sharp-eyed observation of young Jack Aldridge initiated a rapid sequence of events.

Immediately after receiving the call from District Attorney Rodgers, Sheriff Braswell contacted Mississippi Highway Patrol regional headquarters. Leon Turner had been spotted the previous day on a bus near Durant, he disclosed. It appeared that Turner might also have returned to Attala County. Braswell requested that the recently cancelled road-blocks surrounding the Newport area be reactivated.

Roy knew that this was likely his last chance. If the killers weren't found now, he would have to endure the disappointment and embarrassment of calling off the search a second time. He did not want to fail again.

His gut said that he wouldn't. This was it. Roy was confident that the murderers were being drawn back home—so confident that he next called Parchman Penitentiary and asked for the tracking bloodhounds to come to Newport again.

Other related calls took place that night. Lawmen from the disbanded posse were ordered to assemble before dawn just north of Sallis.

Word of the posse's recall made it to the small group of Southern reporters who had brought the Newport murder story to the nation. Having been bitterly disappointed at the apparent escape of the killers, they received the news about the rejuvenated search enthusiastically. As a result, reporters from Jackson, Memphis, and New Orleans joined Billy McMillan of Kosciusko in making their way toward the meeting spot during the night.

Nearly two-dozen armed lawmen and the handful of reporters were at the intersection of Highways 12 and 429 well before dawn. Among them were the three leaders of this new posse: Sheriff Roy Braswell of Kosciusko, Sheriff Dewitt Tyler of Winona, and Inspector Walter Smith of the Highway Patrol's Greenwood district.[2]

Last to arrive was Patrolman Tom Sadler's cruiser from Parchman Penitentiary. With him were Hogjaw Mullen and Parchman's three best bloodhounds. Their appearance sparked a new level of excitement as many curious eyes watched Hogjaw step out wearing a bright red wool shirt, vertically striped pants, and a sweat-stained hat with an upturned brim. Aware of the attention, the flamboyant trusty retrieved his gun belt from the front seat and strapped it around his midsection with a flourish.

Next, he opened the back door of the patrol car. The bobbing, slobbering heads of 'Bama, Nigger, and High Rollin' Red greeted him excitedly, their furiously wagging tails battering the backseat with the chaotic beat of a nervous drummer. Hogjaw attached long tracking leashes to their collars, pulled his charges out of the car, and strutted about the area like a politician.

Mullen's unusual attire and cocksure attitude presented an enthralling site to the assembled newspapermen. One New Orleans reporter described him with the kind of vivid phrasing used for Hollywood starlets at the Academy Awards: "Hogjaw looked like a character out of fiction Wednesday. He stood out boldly against the grim countryside, which was whipped to slush underfoot and blanketed by a butter-milk sky overhead. His red flannel shirt and striped prison pants were in sharp contrast to the terrain and the costumes of the other searchers. A cowboyish hat and a pearl-handled revolver, strapped 'round his waist, and anchored to a thigh, completed the ensemble."[3]

The "buttermilk sky" produced a gray dawn accompanied by a fine mist. With the brightening sky, the search party members lit final cigarettes and checked their weapons. Then they moved solemnly toward the leaders. The scene grew quiet as twenty-two armed men huddled.

Sheriff Roy Braswell broke the silence. In a grave voice, Roy briefed the group on the newly obtained knowledge about Leon's bus ride. Since there had been no additional sightings, the actual location of the two desperados was unknown, he admitted. It was only his guess that the killers would return to their homes, but it was a guess based on sound evidence.

The posse would cover both houses by splitting into two groups. The first—fourteen armed men under Braswell's leadership—would search Leon's home and the surrounding area.[4] The bloodhounds would be in his group. Sheriff Tyler of Winona would lead a second team of eight men covering the Baldridge home.

It was shortly after six o'clock when the briefing ended. The two groups piled into automobiles and headed toward Newport. Twenty minutes later, the cars in Sheriff Braswell's convoy stopped barely out of sight of Howard Turner's shack. Roy got out of his car and stepped forward to view the house. Behind him on the road were clusters of the posse and press. All the newspapermen were there, having chosen to be with the main group.

Standing apart from the assemblage, Hogjaw Mullen leaned against a car fender, left hand holding both a cigarette and the cowhide leashes of his three hounds, right hand dangling a finger's length away from his gun. Next to him waited the dogs, panting and looking almost as relaxed as their trainer.

Daylight came grudgingly while Sheriff Braswell held his men back, monitoring Turner's cabin from a distance while the landscape brightened. While he delayed, the posse grew more and more restless.

Two elderly black men on mules approached from the road behind. Despite siren-topped automobiles and lawmen blocking the way ahead, the riders' slow-speed advance continued. Until, that is, they came to the rearmost group of rifle-toting white men, where they were stopped and questioned.

"Yessuh, we know 'bout de killin's."

"Nosuh, we had'n heard nutt'n 'bout Leon Turna bein' 'roun'."

"Nosuh, we would'n be no trouba; we jus' goin' down de road."

Satisfied that the old men offered neither threat nor information, the officers ordered them to turn around and get going.[5]

At 7:00 a.m., Braswell gave the order to move out. Fourteen lawmen—some with pistols, some with rifles, some with automatic weapons—trudged down the mud road to Leon Turner's shack. Those who had not been there before were surprised to see the decrepit condition of the place. None of these white officers were anywhere near wealthy, but their houses were far better than this one.

Only a few strutting chickens took notice as the posse silently surrounded the home. Braswell and two deputies crept onto the front porch and stood beside the door with weapons cocked and ready. At Roy's signal, a deputy kicked the door open. It yielded easily—a gentle push would have sufficed—and slammed into something inside with a splintering crunch. The men rushed through the doorway and stopped inside, visually sweeping the dark room. Nothing.

Using flashlights, Braswell and his deputies began searching the house. It took only a moment to cover the four cramped and cluttered rooms. Other than a cat under a bed and three clucking hens, the shack was empty.[6] But the sheriff noticed muddy footprints throughout the house that looked fresh. He yelled out the front door for the bloodhounds.

Waiting in the yard, Hogjaw Mullen flicked away his cigarette, gathered in the leashes, and led his hounds into the home.

The dogs picked up a scent as soon as they came through the door. Hogjaw let them wander around, slowly moving them toward the rear of the shack. When the hounds entered the kitchen, their level of agitation increased dramatically. They sniffed at the bottom of the back door and barked. Mullen knew what would come next as he reached out to open the door.

The bloodhounds exploded from the cabin in a run. Hogjaw threw down the slack in the leashes, letting his trackers have the full length, and ran off behind them. The animals bayed loudly as they tore through the backyard, loped up the hill behind the cabin, and dashed into the woods.

After penetrating the tree line a short distance, the dogs began ranging back and forth—they had lost the track. Hogjaw worked them in a wide arc around the shack, searching for the scent. For five minutes the dogs sniffed the grounds, their long snouts barely an inch above the dirt. Approaching the road a hundred yards away from the house, they suddenly erupted into booming howls. Red, Nigger, 'Bama, and their sprinting handler dashed down the dirt road, heading south from the Turner cabin.

The only lawman stationed near the spot where the dogs regained the scent was Attala County Constable Hugh Bailey, at sixty-something the oldest member of the posse. Bailey gave chase as soon as he saw Hogjaw and the hounds take off. Lugging a .30-caliber carbine rifle, Bailey trailed several yards behind Hogjaw. Though his thick spectacles fogged from the exertion, the determined constable kept running. He pushed worn-out muscles to their limits, for this would most likely be the hollow-cheeked old man's last chase. Only by dropping dead would he miss it.

Back at Howard Turner's place, everyone scrambled to automobiles. Sheriff Braswell opened his car door and stepped up on the doorframe to look toward a group of locals. He yelled "You people stay back. We're expecting trouble," then dropped behind the steering wheel and sped off, falling in line with others racing from the shack.[7]

The sight resembled a Keystone Cops chase scene: a dozen cars careening down the slippery road, tires spinning and sliding; wipers beating furiously, spreading mud across windshields, making visibility a rare commodity. More than once a vehicle tried to pass another, only to slide off into a roadside ditch.

Far in front of the pack was the patrol car of Hogjaw's handler, Officer Tom Sadler. Experienced with the unpredictable suddenness of a bloodhound chase, Sadler had been the first to leave once the hounds began baying in the distance. Now, he kept pace a comfortable distance behind Constable Bailey.

Hogjaw and the bloodhounds darted in and out of the woods as they chased the scent. At one point when running along the road toward a single-lane bridge over Seneasha Creek, each hound tried to go a different direction. Hogjaw backtracked until his charges regained a common track, and then started them over. When the animals stayed together on a slightly different path than before, Mullen knew they had the trail. He let 'em run.

Sheriff Braswell furiously chewed on his cigar as he fought to maintain control of the car. Clenching the steering wheel tightly with both hands, he stared straight ahead. He was in the middle of the pack, struggling to keep pace with the hounds. Though vision was poor, Hogjaw's red wool shirt acted as a distant beacon.

Once past the Seneasha bridge, the bloodhounds ran full bore along the road as Hogjaw held the taut leashes securely. Constable Bailey, wheezing but still keeping up, glanced over his shoulder at Sadler's car fifty yards behind. Then he returned his gaze to the man in striped pants running ahead.

Hogjaw did not look rearward; his concentration was solely on the hounds. All three were baying excitedly, running as fast as their handler could manage. The track was sure; Hogjaw knew they were close. Suddenly, the dogs veered off the left side of the road.

It was nearly 9:00 a.m. Having tracked some two miles since leaving the Turner shack, the bloodhounds were headed up a small hill, passing through high weeds and underbrush.[8] At the top of the rise, the ground cleared and a farm loomed ahead. The hounds were silent as they headed toward two wooden sheds.

As their trainer, Hogjaw knew the dogs' behavior meant his quarry was near. He stopped them by yanking hard on their leashes and waited on Constable Bailey. Experience had taught him the value of having a backup in a dicey situation. He lit a cigarette.

Constable Bailey caught up, his face strained from the exertion, and the two men discussed the situation in a whisper. Leon was surely close by. He probably wasn't aware that he was being tracked; otherwise, he would have opened fire by now. Soon, though, he would find out, and things would get dangerous. The two trackers decided to split up, with Mullen advancing while Bailey covered him.

The constable ducked behind the trunk of a large oak tree. Once in position, he waved Hogjaw forward. Mullen started moving toward the two buildings. Holding the dog leashes in his left hand, he drew his .38 from its holster with his right. Then he dropped the straps.

The well-trained animals advanced slowly toward the potato shack, approaching from its left side. A few feet away, Nigger and Bama held back while Red continued onward. At the front corner of the small building, he stopped and stuck his head inside.

The result was an immediate *"ROWF!"*[9] Hogjaw knew the single bark meant someone was inside.

It had been a long night for Leon Turner—his damp blanket atop smelly, half-decayed straw provided little comfort or warmth. Leon had struggled through periods of sleep and wakefulness the whole evening. At the moment, he was half awake.

Out of nowhere, a dog barked. It sounded close, like the animal was inside the shed. Leon opened his eyes and looked around, but he saw nothing in the cramped space other than Windol Whitt sleeping a foot away. Turner yawned and sat up.

Crouched outside the shed's front corner, Hogjaw jutted his head into the opening just enough to glance inside. He spotted Leon Turner sitting against the right wall. Hurriedly, Mullen pulled back from the opening and signaled to Bailey that someone was inside.

"All right, Turner, come on out!" he shouted.[10]

Leon reacted instantly. Fishing his pistol out of the hay, he replied "Yeah" and fired two shots out the front.

Hogjaw scurried a few steps away and then stopped and fired his weapon wildly into the shed's sidewall. Six quick shots bored into the wood. Constable Bailey stepped forward and poured two more rounds into the shed.

"Leon, this is Hogjaw Mullen," Hogjaw yelled. "You know I'm badder than you. Come on out."[11]

Inside the shed, Leon cursed and told Windol that he'd never give up. Windol, for his part, was anything but belligerent. He wanted to surrender. They argued.

Hogjaw couldn't make out what the voices within the shelter were saying. That he could hear a discussion presented a rather significant problem, for Hogjaw was out of bullets. He had emptied his weapon into the shed in a bid to end the situation once and for all; but the gamble had not paid off, and now there was no more ammo. Although being a convict trusty allowed him to carry a fully loaded pistol, the State of Mississippi did not trust him enough to allow reloading.

But Hogjaw hoped Leon Turner didn't know that, for there was only one play that Hogjaw could make. If this didn't work, everything would be up to old Constable Hugh Bailey.

"Come on out of there crawling or I'll let you have more!" Hogjaw bellowed.[12]

But all that came from the shed was silence.

A long moment passed. Running out of options, Hogjaw prepared to yell another bluff threat, but then he saw motion at the potato shed opening.

Twenty yards away, watching through the sight of his rifle, Hugh Bailey also saw the movement. The constable held his trigger finger ready but did not fire as Leon Turner emerged into view. His hands appeared to be empty.

Hogjaw aimed his revolver at Leon's head, and in a tone that made it clear he would shoot without hesitation, ordered his adversary to crawl. Leon slowly dropped to his hands and knees on the rain-soaked ground and continued coming. The brim of his hat blocked his face. It was a tense moment for Mullen, for he could not see the eyes of this unpredictable killer. Standing in the open, completely exposed should Leon make a sudden move, Hogjaw was in a dangerous position.

A noise from the left drew a quick glance from Hogjaw. Reinforcements.

"Mr. Sadler, come here," Hogjaw shouted. "Mr. Sadler, come here," he repeated.[13] From the road, Patrolman Tom Sadler rushed toward the scene with pistol drawn.

Leon was on all fours a few feet in front of the shed. Hogjaw walked up to him, put his foot on the killer's back, and pushed him down into the mud.

Windol Whitt scrambled wild-eyed from the interior shadows of the potato shed and threw himself on the ground near Leon. He laid stomach down, arms extended.

Sadler arrived to see Parchman's Main Mos' Dog Boy squarely in control. Hogjaw looked at him with a hint of a smile, and he winked. Constable Bailey moved in closer, his carbine trained on the two figures sprawled on the ground. Seconds later, two dozen men came charging onto the farm.

The swarm rushed forward to witness an unforgettable spectacle. Hogjaw, in his up-and-downs, stood legs apart, pointing a pearl-handled pistol at the two spread-eagled fugitives at his feet. Close by, Bailey and Sadler had weapons pointed at the men on the ground.

Excited lawmen surrounded the captives with an arsenal of rifles and pistols. Adding to the increasingly chaotic mix, press photographers vied for an angle, capturing the dramatic events on film.

Into the jostling crowd strode Sheriff Roy Braswell. With tan coat over open-collared white shirt, cigar in hand, and controlled demeanor, his air of authority had an immediate calming effect. Firmly taking command, he ordered the prisoners searched for weapons. Tom Sadler moved to Turner and straddled him at the waist. Handing his unfired pistol to Hogjaw Mullen, Sadler squatted and began frisking Leon. A few feet away, another patrolman patted down Windol Whitt. Braswell also crouched down and searched Whitt. All the while, Hogjaw Mullen remained planted between the captives, calmly smoking his cigarette. In his hands were two pistols—only one of them loaded.

Photographer Billy McMillan maneuvered about the scene, shooting photos as rapidly as he could, hoping his film and his focus would adequately capture the action.[14]

Leon Turner turned his head sideways and looked up at Hogjaw. "What you shootin' at me for? I ain't done nothin' but broke jail."[15]

The realization struck Hogjaw that, although someone had shot at him, Leon hadn't carried a gun when he came out of the shed. Sadler's inspection hadn't found anything.

"Where's your pistol?" Mullen asked.

"What you talkin' about?" Turner replied.

"Where's that gun?" Hogjaw repeated angrily.

"Ain't got no gun."[16]

During the verbal exchange, Nigger walked up and stood docilely at his trainer's feet. Seeing the bloodhound's leather leash trailing on the ground, Hogjaw handed back Patrolman Sadler's gun and picked up the strap several feet from its end. In a burst of anger, Hogjaw swung it hard across Leon's back.

Once more, he asked about the gun.

Leon looked up at Mullen with flared nostrils and again denied having a pistol.

The strap lashed at Leon a second time, striking home with a loud *pop!* Hogjaw swung again and again, flogging Turner viciously.

Leon rolled to his side and reached out to grab Mullen's leg, but Hogjaw nimbly stepped out of reach. With a grunt, Leon started to get up, but several lawmen jumped on him, beating him brutally about the head and face and kicking him in the side. Leon thrashed about wildly, fighting the attackers with every muscle of his considerable strength. But there were too many of them. They forced Leon back onto his stomach and shoved his face into the mud. Two officers twisted his arms behind his back, and a third slapped on a set of handcuffs. At last, Leon stopped struggling. It was over.

Inspector Smith of Greenwood had noticed a photographer taking pictures during the beatings. With Leon now restrained, Smith walked over to the journalist and jerked the camera out of his hands. Popping open the camera back, Smith yanked out several feet of film with a sickening whir. A treasury of precious photos lay in a snake of ruined celluloid at the inspector's feet as he thrust the empty instrument into the hands of its stunned owner. No words were spoken; the lawman's fiery eyes said enough.[17]

Where Leon Turner had fought being subdued like a trapped bobcat, Windol Whitt accepted arrest submissively. He lay in the mud and passively allowed himself to be cuffed. A patrolman asked Windol where Leon Turner had hidden the gun. Whitt replied that he didn't know, but Hogjaw Mullen didn't buy it. Still grasping the leather strap, he whipped the handcuffed captive. Four licks later, Windol's pants and underwear were ripped through.[18] Still, Whitt said nothing.

Once the beatings and lashings were over and all was calm, Sheriff Braswell directed his men to get the captives to their feet. Two deputies grabbed Windol by the arms and roughly yanked him up. The procedure was repeated on Leon, but more brutally.

Noticing blood on Leon's shirt, the deputies turned and probed their prisoner, inspecting him like a slab of meat. Lifting his shirt, they found a wound kidney-high on the right side of Leon's back. A bullet had ranged laterally from right to left just under the skin, leaving a visible bulge where the slug stopped six inches to the left of Leon's backbone.[19] The remarkable sight drew oohs and whistles from the lawmen. They cracked jokes at Leon, calling it his lucky day. Further inspections revealed that Leon had also been struck above the right knee—a superficial gash of little consequence.

Amazingly, Windol had come through the fusillade of bullets unscathed.

Sheriff Braswell and Inspector Smith began questioning the pair about the murders. Not surprisingly, Leon and Windol both denied having anything to do with them. Turner insisted the wrong men had been captured; his only crime was breaking out of jail.

During the interrogations, deputies searching the potato shed found Leon's gun buried in the hay bed. Sheriff Braswell removed a bullet from its chamber and retrieved from his pants pocket a spent shell recovered from the Harris home. He compared the two pieces of copper side by side. They looked identical.

The gathering at the Albin farm quickly increased in size as local citizens showed up to witness the capture of Leon Turner. It was the kind of affair that would be retold within families for generations. Relaxed but weary lawmen mingled with the crowd. Relieved by the successful conclusion of a fifty-seven-hour manhunt, they were more than happy to chat about their experiences with interested spectators. Likewise, they gladly obliged members of the press with interviews and poses.

Turner and Whitt were put on display. Leon—face puffy and bleeding; wrists handcuffed behind his back—remained docile as deputies lifted his shirt and pointed out the bullet in his back. Windol merely stared at his feet, suffering through the indignation of being on exhibit. Neither man uttered a single word.

The same cannot be said for Hogjaw Mullen. As the story of his daring gun battle circulated and he became the center of attention, the cocky trusty was not shy in telling of his brave deeds. Hogjaw was a hero in his own mind, and the crowd ate it up. To thank him for collaring the criminals, grateful members of the posse and Newport-area residents gave him money, which Hogjaw stuffed in his shirt pockets.[20]

The press was especially drawn to Hogjaw, and he did not disappoint. Several of his homespun words of wisdom would grace stories of the capture in tomorrow's newspapers. One reporter asked why his bloodhounds had run away when the shooting started. These dogs were Mississippi's finest tracking animals, Hogjaw explained, trained by the state's best trainer—himself. Because of their high value to the state in catching criminals, they were taught to retreat to safety at the first sound of gunfire. "You know, those dogs have got more sense than some folks I have seen today," reflected the convict-turned-sage.[21]

When asked why he had come such a distance and endured the cold, wet conditions to join the hunt, Hogjaw looked the questioner squarely in the eyes and delivered his most convincing performance: "I was out here because I want to make something of myself beside a number at Parchman."[22]

Sheriff Roy Braswell stood at the outskirts of the activity with a freshly lit Roi-Tan, patiently enduring the celebration. His men had earned the right to bask in their triumph. Unlike the loquacious tracker from Parchman who spoke with anyone and everyone wanting to be the man of the hour, Braswell said little. He was tired and ready to get home to Inez.

After half an hour, he called an end to the affair.

A rare backcountry traffic jam formed as trucks, mules, wagons, and horses returning to Beat 4 homes mixed with law enforcement vehicles heading toward Highway 14. Sitting handcuffed in the backseats of separate Highway Patrol cars were Windol Whitt and Leon Turner.

The official entourage traveled to Durant, where Turner and Whitt were temporarily held in jail while Malcolm Whitt and Caesar Young were brought in from nearby Lexington.[23] Once all four suspects were gathered, they were whisked away. Nearly a thousand curious onlookers gathered along Highway 51 to view the procession as it headed south out of Durant toward Jackson.[24]

During the excitement, another Highway Patrol car passed through Durant going in the opposite direction. Inside, three bloodhounds smeared red mud across the backseat as they and their colorful handler headed back to Parchman.

At three o'clock that afternoon, Wednesday, January 11, 1950, a funeral was held at the Pleasant Grove Church Cemetery west of Newport.[25] Mournful Negro spirituals filled the air as three children were laid to rest. Sisters Mary C. Burnside and Ruby Nell Harris, dressed in their finest Sunday dresses and shoes, lay next to each other in the same casket. Buried nearby in his own coffin was their brother Frankie Thurman, wearing his cherished aviator cap.[26]

Several miles away, the children's seriously injured father and older sister lay in the Kosciusko hospital, unable to attend the services. Their mother, emotionally debilitated by the tragedy thrust upon her family, also was not present.[27]

The capture. Leon Turner, on the ground wearing hat, being frisked by Tom Sadler. Hogjaw Mullen standing. Windol Whitt is on the ground in rear being searched by Sheriff Roy Braswell, right.

After the capture. L to R: Hogjaw Mullen and his bloodhounds; Constable Hugh Bailey in checkered shirt, Sheriff Braswell in coat and white shirt; Leon Turner, face battered and bleeding; Windol Whitt.

Part 3

Chiseled in Vermont marble over the west façade of the United States Supreme Court building, the words "Equal Justice Under Law" represent an ideal upon which the nation was founded. Unfortunately, the ideal will never be fully achieved, for the judges, lawyers, and jury members that constitute the system of justice are imperfect. While the legal actions and judgments of these individuals are for the most part honest and moral, they occasionally fall short. Whether twisted by defects of personality or blurred by unjust precedents, biased and unfair judicial rulings do occur.

During America's era of slavery, the State of Mississippi, among other Southern states, failed to secure equal justice for all. Long after emancipation, African Americans remained subject to inequality before the law and were often victimized in society. In 1950 the trial of three accused child-murderers provided an opportunity for Mississippi to etch its own commitment to "Equal Justice Under Law." The nation was watching.

Chapter 16

Public Reaction

Twelve days after escaping from the Attala County Jail, Leon Turner, Malcolm Whitt, and Windol Whitt were in the Hinds County Jail in Jackson, Mississippi. So was Caesar Young.

When news of their capture first reached the citizens of Beat 4, the reaction was a collective sigh of relief. But as the distance from Newport increased, reactions transitioned, hardening from relief to anger. Mississippians were outraged. Among white citizens, feelings of racial prejudice were pushed aside by the utter brutality of the crime. Gone was any apathy toward white-on-black offenses. Three little children had been slaughtered; the color of their skin wasn't a consideration.

In Jackson, state leaders considered the crime a disgrace to humankind in general and to Mississippi in particular.[1] Well aware of the adverse publicity that had been heaped upon their state by the disappointing early reports from the manhunt, politicians were primed to respond to the good news of the suspects' arrests. They reacted quickly.

The slayings had occurred within the district of State Senator Stokes Sanders, a senior member of the Mississippi Legislature.[2] A retired U.S. Army colonel, former mayor of Kosciusko, and owner/publisher of the *Kosciusko Star-Herald*, Senator Sanders was dismayed at the blight cast upon his normally tranquil district by this monstrous event. Never in Attala County's 117-year existence had it received such widespread negative attention. Determined to demonstrate the disapproval felt by his fellow Attalans, Sanders submitted a concurrent resolution three hours after the arrests that praised the capture and condemned the crime.

"Be it resolved," stated the resolution," that we, the Mississippi State Senate . . . deplore this unfortunate occurrence, and . . . express the hope that these culprits . . . will be brought to justice, and be required to pay a penalty in keeping with the laws applied to the willful, malicious, unlawful, and felonious crime of murder."[3]

Governor Fielding L. Wright also quickly released a statement proclaiming, "The recent dastardly crime occurring in Attala County wherein three children were killed has shocked the entire citizenry of Mississippi. . . . The laws of Mississippi stand as a shield to protect and preserve the rights, the lives, and the property of all our citizens, whatever their race may be."[4]

While resolutions, speeches, and statements may unburden the consciences of elected officials responsible for ensuring the public safety, in practical terms, they do little to help the victims of a crime. Realizing this, various groups throughout the state mobilized to provide financial compensation for the surviving members of "The Attala County Massacre." The Kiwanis Club of Hattiesburg contributed $125 as a "gesture of sympathy expressing the shame that Mississippi white people feel over the crime committed by members of their race." The students of Mississippi State College in Starkville placed a collection box in front of the YMCA and held a benefit concert.[5] They raised $65.71.[6]

Kosciusko's mayor proclaimed January 20 as "Thomas Harris Day," when an effort would be made to collect donations nationwide.[7] The Chamber of Commerce of Kosciusko, which condemned the crime as "brutal, malicious, sordid and atrocious," issued a notice that contributions to the fund could be sent to the chamber's secretary.[8] Donations ultimately exceeded $2,000.[9]

By telephone, telegraph, and wire service, news of the daring capture flew within hours from the few reporters on the scene to the nation's major newspapers. The following morning, dozens of headlines proclaimed the capture of the Mississippi child killers. Several elements of the captivating story guaranteed public interest: an innocent Negro family terrorized; the lives of three children cut tragically short; their father and older sister seriously wounded; a despicable group of hate-filled white men caught; a heart-wrenchingly futile search turned overnight into a gloriously successful capture—all happening within a matter of days. It was the perfect news event.[10]

Leon Turner was reviled in the published accounts. Described in such terms as "mad-dog killer," "drunken marauder," "raging maniac," "cowardly killer," "drunken bully boy," and "circus wildman," he became the country's number one villain.

At the opposite end of the popularity chart, Hogjaw Mullen achieved near-sainthood status. The riveting account of his role in the gun battle and of his bold capture, without ammunition, of the two dangerous killers made Hogjaw an instant national celebrity.

Citing the Mississippi custom whereby a prison trusty who captured an escaped criminal was traditionally given highly favorable consideration for parole, newspapers suggested that Hogjaw may soon win freedom.[11] Parchman Penitentiary Superintendent Marvin Wiggins, who would have to initiate the clemency process, related that Hogjaw had gained freedom under similar circumstances once before, but had eventually been reincarcerated after running afoul of the law. "He's a model prisoner," Wiggins said, "but he can't seem to stay out of trouble on the outside."[12]

The press dogged local officials, eager to obtain their comments about the case. Asked to provide a possible motive for the senseless murders, District Attorney Henry Rodgers offered that the three white men had been arrested during a previous visit to the home when they had tried to rape Mrs. Harris and her teenage daughter. Somehow blaming the Harris family for the sheriff's arrival and their being taken into custody, the men broke out of jail and returned to the home in a "drunken orgy of revenge."[13] The killings thus took on a name. The press began calling the crime the "revenge murders."

When quizzed about allegations being considered against any others, Sheriff Roy Braswell explained that charges of "some sort" might be filed against Howard Turner and Parvee Rutherford. The Whitts' mother and stepfather, along with five children of Howard Turner had been released, he noted.[14]

Kosciusko mayor Alton Massey, a thirty-nine-year-old attorney in his second term of office, became the de facto spokesman for his increasingly publicized town. Soft-spoken in his day-to-day speech, Massey could be a vigorous orator when soliciting votes, bragging about his alma mater, Ole Miss, or defending his community. As a former state senator, district governor of the Lions Club, and district commander of the VFW, Massey was used to taking center stage.[15] He now did so with gusto.

With his city teetering at the edge of a public relations cliff, Mayor Massey sought to push someone else over. The obvious choice was, of course, the three killers. As there was no question of the guilt of these bad apples, it was easy for the mayor to lay the blame entirely on their shoulders. And he did—constantly. At any gathering, to any willing ear, Massey publicly lambasted the guilty trio. Don't blame Kosciusko for the dead children, he railed; this was strictly the work of three evil murderers.

Mississippians soon learned that even more fuel was about to be heaped on the fire beneath their state's reputation. The death of the Harris children was being considered for classification as a lynching.

To many, "lynching" entails a killing by hanging. The actual definition, however, specifies more the participation and motive than the method. Tuskegee University (formerly the Tuskegee Institute) in Alabama, recognized since 1882 as the nation's organizational expert on lynchings, classifies it as meeting the following conditions: "There must be legal evidence that a person was killed. That person must have met death illegally. A group of three or more persons must have participated in the killing. The group must have acted under the pretext of service to Justice, Race, or Tradition."[16]

White-on-black lynchings of the past had imposed a dark stain on the history of Mississippi, a legacy of which good people of the state were not proud. They could boast, however, that the lawless practice had meaningfully declined over recent decades and, by 1950, lynchings were nearly eradicated. Thus, state leaders were highly sensitive to anyone's calling the Harris family murders a lynching. Pulitzer Prize winner Hodding Carter Jr., editor and publisher of the *Greenville (Miss.) Delta Democrat-Times*, editorialized, "Should it be that these killings are to be classified as lynchings, we wonder what account will be made of the feeling of the citizens who evidenced such anger that one of the prisoners had to be hidden?" Expressing the emotions of his fellow Mississippians, he added, "There was no color issue in this at all. People were outraged by the wanton murder of three children, just as people would be anywhere had this thing happened to any children."[17]

In the end, the arguments went for naught. The deaths of Freddie, Mary, and Nell were added to the national list of lynchings.[18]

Publicity surrounding the apprehension of the "revenge murderers" leaned positive at first. The good news of the capture was viewed with relief; printed accounts and descriptions were accepted at face value. Unfortunately, the nation did not take long to get over the exhilaration.

Three days, to be precise.

Clarence Grammer's masquerade as boxer Hogjaw Mullen had been successful due to the limited visibility within Parchman Prison and the Mississippi law enforcement community. This obscurity disappeared with the capture of Leon Turner, when newspapers in every state extolled the manly exploits of a Mississippi prison trusty named Hogjaw Mullen. The stories naturally provided a paragraph or two on Hogjaw's background—the background as told to reporters by the hero himself during the heady moments of backslapping celebration following the arrests. Biographical snippets related that Hogjaw had once been a respected Mississippi boxer; he had even won the world light-heavyweight championship from Tiger Burns in 1939.[19]

One particular reader found Hogjaw's "biography" especially interesting. In Beaumont, Texas, thirty-nine-year-old

Curtis Mullen made his living as a route man for a dry cleaning business. Curtis had not always lived in Beaumont; he was originally from Greenwood, Mississippi. And he had once been a boxer. In fact, he had used the ring name "Hogjaw" Mullen when he boxed the Mississippi circuit in the late 1920s.

When Curtis "Hogjaw" Mullen read about Clarence "Hogjaw" Mullen, he went to the Beaumont newspaper office with a fascinating bit of information.

News of the "real" Hogjaw broke nationally via the United Press International syndicate on Saturday, January 14, 1950. In his identity-revealing interview, Curtis Mullen claimed to be the 1928 welterweight champion of Mississippi; although, he noted, his current weight put him far outside the welterweight class. Of Clarence "Hogjaw" Grammer, Curtis admitted, "I heard of that Mississippi man once. We never met, but I got reports about him. I think he did do a little fighting." Curtis found it a "peculiar coincidence" that Clarence used the name Hogjaw Mullen.[20]

The Hogjaw revelation provided the first trickle of negative publicity. Over a week later, the trickle turned into a flood. Old, simmering tensions between the North and the South surfaced when certain publications north of the Mason-Dixon Line began to criticize aspects of the capture.

TIME Magazine fired a surprise volley in a January 23, 1950 report entitled "Shooter's Chance" in which they slammed Mississippi's penal system as "earthy and antiquated." TIME criticized Parchman Penitentiary's system of using "shooter trusties" to capture escaped convicts, calling these trusties "bad actors ... equipped with rifles and vertical stripes." Attacking Hogjaw personally, TIME ridiculed that his qualifications for "shooter" were "thirteen years of crime" and "other good qualities: he beat up fellow prisoners and talked politely to the guards."[21]

Kosciusko's Mayor Massey, incensed by the unprovoked criticism, penned a rebuttal letter that was published in the February 20, 1950, issue of *Time*:

> "Shooter's Chance," like most other articles I have read concerning Mississippi, is obviously indicative of the highest type of prejudice. . . .
>
> This statement, "Under Mississippi's earthy and antiquated penal system, the tougher and more ruthless a convict is, the better off he is" comes from not only a prejudicial mind but one that . . . apparently is not interested in obtaining the true facts. . . . The Mississippi Penal Farm may be in some degree "earthy" but it is not "antiquated." The history of the state prison at Parchman, Miss. has shown marked improvement through the years, and it is now and has been for a long time modern.
>
> Your statement, "Hogjaw, who had also shot (but only wounded) another fleeing prisoner last August, was obviously the type of man that some Mississippi law enforcers admired," is another that carries with it every implication short of libel. . . . This is another subject which you . . . know nothing about. Most of our law-enforcing officers in Mississippi are high type gentlemen. . . .
>
> Alton Massey
> Mayor, City of Kosciusko[22]

Time responded:

TIME still considers arming a convict to catch a criminal an odd and antiquated practice. But TIME has only admiration for Mayor Massey and the people of Mississippi for their generous reaction to the murder of three Negro children.—Ed.[23]

The mayor's retort was an unabashed hit among friends of Mississippi. Congratulatory letters poured into his office from supporters all over the South:

From a lawyer in Philadelphia, Miss.: "TIME is under an obligation to the general public of the US to present a true interpretation of any local situation, without bias or prejudice. . . . TIME did not live up to this obligation."

From a homemaker in Louisiana: "We need more Southerners who will take issue with articles representing the South as backward and feeble."

From a businessman in Texas: "I am glad to see someone with guts to call that TIME magazine's hand on the article. . . . They must have a yankee or Negro correspondent writing those articles over there."

From an attorney in Texas: "I was glad to see you taking to task that Little Lord Fauntleroy of the magazine world through your letter. . . . Obviously, they are deliberate in coloring their stories through a careful selection of words and employment of a descriptive style all their own."

From a professor at the University of Virginia: "It is necessary that the frequent misrepresentations by news reporters be properly refuted by the intelligent leadership of the state."[24]

The *Boston Globe* also released an unfavorable story. In an editorial, the *Kosciusko Star-Herald* responded:

> Another smear appeared in the BOSTON GLOBE, and along the same lines. "It happened in Mississippi in a place called Kosciusko," says the Globe. "Two men suspected of killing three Negro children of a share cropper were on the lam. . . . They had not been convicted or even tried, but the authorities wanted them. As the fugitives were dangerous, state officials felt it wise to send a convicted murderer out to catch and kill others on whom the law frowned."
>
> That latter statement is as libelous as it is untrue.
>
> Naturally the men had not been convicted or even tried. They had to be apprehended first, arraigned, and then go through other legal procedures.
>
> The Globe concludes [about Hogjaw], ". . . this killer . . . caught up with the men he trailed . . . one of them he shot . . . the other surrendered. So, in the Mississippi view, justice has been done."
>
> Just where they get that last statement, we do not know, or what they base it on. Not knowing Mississippi, its people, nor even justice, is the only way we can account for it.[25]

Not all national publications turned negative. This same *Star-Herald* editorial gave credit to *Newsweek*, which "gave a rather fair account of the entire case."[26]

Once the editorial salvos finally ceased, it was fortunate that only words had been used as weapons. The notoriety of the capture abated, and each side was able to return to its normal business having suffered nothing more than hard feelings. Weeks passed with no significant news updates about the case. Nationally, interest in the story went into hibernation. Locally, though, effects from the bout of negative publicity lingered. The war of words had left no doubt that Attala County was under the nation's microscope. No longer were residents free to confront homegrown problems without interference. Every action they took concerning Turner and the Whitts would be scrutinized and criticized by a national audience.

Barring any exceptional incidents, such as a second jailbreak by the now well-guarded suspects, the next newsworthy events would be their trials. As these proceedings were expected to again swing the national spotlight to Attala County, preparations were conducted cautiously, without haste.

Besides the necessity of being careful, there was another good reason to go slowly: the witnesses' health. Even though Mary Ella Harris was physically ready to testify about her experiences that tragic night, she had not directly observed the murders. The only living witnesses to the shootings were in the hospital. The testimony of Thomas Harris and Verlene Thurman would be crucial to the prosecution. Encouragingly, Verlene was showing signs of improvement from her two gunshot wounds. Her stepfather's injuries, on the other hand, were more life threatening. Thomas needed time before being able to testify. A distinct possibility existed that he wouldn't heal, in which case the additional time would find a fourth murder added to the charges.

Verlene and Thomas lay in the Montfort Jones Memorial Hospital on East Adams Street a few blocks from downtown Kosciusko. The black section of the hospital—racial segregation in all public facilities being the law—was adequate to provide for its patients, but it was not as well apportioned or maintained as the white section. Since the town had no black doctors, white physicians attended equally to both races.

Fourteen-year-old Verlene remained quiet and still beneath fresh white sheets that contrasted sharply with her dark skin. Her chest and right arm wrapped heavily with gauze and bandages, she was gradually improving. Her injuries were serious and painful, but they would not cause her to succumb to Leon's murderous intentions. She and her unborn baby, as surviving members of the Harris family tragedy, were being well cared for by the hospital staff.

In a nearby room, Thomas was not improving. He lay on his side in a hospital gown spotted with bloodstains. Behind him, a window with a torn shade leaked cold air into the room. From a transfusion bottle high over his head, a blood-filled tube drooped downward, snaked along the mattress, and disappeared under gauze wrapped around his right elbow.

Thomas drifted in and out of consciousness. He was awake for the moment, eyelids half open in a morphine haze. Occupying an uncomfortable metal-back chair beside his bed, Mary Ella sat mutely with hands clasped, expressionless, eyes fixed on her husband. She reached out and wiped away a tear running down his nose. Thomas did not flinch; he merely stared toward a distant spot on the floor, gazing in despair at nothing.

The doctor had left a half hour ago. Dr. Frank Lacey had delivered the news gently and respectfully, but his prognosis had been devastating. In all likelihood, Thomas would be permanently paralyzed; he would never walk again.[27]

Mary Ella was filled with hopelessness. Despite all that her family had been through, the nightmare was not over. It might never end. She recalled the conversation with her husband months ago when he was stubbornly hanging out with Leon Turner and his group of white friends. She had warned Thomas that nothing but bad could come of his association with Leon. She had been right. Now, as Mary Ella sat next to her helpless man, she did not remind him of her warning. There was no need. Thomas was desperately ill, and three of his children were dead. Nothing she could say would change those facts; nothing she could do would hurt him more. She remained silent.[28]

Chapter 17
Preparation for Trial

The triple murder of children had been the most
disturbing crime in Mississippi within memory.
Everyone had followed the progress of the ensuing
manhunt. Now that it was over and the killers were behind
bars, citizens turned their attention to the upcoming trials.
Lawmen, however, had already taken actions with a view toward prosecution. Their work had begun shortly after the
surrender of Malcolm Whitt at his mother's house.

When news of Malcolm's arrest reached Jackson, officials
at Mississippi State Highway Patrol headquarters immediately
dispatched an interrogation expert to Kosciusko. Investigator
Mike Nichols of the Highway Patrol Identification Bureau
was a specialist in obtaining statements and confessions.[1]
Within hours of Malcolm's capture, he joined Sheriff Roy
Braswell and District Attorney Henry Rodgers to question
Malcolm in the sheriff's office.

The suspect needed no threats or persuasion to talk—
his cooperation began immediately. Malcolm told of his and
Windol's first encounter with Leon Turner at the Newport
store, then detailed the troublesome days that followed.
Malcolm emphasized throughout his admission that Leon
had been the one calling the shots. From the pre-Christ-
mas harassment of Sally Ward and Mary Ella Harris to the
jailbreak a few days later; from the shootings at the Harris
cabin to the escape through the Delta. Turner had been the

ringleader and triggerman; in Malcolm's eyes, he and his brother had done nothing wrong.

Night had fallen by the time questioning was completed. Less than twenty-four hours after the murders, Sheriff Braswell had a somewhat plausible version of the killings and a rough idea of where Leon and Windol were headed. He decided to trace their escape route in search of more evidence.

Braswell, Nichols, Rodgers, and Whitt piled in the sheriff's car and drove to Newport. From there, they headed west, following Malcolm's recollection of the way taken in Caesar Young's waylaid pickup.

In Belzoni, the first firm confirmation of Malcolm's story came when he recognized the Gulf station where the escapees had stopped to get gasoline. Luckily, Lloyd Turner was there, working the night shift as he had the previous evening.[2] The chain-smoking attendant remembered Malcolm and the threatening carload of men with him last night.

The sheriff's group continued to wander through west-central Mississippi, arriving late in the evening at the Greenwood store where Malcolm and Caesar had split from Windol and Leon. Here, the trail went cold. Gaining no further clue about the fugitives' whereabouts, they followed Malcolm's return path home.

Two days later, Leon Turner and Windol Whitt were captured and taken to Durant. After Malcolm Whitt and Caesar Young were brought in, the four suspects were transported in separate patrol cruisers to Jackson. The caravan of black-and-white vehicles with emergency lights flashing was an impressive sight as it made its way south on the hour-long trip.

Once they reached Jackson, the convoy split up. Windol and Malcolm Whitt and Caesar Young went to jail. Leon

Turner was driven to Charity Hospital to have his injuries assessed.

Waiting in a hallway wheelchair for X-rays to be taken, Leon presented a curious sight to the hospital staff. The clean white scrubs temporarily replacing his filthy clothes contrasted sharply with his shaggy, unkempt hair. Dark lines of dried blood streaked the left side of his unshaven face, a face purple and swollen from the struggle during his capture. More blood from a split lower lip smudged his chin.[3]

Despite being surrounded by armed lawmen, Leon jabbered cheerfully with onlookers. He was especially playful with the nurses, one with whom he shared a connection: he had shot her roommate's brother-in-law, Buddy Gowan, at the Sallis house dance in 1940.[4]

Leon continued the good-humored banter while being poked and prodded by a young doctor. The examination determined that none of his injuries were serious—even the lead slug in his back could wait to be removed. With the bullet wounds bandaged and facial lacerations cleaned, Leon was whisked away to jail in the back of the patrol car wearing his old clothes.

Formal examination of the suspects began the day they arrived in Jackson. Led by Investigator Nichols, the interrogations were serious and sometimes severe, but never abusive. Some of them were recorded using the latest technology, a Prestwood brand wire recorder.[5] Unfortunately, the questioning produced no confessions to the killings. The suspects' stories had differed greatly—an inconclusive mixture of truths, half-truths, omissions, and outright lies. But there was one consistent detail in all the narratives: Caesar Young.

Each of the white prisoners had truthfully recounted the role of the Negro owner of the commandeered Studebaker pickup truck. He had been but another victim of the crime spree. Caesar Young was soon cleared of all charges and released.

The upcoming trials of the accused murderers fell under the jurisdiction of Mississippi's Fifth Circuit Court, presided over by the Honorable John Plemon Coleman. This was the same J. P. Coleman who, as a prosecutor in 1940, had sent Leon Turner to prison for ten years.

At age thirty-six, Coleman was clearly an up-and-comer, and his sights were aimed high. Lean, well groomed, and nattily dressed, the Ackerman, Mississippi, native had been elected district attorney in 1938 at age twenty-five—the youngest allowed by the Mississippi Constitution. In 1946 he was voted to the bench of the Fifth Mississippi Circuit Court. This prestigious assignment would be intentionally brief, as Coleman had announced that he would not seek re-election in 1950. Speculation was that he would make a run for governor.[6]

Coleman's judicial domain covered seven Mississippi counties, including Attala, and court proceedings rotated among the various county seats. The seven-county rotation was completed in six months, with two cycles occurring each year. Accordingly, the Attala County Courthouse in Kosciusko hosted the Fifth Circuit Court every March and September—a schedule that continues to this day.

Two days after the killers' arrests, the Mississippi House of Representatives unanimously approved a declaration that called for swift punishment by soliciting the Fifth District circuit judge to convene a special court session at once to try the three accused men.[7] It was a call to action for Judge Coleman, but it presented a problem. Coleman informed the House of Representatives that Mississippi law required that the public be notified via newspaper or other publication at least twenty days before a special court term could be called.

"If that is done, the earliest possible date would be February 13 for a special session in Attala," the judge noted. However, a regular court term was scheduled to begin February 20 in Choctaw County, and Coleman doubted that the one week beginning February 13 "would be sufficient to hear the trials of the three alleged slayers. Furthermore, there is a regular term of Fifth District Circuit Court March 6 in Attala." He concluded that "it would be better to wait the 21 days from Feb. 13 to March 6 until the regular Attala court term."[8]

The judge's logical argument was accepted; the rush to trial was not to happen. Nearly two months were to pass before the legislature would get its wish for punishment.

Prosecutor for the upcoming trials would be Henry Lee Rodgers, district attorney for the Fifth Mississippi District. An experienced trial lawyer from Louisville, Mississippi, Rodgers had succeeded Coleman as district attorney when the latter was elected circuit court judge. A World War I veteran and graduate of the University of Mississippi Law School, Rodgers had originally been a defense attorney, having defended fifty-two death penalty cases. Since becoming district attorney, he was well on his way to racking up an equally impressive number of capital prosecutions.[9]

To make it clear that the State of Mississippi was dead serious about bringing the child killers to justice, Rodgers filed a weighty set of charges against the three defendants:

first-degree murder on three counts; burglary with firearms; possession of whiskey; attempted rape of Sally Ward and Mary Ella Harris; and pointing a loaded pistol at Sally Ward and Verlene Thurman.[10]

Once court convened, it would mark Attala County's first ever trial of a white man for murdering an African American.[11] But it wasn't enough. In a startling announcement, Rodgers declared that the State of Mississippi would seek the death penalty against each of the accused men.[12] Court watchers scoured the state records for any precedent. Unexpectedly, they found one. In 1890 a white storekeeper in Grenada County had been sentenced to death and subsequently hanged for the slaying of a black man.[13]

The people of Kosciusko got their first glimpse of the criminals at a preliminary hearing on January 20. Justice of the Peace Solon Black would here determine whether or not reasonable evidence existed to try the men.

A large crowd was gathered outside Judge Black's courthouse office when the trio arrived from Jackson.[14] Excited and boisterous prior to the appearance, the onlookers quieted to hand-over-mouth whispers at the sight of the escorted prisoners. Bound in handcuffs and ankle chains, still wearing the clothes in which they had been captured, Leon, Malcolm, and Windol shuffled awkwardly down the courthouse hallway. Only the clanking of chains against the marble tile floor pierced the silence. Women drew back as the mass murderers passed by within arm's length. Some little boys lunged forward trying to touch them, only to be yanked back by their mothers. Few in town had ever witnessed such a sight. Here were the cold-blooded monsters who had dominated all news and gossip for the past two weeks.

Some onlookers were surprised by their age differences. Leon Turner, being over a decade older than the Whitt brothers, looked it. Years in one of the nation's toughest prisons had given him a hardened appearance that, by contrast, made the Whitts look like altar boys.

As the men were led into the courtroom, the differences in their demeanor were striking. The Whitt brothers hobbled into the chamber silent and miserable, staying close to each other, shying away from attention, talking only to their mother. Each clutched a crumpled brown paper sack containing clean clothing and a small amount of cash that Birdie Bell had been allowed to bring her sons.[15]

Leon Turner, for his part, was in an outwardly jolly mood. Though moving with a touch of stiffness—the slug still lodged in his back would not be removed until after the hearing—he seemed to enjoy all the attention.[16] Nodding and smiling to spectators, he spoke loudly with relatives in the crowd and posed willingly for photographers.

Suddenly, a murmur erupted in the crowd. Heads turned to see an ambulance stretcher being rolled into the room. On the stretcher, covered by a white sheet up to his neck, lay Thomas Harris. His eyes remained closed as he was wheeled through the crowd and positioned next to Justice of the Peace Black.

After gaveling open the preliminary hearing, Judge Black stated that public defenders had been appointed for each defendant. He motioned for three men in suits at the rear of the room to approach. The lawyers stepped forward and stood beside the defendants. Allowing a moment for the lawyers and their clients to confer, the judge asked Leon Turner how he pleaded to the crime of murder. Without hesitation, Leon loudly announced, "Not guilty."

The question was repeated for Malcolm and then Windol Whitt. Each echoed, "Not guilty."

At that point, the defense lawyers requested to postpone the preliminary hearing for two weeks so they could prepare. Judge Black granted the delay until February 3 and then closed the proceedings.[17]

Three well-known Kosciusko attorneys were now duly appointed to represent the accused murderers. None had asked for the job, but none backed away from the task once selected. Each lawyer had a good record and an unblemished reputation, attributes required for the assignment by Judge J. P. Coleman, who was fully aware of the intense scrutiny that would accompany this trial.

Picked to defend Malcolm Whitt was thirty-one-year-old David E. Crawley Jr., a Kosciusko attorney who had distinguished himself academically at the University of Mississippi.[18]

In a twist of irony, the lawyer appointed to represent Windol Whitt turned out to be Kosciusko's mayor, Alton Massey, who had spent the last week and a half railing against the no-account murderers who had besmirched the good name of his city.

The toughest assignment, handling the defense of Leon Turner, was given to young Claude Woodward. Woodward had a solid reputation as a defense attorney, even though his law practice had begun only two years earlier after his graduation from the law school at Ole Miss.[19]

Howard Turner was still being held in the Attala County Jail, although the appearance of the hardworking logger was actually improved from the day he was arrested. Even in the barely tolerable stench of the old jail, Howard's aroma had stood out. Unable to stand the smell of him, fellow inmates had made him bathe, shampoo, and shave. Then they had chipped in to buy him a new set of blue denims.[20]

Howard was not at all happy about being locked up. With his elderly mother staying with relatives in another county until the matter was settled, his children were left at home to fend for themselves. In a jailhouse interview, Howard complained, "It's hard on a man being kept in here when everything he's got's just going to rack. Plumb going to rack."[21]

By Friday, February 3, when the rescheduled preliminary hearing was to convene, the defense attorneys had spent two weeks assembling the facts of their cases. They had found it painfully obvious that overwhelming evidence existed to warrant pressing ahead to trial. As a result, in a short meeting with District Attorney Rodgers and Judge Coleman, all three counselors waived their clients' right to a preliminary hearing.[22] In response, Judge Coleman announced that each defendant would be tried separately, and the trials would be held one week apart. The case of Windol Whitt would be heard first on March 15, followed by those of Leon Turner and then Malcolm Whitt.

Furthermore, each of the accused would go to trial for the death of four-year-old Ruby Nell Harris only. Rodgers had chosen this strategy so that, in the event of an acquittal, the offender could then be tried again for the murders of the other two children.[23]

After the meeting, two men walked to the small courthouse room that served as the private office of the visiting circuit judge. Judge Coleman entered his cozy, familiar conclave, where hundreds of leather-bound books of law neatly lined the walls, and sat in a leather chair behind a well-organized desk. Removing his black-rimmed glasses, he massaged his eyes as newspaperman Billy McMillan settled into a chair on the other side of the desk. The topic to be discussed by these acquaintances was not the guilt or innocence of the accused murderers. This meeting was to address a bedrock of democracy protected by the United States Constitution—freedom of the press.

Without question, the upcoming trials would be of huge interest to people across the nation. The press would be present in force to cover the proceedings. Fearing a disruption caused by too many media representatives, Judge Coleman had already ruled that only working reporters, not photographers, would be allowed into the courtroom while court was in session. In making this edict, Coleman was merely following the status quo; the "no photographers" policy had been the standard protocol followed by judges nationwide for more than a decade. It had resulted from one of the most publicized crimes in American history, the Lindbergh kidnapping.

Charles A. Lindbergh became an international celebrity in 1927 when he flew solo across the Atlantic in a single-engine airplane. Five years later, the one-year-old son of Colonel Lindbergh was kidnapped from the second-floor nursery of his home. Charley Lindbergh's body was later found buried in the woods nearby. Bruno Richard Hauptmann, an illegal German immigrant, was eventually arrested and charged with the murder.

Hauptmann's trial began January 2, 1935, in Flemington, New Jersey. Drawing upwards of seven hundred writers and broadcasters, and one hundred still and newsreel cameramen, the affair became a media circus. Photographers took pictures of Colonel Lindbergh with flash cameras whenever he testified. A remote control movie camera with hidden microphone captured the testimony of witnesses. Newsreels resulting from this arrangement were shown in moviehouses while the proceedings were yet ongoing, forcing the furious trial judge to shut down the operation.[24]

This unprecedented intrusion into the "trial of the century" by modern instruments of mass communication produced a backlash that lasted for decades. In direct response to this trial, in 1937 the American Bar Association approved Canon 35 of the Code of Judicial Conduct banning photographers, cameras, and broadcasting from all federal and most state courts.

Canon 35 was a bitter pill to news photographers. They were denied the right to cover courtrooms where reporters were permitted, effectively relegating them to second-class journalistic status. But Canon 35 was custom not law; the ABA had no official powers to impose its rules. The final decision was left up to the individual trial judge. While the courts of most states overwhelmingly adopted the ABA protocol, there were rare instances where judges allowed cameras into the courtroom. The key was convincing them that trial photography could be unobtrusive.[25]

Billy McMillan, photographer for the *Kosciusko Star-Herald*, wanted a chance to convince Judge Coleman.

McMillan knew that much of the nation believed the South had two different kinds of justice: one for whites and one for blacks. He felt that the best way to show that modern Mississippi could deal equitably with all its citizens was to give this case extensive visual coverage in the national press. But not by the typical courtroom imagery of the day, which consisted of artists' pencil or charcoal sketches of a trial's participants or setting—renderings that were often too artificial to generate much interest or contemplation by the reader. To grab and hold maximum public awareness of the upcoming Attala trials, newspaper stories needed to be accompanied by photographs. But to enable this, Judge Coleman's previous ruling against photography in his courtroom would have to be reversed.

Prior to his appointment with Coleman, the small-town newspaperman assembled newspaper and magazine clippings of stories and editorials about trials where cameras had been satisfactorily used. As McMillan now waited quietly, Judge Coleman scanned each clipping. Once Coleman put the last one down on his desk, McMillan proceeded to give a thorough lecture on modern cameras and film, explaining how techniques had changed since the Lindbergh trial; it was now possible to take courtroom pictures without the use of flash equipment or noise.

For his final argument, McMillan made a play on Coleman's known intent to ascend to higher office. He pointed out that the judge himself would be featured in many of the resulting trial pictures, and these would be printed in newspapers everywhere. Every voter in the state would know J. P. Coleman's name and face. Next to the governor, Judge Coleman would become the best-known public official in Mississippi.

Coleman leaned back in the chair with interlaced fingers behind his head and stared at the ceiling. After a long moment of contemplation, he looked at McMillan and declared that he would reverse his previous decision. Photographers would be allowed in his courtroom, but they would have to abide by a strict set of rules that he proceeded to list, tapping his desk with a finger as he voiced them.

1. Photographers would make every effort to maintain the decorum of the proceedings.
2. No flashes would be permitted.
3. Photographers would be located with reporters in a designated area of the courtroom.
4. Photographers would not be able to talk or move about during the proceedings.
5. They would not be allowed to smoke.
6. They would not take close-up pictures of the jury.[26]

In the fifty years since the courthouse had been built to replace its burned-to-the-ground predecessor, few improvements had been made. With the huge tidal wave of attention coming to town, city leaders funded a major spruce-up of the stately, but drab, main courtroom.

Incandescent lights hanging from the high ceiling were replaced with fluorescent fixtures. Potbellied stove heaters on the floor were removed in favor of overhead electric heating units. Battered furniture was revarnished; wooden floors were refinished; and trim work was repainted.[27]

A special area for the press was configured at the front of the courtroom gallery. By using the courtroom's ornate mahogany railing as the forward boundary of the area and enclosing the other three sides with unstained pine two-by-fours, a functional—though not overly attractive—press corral was created.

The Attala County session of the Fifth Circuit Court of Mississippi was called to order on Monday, March 6, 1950, a full week before the Harris murder trials were to start. This first week of court involved the business of grand and petit juries and the hearing of civil cases. Thus, it was unexciting and uneventful inside the courtroom; but outside, the atmosphere was heating up.

Strangers began filtering into town. Reporters and photographers from big-city Southern newspapers and national news services began strolling around the square, wandering through shops, and interviewing townsfolk. One visiting reporter asked eighty-one-year-old J. M. Knotts if he thought an all-white jury would sentence a white man to die for killing a Negro. Knotts replied, "I believe, without exception, everyone that I've heard discuss the case is hoping that Leon Turner gets the chair."

"I have lived here all my life," drawled the old-timer. "I know Kosciusko. We have never had any serious misunderstandings between Negroes and white people. Our relationship has been good. The general belief among Negroes is that Turner won't get the chair. They don't say much, it's hard for them to talk, but I'm certain they don't believe Turner will be executed. I think he will be. No doubt, if he isn't, it would shake the Negroes' faith in the whites."

"It's not only the Negroes, though. I've heard many people say if Turner doesn't get the chair, we might as well burn it. That's the general feeling among the better people of this county."[28]

In another interview, Sheriff Roy Braswell said, "Mr. Knotts is right about it being mostly a gentle town. I've only got about seven prisoners now. Never have too many. Somebody gets drunk. Somebody pokes somebody. That's all."[29]

Even inmates at the "curiously friendly" jail seemed content to the out-of-towners. They smiled when Inez Braswell brought a newspaperman in for a tour.

"You boys mind if this man comes in and looks at you?" she asked.

"Not at all. But bring us a broom and let us sweep up first."[30]

Of course, not everyone took the attention well. In a hardware store on the square, a man flushed when asked about the trial. "There's been too much talk already," he grumbled. "Too much writing in the newspapers. I don't like it."[31]

T. J. Breazeale, a seventy-two-year-old deputy sheriff, groused, "People making too much of this up north. Making more of it than we are right here in Kosciusko. Why, I got a son—T.L.—in the state of Washington. He says they write something in the papers about it every day. It ain't right."[32]

Because of the influx of reporters to Kosciusko, stories about the upcoming trials began flooding newspapers throughout the country. Public interest in the sensational child murder case awakened after lying dormant for nearly two months. Newspapers began speculating on defense strategies for the upcoming Windol Whitt trial. "It is rumored Windol Whitt will claim he was drunk when he went to the Harris home," one story reported, "but sobered up and left before the slayings."[33]

In a pretrial question-and-answer session with reporters, Windol said, "If Leon Turner tells the truth, I'm not worried. I swear I'm innocent of murder. . . . I'll tell you this again: I'm innocent of murder and all I ask is for Turner to tell the truth."[34]

A daunting task faced Windol's defense attorney, Mayor Alton Massey, for all evidence pointed to his client's culpability. And Massey had an additional cross to bear—the damning statements he had made about his future client following Windol's capture. The press learned of these statements and reported that Massey, "as a city official . . . had a great deal to say about the case in the past."[35]

Forced to initiate damage control, the mayor admitted making negative statements about the three accused men, "some of which might be considered derogatory to the defendant." But these would not affect his tenacity in defending his client, he promised.

"To avoid any possible charge of inconsistency on my part, I would like it to be understood that my motive in defending Windol Whitt is entirely professional and that Windol Whitt will receive the fullest extent of my ability as a lawyer. He will be diligently defended."[36]

Further stirring the pot of controversy, reports circulated that the defense lawyers were battling one another. It was rumored that Alton Massey wanted to call Leon Turner to the stand but that Claude Woodward would refuse to allow his client to testify for Whitt.[37] Coincidentally, Mr. Woodward had recently announced that he would be running against Mayor Massey in the upcoming mayoral primary.[38]

The swarm of reporters and photographers snooping around and requesting interviews caused major disruptions in Judge Coleman's office, and the judge knew it would only be worse for the Leon Turner trial. Accordingly, he asked Billy McMillan to be his intermediary with visiting pressmen.

McMillan relished the role. An energetic and innovative reporter, his vision was usually confined by the close horizon available to him in Kosciusko. Now he was on a tower with the big boys, getting a more distant view.

Press representatives already in town or soon expected to arrive included personnel from the *Memphis Commercial Appeal*,

Jackson Daily News, *Jackson Clarion-Ledger*, *New Orleans Times-Picayune*, *St. Louis Post-Dispatch*, Associated Press, and United Press International. Others might show up unannounced. The daily need of these writers to transmit stories to their home offices would surely overwhelm the town's small telegraph office. To compensate, McMillan persuaded Western Union to assign three extra telegraphers to duty.[39]

On Monday, March 13, Judge Coleman opened the second week of the circuit court's session, the much anticipated week of Windol Whitt's trial. Legal maneuvering began right away, but it was not Windol's defense lawyer that made the initial move. Instead, Leon Turner's attorney, Claude Woodward, stood and requested a six-month delay until the next term of the court. Claiming "ill feeling and grudge" in the area due to "temporary public excitement," Woodward stated it would be impossible to obtain a fair, impartial trial during this court term.[40]

Woodward laid a stack of papers on the bench in front of Judge Coleman. Presented as evidence were newspapers from Kosciusko, Jackson, Memphis, and New Orleans, as well as the "Shooter's Chance" article from *Time* magazine. Motioning to the pile, Woodward claimed that the large amount of publicity given the case had biased the citizenry.

He proceeded to call witnesses to the stand. Five men gave sworn testimony that they believed prejudgment toward the defendants existed in Attala County. After Woodward finished questioning each witness, District Attorney Henry Lee Rodgers performed a cross-examination. His tactic was not to show a lack of knowledge of the case by the adults of Attala County—an impossible task—but rather, to point out that they could judge fairly in spite of it. In the end, all witnesses admitted to Rodgers that they believed twelve impartial men could be selected for a jury in this place at this time.

Once both sides finished their arguments, Judge Coleman ruled for the prosecution, saying that no grudge existed that would prevent a fair trial. About the stack of publicity, Coleman remarked, "The purpose of a newspaper is to print the news. What the general public thinks will have no bearing on this case. The jury will decide."[41]

Wrapping up, Judge Coleman ruled that the defendant had adequate counsel and that adequate time had been given for preparation. The request for a delay was denied. The trial of Leon Turner would begin next Monday at 9:00 a.m.

With that business concluded, attention again focused on the trial that would commence in two days. Windol Whitt would be tried on the charge of murdering four-year-old Ruby Nell Harris. It would be among the most closely followed events in the history of the state.

Chapter 18

The Windol Whitt Trial

"Large" was the usual first impression of the main courtroom of the Attala County Courthouse. The room seemed far bigger than necessary for a small town in a rural county. But with few other sources of public entertainment available in Kosciusko, a good trial was typically well attended.

Located on the second floor of the courthouse, the courtroom had bare white walls, wood floors, and a twenty-five-foot ceiling. Seven tall windows, extending from the floor to the ceiling, filled the back wall. Entry doors midway on both sides of the chamber contained clear glass in the upper half, allowing spectators in the outside hallway to peer inside. At the front of the room, steep stairways on each side climbed to the third-floor courthouse attic.

The courtroom was divided into two main sections, the gallery and the bar. The gallery occupied the rear two-thirds of the room and was filled with long rows of unpadded wooden benches. Three interior aisles provided easy access for the six hundred spectators the benches could seat. Defining the forward boundary of the gallery was a waist-high mahogany balustrade running the width of the room.

The bar was the front third of the room where proceedings were conducted. Its focal point was the judge's bench, a wide, richly paneled, elevated mahogany dais centered along the courtroom's front wall.

To the left inside the bar was the door to the witnesses' waiting room. At the right stood the jury box with its three rows of four swivel chairs. An adjacent door opened to the jury assembly room.

Four feet from the left front corner of the jury box, a small, elevated witness stand was positioned next to the balustrade. From its center rose a chair mounted on a chrome pedestal, not unlike a barbershop chair. Instead of being protectively snuggled next to the judge as in many courtrooms, this isolated witness chair faced the judge and jury as in an inquisition.

Ordinarily, a felony trial in Attala County Circuit Court used a panel of twenty-four men to eventually select the twelve jurors. But this trial was anything but ordinary; this was the case of accused mass murderer Windol Whitt. Suspecting that a fair, unbiased jury may be tough to find, defense attorney Alton Massey had requested and received a venire of one hundred lawful candidates—"lawful" at the time meaning white male citizens of Attala County over twenty-one years of age.[1]

Despite the number of panelists, voir dire moved along rapidly, and twelve duly sworn citizens filled the jury box by noon on Wednesday, March 15, 1950.[2]

Judge Coleman called for a recess until 1:30 p.m., and the bailiff opened the courtroom doors. A crowd was waiting for this moment. No spectators had been allowed in court for the morning's proceedings, but dozens of people had shown up nevertheless, chatting on the courthouse lawn, loitering in the halls, gazing through the glass of the courtroom's side doors. With the doors now open, these early birds began filing into the gallery to choice seat locations.

Joining the throng were a small group of men who did not need to jockey for seats, for a folded sheet of white paper printed with the words "RESERVED FOR WORKING PRESS" identified their table. Having been prevented from covering the jury selection, the visiting newspapermen had kept close to the courthouse, flocking like pigeons to any crumb of news.

Most journalists are an independent sort. Used to jostling with their peers for the best angle, the best lighting, the best anything that might give them an advantage on a story, they are not easily herded into conformity. Billy McMillan, however, was proving to be a more than adequate shepherd. Appointed by the judge to take charge of the visiting reporters and photographers, he ensured that his cohorts were credentialed, familiar with the media rules imposed by Judge Coleman, and properly settled in place. The big-city media reps had no problem following their small-town counterpart's lead; all wanted to cooperate with the bold judge.

As the reporters and photographers claimed a spot in the press area and spread out the tools of their trade, the nine members of the media who attended this first day of the trial were in high spirits.[3] Recognizing both the historic rarity of their invitation into the courtroom and the influence that their success could have upon future trial coverage, they referred to their little fraternity as the "charter members."[4]

By 1:25 p.m., six hundred chattering souls filled the courtroom benches. As was customary in any such Southern gathering at the time, the crowd was divided by color. Two hundred black men and women occupied the court's rear seats;[5] four hundred whites sat nearer the front. Everyone was dressed in their Sunday best, all with something in their laps: the women had their purses; the men, their hats.

Inside the bar, attorneys Alton Massey and Henry Rodgers sat at unpretentious rectangular tables directly in front of the judge's bench. At an identical table to the right of the judge, longtime court reporter Wiley DeLoach massaged his writing hand, readying to record the proceedings in shorthand. The dozen selected jurors waited in their seats of judgment. In contrast to the excited nature of the gallery crowd, these men were serious and composed, talking quietly among themselves.

Sitting within the bar next to the balustrade, a dozen court officials and county VIPs bided time. There among them was the defendant.

Windol Whitt was three chairs away from the witness stand. Dressed in a lightweight tan jacket over an open-collared shirt; hands in his lap, motionless, gazing downward, he looked pitifully alone. No one spoke to him; no one paid him any attention. Even his estranged wife, sitting three rows back with their two squirming children, kept her physical and emotional distance.[6]

Everyone paid attention to the door directly behind the judge's chair. It was easy to notice. This door to the judge's chamber was framed on each side by two dark-wood Greek Ionic columns, atop which rose a massive, carved entablature that reached almost to the ceiling. Promptly at one thirty, hundreds of conversations instantly silenced as the door opened and Fifth Circuit Court Judge Coleman entered. Coleman settled into his high-back leather chair, removed his glasses, and gaveled the court to order.

Most of the audience had never before laid eyes on this black-robed magistrate. Tall and aristocratic, J. P. Coleman dominated any gathering, not only by his regal looks and purposeful manner, but also by his strong personality and sharp mind.[7] Possessing the crowd-manipulation skills of a good politician, Coleman could in turn act the part of a serious, stern overseer or a friendly country neighbor.

As he began his introductory remarks, the folksy side emerged. Bantering like the master of ceremonies at the Attala County Forestry Queen beauty contest, he laid out his rules of conduct for court observers. One dictum prohibited smoking: "I got some of my favorite cigars with me, but I'm going to make myself do just like I'm telling you. I won't smoke either."[8]

Frowning at the assorted VIPs scattered along the railing nearby, he instructed, "I'm not pickin' on anybody, but every man who isn't an officer has to get out from behind the bar of this court."[9] The sound of scraping chairs erupted as some of the town's most recognizable personages retreated into the commoners' arena, somehow squeezing into the mix.

When the commotion was over, Judge Coleman donned his glasses, rolled his chair back a foot, leaned back, crossed his legs, and began.

"The prosecution may call its first witness."

District Attorney Henry Lee Rodgers stood and trumpeted, "The State of Mississippi calls Thomas Harris to the stand."

The witness room door at the front left of the courtroom opened and an ambulance gurney was rolled slowly into the room. Lying atop its sheet-covered mattress, propped up on a pillow with a blanket covering him from the waist down, was Thomas Harris. Dr. Frank Lacey carefully pushed his patient the width of the room as tables and chairs were moved aside.

The wheeled stretcher was positioned with Thomas facing the jury, his toes a yard from the nearest juror, his head five feet from Windol Whitt. Henry Lee Rodgers took a seat in the witness chair, allowing him to look down into the pitiable eyes of the very sick man.

"Thomas, I understand you have been shot," Rodgers began.

"Yes sir."

"Where were you shot?"

"In the back." Thomas's voice was weak. People strained to catch his words in the quiet courtroom.

Thomas began to tell the events of that tragic night. "Leon came in the house and walked back there to the bed where I was, and I jumped out the bed and my wife jumped out her bed and we all run back in the kitchen and tried to get out the back door."

"And what happened?" Rodgers asked.

"Mr. Windol was standing there with a shotgun."

"And what did he do?"

"He was standing there with a shotgun and told me if I run out he would shoot me."

When the prosecution finished, Alton Massey stepped next to Thomas. "Now at what point in the progress of this killing did you hear Mr. Windol Whitt speak?" he asked.

Harris thought for a moment. "When I opened the door, he says, 'You better get back or I will shoot you.'"

"Was he pointing the gun at you?"

"Yes sir."

"What kind of gun was it?"

"A shotgun or something. I reckon it was a shotgun. It was a long gun. I couldn't say now whether that was a Winchester or something like that, but I say it was a shotgun."

Massey looked toward the jury. "He could have been pointing a broomstick at you and you would still have thought it was a gun because you were scared of Mr. Leon, weren't you?"

"Yes sir, I was scared of all of them."

Next to testify was Mary Ella Harris. Her gaunt face reflected the stress of the last two months. She sat erect in the witness chair, interlaced fingers resting calmly in her lap as the district attorney asked questions.

"Did anything disturb you all there at home on the night of January 8, 1950?"

"Well, somebody come up and knocked on the door, and nobody didn't answer, and I heard the foot steps went toward the door—come to the door and knocked, and I heard the foot steps when they went back toward the door steps, and somebody mumbled something but I couldn't understand what they said, and at the time somebody hit the glass window."

"What happened then?"

"Well, when they hit the glass window, I jumped up out of the bed and took Ruby Nell up and I went on through the kitchen."

"Then what did you do?"

"The kitchen door was open some, it wasn't open wide; but I didn't stop at that door, I went on in the side room."

"Tell me what you did."

"Well, when I got in there I was intending to go out that door, but somebody on the outside says, 'Shut that door, don't come out.'"

To Mary Ella's left, Windol Whitt shook his head as the witness quoted him.

Mary Ella told of running, making a complete circle through the house until she saw Leon Turner in her bedroom.

"He was just there in the middle of the floor. When I got in there and seen him, I just rushed on out."

"Did you have any children with you?"

"I had the baby."

"What had become of Ruby Nell Harris?"

Mary Ella paused for several seconds; her eyes filled with tears. Finally, her voice quaking, she spoke. "When I got back in the bedroom and saw Mr. Turner, I got frightened and turned her loose. I went out on the porch and went down the door steps."

"Then what happened?" Rodgers asked tenderly.

"I started toward the road, toward the next house, and somebody was out there with a shotgun or rifle one. I caught the barrel and he was going along beside me telling me I better get back in the house or I would get shot, and I caught the barrel of the gun with my right hand and he pulled it back and forth until I turned the barrel loose."

"Did you know the man that had the gun in his hand?"

"I didn't just know him good, but he looked like the largest Whitt boy."

Mary Ella told of being forced back toward the house. Through the open front door, she saw Frankie and her two little girls huddled by the fireplace. As she watched Frankie, she heard a shot.

"I heard him hollering, 'Oh!' and he fell over against the wall, and I whirled and run back off to the next house."

"Did you see anything else that occurred after you turned and ran away from that house?"

"No sir."

"That's all, Your Honor."

Walking slowly back to his seat, Rodgers glanced at the audience. Scattered about were women clutching handkerchiefs to their faces, sniffling quietly.

Mayor Massey saw the same thing as he stood to question the witness. His counter was to suggest that Thomas may have brought on the calamity by his dealings with Leon. Mary Ella admitted that she and Thomas knew Leon "pretty well" and that he sometimes dropped by her house. But she didn't know why.

"You don't know why he came, he just came?"

"No sir, I don't know."

Verlene Thurman took the stand next with her right arm in a sling. Although she looked calm, a slow back-and-forth twisting motion of the swivel chair gave away her nervousness. Henry Lee Rodgers gave the fifteen-year-old his best "Everything will be okay" smile, then asked her to describe the events of the night. Verlene took a deep breath and hurried out her story like water through a breached levee.

"We had gone to bed and heard footsteps come up on the porch and knocked on the door and didn't nobody say nothing and then we heard footsteps go back to the door steps and heard somebody mumbling something and then the footsteps come back to the window and hit on the window and broke the glass window pane and we all jumped up out of the bed and went running through to the kitchen and . . ."

Rodgers moved in front of her, "Wait a minute now. Don't talk quite so fast. Talk so the jury can understand you."

Verlene took a couple of breaths and described her attempt to run out the back door. "The little Whitt boy was standing at the door and told me to go back in the house."

"What do you mean by that when you say 'the little Whitt boy'?"

Verlene pointed at Windol. "Windol Whitt. Told me to get back in the house or he would shoot me."

Nearby, Windol chewed furiously on a piece of gum and glanced back at his wife. Helen returned his gaze, but her eyes showed no pity, no sympathy, no love.

Continuing her testimony, Verlene described hiding under the porch and being forced out by Windol. She proved to be a very damaging witness for the prosecution.

During cross-examination, Massey stressed uncertainty about Windol's gun due to the darkness.

"He was pointing the gun at you, was he?" asked Massey.

"Yes sir."

"As a matter of fact, you don't know whether that was a gun or a broomstick, do you?"

"It was a gun. I recognized the barrel."

Massey achieved a small gain by getting Verlene to admit that although Windol had plenty of opportunity to shoot her, he had not done so.

She was released just before four o'clock.

Although it had been two and a half hours since court convened, Judge Coleman did not stop for a break. Other witnesses now filled in the events surrounding the murders.

Sheriff Roy Braswell described the crime scene in shocking detail. John Wiley Brown, the ambulance driver, testified about transporting Thomas Harris to the hospital and returning to pick up the dead. Dr. J. L. Turnage described examining Ruby Nell's body at the mortuary.

Roosevelt Whitcomb recalled cooking "flapjacks" for Leon Turner and two other men after their December jail escape. Caesar Young recounted being kidnapped by the trio of white men and then driving through the Delta all night. Farmer Oscar Sibley told of being robbed by Malcolm and Leon at his home in Louise.

After this parade of adult witnesses, eleven-year-old Jack Aldridge of Winona came to the witness stand. The district attorney first provided a brief lesson on the importance of telling the truth in court.

"What will happen if you don't tell the truth?" asked Rodgers.

"You will go to the bad man," replied the youth.

Jack proceeded to give his totally honest account of watching Leon and Windol board the Trailways bus just outside Winona. The men rode only a short time, he said, before mysteriously getting off in the middle of nowhere.

Testimony then shifted direction to Windol Whitt's post-capture questioning in Jackson. Sheriff Braswell, recalled to the stand, testified that Windol confessed that he, Malcolm, and Leon had weapons at the Harris place. Highway Patrol Identification Officer Mike Nichols next told how Windol admitted firing a pump shotgun "two times away from the house towards some trees that were up on the hill behind the house."

The time was 5:30 p.m. when Nichols left the stand. Having scampered through seven witnesses in the hour and a half since Verlene finished, Henry Lee Rodgers announced that the State of Mississippi rested.

It seemed a logical time for court to adjourn until tomorrow. Several men and women in the gallery began fiddling with coats and purses, preparing to leave. But Judge Coleman did not so much as take a brief recess. To the disappointment of restless spectators, he pressed ahead by directing Alton Massey to summon his first witness for the defense.

Massey called Malcolm Whitt.

As Malcolm walked from the witness room to the witness stand, he passed in front of his brother. The two exchanged sad glances. Testifying was a gamble for Malcolm as he himself would face trial on the same charge in two weeks. But his attorney, David Crawley, had agreed to let Malcolm try to help Windol.

Under Alton Massey's mild questioning, Malcolm described the events of the December day when he and Windol first met Leon Turner.

"You met Leon Turner one afternoon and got in jail that night?" Massey summarized for the jury.

"Yes sir."

"Now, why did you break out of jail?"

"One thing because we wasn't getting enough to eat, and I was there for something I didn't think I should be there for."

Massey's remaining questions focused on the day of the murders. Malcolm told of making moonshine to sell and Leon saying he knew where they could get rid of it. The men walked a ways to Thomas Harris's house, when Malcolm quoted Leon Turner as saying, "You all better stay out here in the yard. The man don't know you and he might be afraid."

He and Windol "stopped there in the yard," Malcolm explained, "and Leon went up and pushed the door open and went in and knocked some chairs over or something and some women started hollering and when that happened we started towards the road and about the time we got two-thirds of the way to the road from there the gun started firing and we kept going about a block down the road and Leon come running and called and told us he had killed the whole damn bunch of them, and then from there we went to his daddy's house."

The attorney turned away from Malcolm and walked toward the jury as he asked, "You deny taking any part in this killing down at Thomas Harris' house?"

"Yes sir," Malcolm answered.

Henry Lee Rodgers flipped through his legal pad as he rose and continued to do so as he ambled slowly toward Malcolm Whitt, drawing an over-the-glasses look from Judge Coleman. Rodgers seemed to find what he was looking for right as he stopped in front of the fidgety witness. Lowering his yellow pad, Rodgers looked coldly at Malcolm and launched right into it.

"Isn't it the truth, sir, that you and Leon Turner and Windol Whitt agreed to go down to the Harris house to have sexual intercourse with his women folks?"

"No sir."

"And you had in your hands at that time a .22 rifle?"

"No sir."

"That's what you told me, isn't it, Mr. Whitt?"

"No sir."

In fact, Malcolm had divulged these pieces of information soon after giving himself up. Rodgers now tried to jog Malcolm's memory.

"Were you down here in the sheriff's office in the presence of a great number of officers including the sheriff, Mr. Roy Braswell, Mr. Mike Nichols, and others when I talked to you?"

"I don't remember."

"Do you remember seeing me the night you were captured?"

"I don't know as I do or not."

"Didn't you tell me, please, sir, that when you got to the front door and started up in the house that Leon Turner turned to you and that you were at the front door with a .22 rifle in your hand and he said, 'We are going in that house and have intercourse with those women'? (The word 'intercourse' I am using for another word.) That 'we are going to have intercourse with those women or kill the whole damn pile'?"

"No sir."

"Didn't you tell me that your brother had a .12 gauge shotgun you had got from Parvee Rutherford and that he went around to the back door of the house?"

"No sir, I did not."

Rodgers next used Mary Ella's totally believable testimony to show Malcolm's veracity.

"Mr. Whitt, were you the one in front of the house during the time the shooting was going on?"

Malcolm looked toward his brother. "Me and him both was in the front yard."

"Did you see anybody come out?"

"No sir."

"Didn't see a Negro woman run out with a baby in her hands and you take your gun and try to make her go back in the house?"

"No sir."

The district attorney stared silently at Malcolm for a moment and then turned toward the judge. "That's all."

Malcolm left the witness stand at 6:30 p.m.

Throughout the courtroom, people were squirming in their seats—several hours on hard wooden benches were tough on good backs and nearly unbearable on bad ones. Full bladders and empty stomachs added to the discomfort. Mercifully, Judge Coleman finally allowed a recess. Relentless in his push to move the trial along, he announced the break would only last an hour.

When court reconvened at seven thirty, Mayor Massey called his second witness to the stand. Windol Whitt shuffled to the witness chair with a reluctant, hangdog look that projected quite the opposite impression of what his lawyer would have wished. Windol further compounded his show of hopelessness by talking so softly that Massey had to ask him to speak up.

Windol told his version of the events leading up to the murders, and it was not surprising that his story closely paralleled his brother's. He covered everything from meeting Leon to the shootings. He traced the route taken by him and Leon on their journey through the Delta and subsequent return to Attala County. He spoke of convincing Leon to let Malcolm go free in Greenwood by telling the killer, "If you leave my brother alone, I will go with you."

"Why did you tell Leon that?" asked his attorney.

"I was scared he was going to shoot my brother."

During cross-examination, Windol again parroted his brother by denying having any weapons on the night of the shootings. Even when the district attorney pointed out that he had admitted having guns during questioning at Jackson, Windol disavowed it. Windol left the stand at 9:00 p.m.

Despite the late hour, Judge Coleman directed the defense to call its next witness. A fatigued Alton Massey—his face, like his suit, considerably more wrinkled than earlier in the day—brought forward a surprise witness, a white man from Thomastown named Allie Ellington. Ellington explained that he had been in the hospital visiting his sick wife and had talked to Thomas Harris while there. As he paused to take a breath, Rodgers objected. Judge Coleman sustained, explaining that the witness could not yet go down this path of evidence since Massey "did not lay the predicate to impeach his testimony when Thomas Harris was on the witness stand."

Massey's shoulders drooped. "Well, we better get him back up here then, because I sure want to impeach him."

Knowing that Thomas Harris could not be recalled from the hospital at this late hour, Judge Coleman ruled that Thomas would indeed be brought back as a witness, but it would not be tonight. "It now being 9:15 p.m., court now stands adjourned until 8:30 o'clock tomorrow morning."

Hundreds of weary people struggled to their feet and slowly began to leave. A conspicuous few, however, hurried to get out. Reporters and photographers were still on the clock. They speedily gathered their equipment and rushed a block northwest to the two-story Star-Herald Building. Billy McMillan turned on the lights and led everyone inside. As a professional courtesy to the visitors, the local newspaper had made desktop space and darkroom equipment available.

The heavy tapping of several manual typewriters filled the smoky room as reporters bylined tomorrow's stories. Then they rushed to the nearby telegraph office, with its own clamor of teletype keyboards, to send the articles to home newspapers in time to make morning editions. It was a good thing that extra telegraph employees had been hired, for the Western Union office in Kosciusko, which normally sent about 200 words a day, moved 11,000 words on the trial's first day. Another 8,000 words would be transmitted the second day, making the equivalent of three month's wordage in two days.[10]

The courtroom was packed well before half past eight on Thursday morning. In addition to hundreds of adults, a teachers' convention allowed several children to attend.[11] Members of the press occupied the same spots as the day before, though their number had grown by one. Pulitzer Prize–winning reporter Hodding Carter Jr. of the *Greenville Delta Democrat-Times*, had driven in earlier that morning.[12]

Sitting in the row directly behind the press box, Helen Whitt talked with a reporter. "My husband is innocent," the young Alabama brunette proclaimed. "I just don't think he done any of it." Asked what she and her husband would do if he were acquitted, Helen replied, "I reckon we'll live here in Attala County."[13]

After Judge Coleman brought the court to order, Alton Massey called Thomas Harris to the stand. The ailing gunshot victim, and father of the girl for whose murder Windol Whitt stood trial, was once again rolled in on the ambulance gurney.

Massey jumped straight to the subject of Allie Ellington. Thomas stated that he did not know the man, but it was possible that he might have talked to him in the hospital. He had been "under the influence of medicine—morphine and stuff" and did not know what he may have said.

"You don't remember telling Mr. Ellington that you didn't know who shot you?" asked Massey.

"No sir, I don't remember telling him, but I won't say now I didn't tell him. No sir, I won't say that."

Massey next recalled Allie Ellington to the stand, but before the witness could report anything, Rodgers objected. The judge sustained, explaining that Thomas had admitted just now that he might have told Ellington he didn't know who shot him. Therefore, Allie Ellington could add nothing more, and his testimony was unnecessary.

The exasperated defense attorney tried twice more to have Ellington answer questions, but Coleman nixed both attempts.

Massey was done. "The defendant rests."

Rebuttal witnesses for the State appeared next. First came Mike Nichols carrying the Prestwood wire recorder that had captured the January 17 jailhouse statements of Windol and Malcolm Whitt. The crowd buzzed with excitement as Nichols set the device on a table and plugged it in. Judge Coleman then made an announcement that disappointed many.

"The district attorney advises me that there is language in that record that is not at all becoming for a lady to hear, nor for any young children to be hearing. I regret the necessity of asking them to leave the courtroom, but I don't want any language like that being bandied about in my court for ladies to listen to. I am going to ask all ladies to leave the courtroom, and I ask the sheriff to see that all children under 18 years of age leave the courtroom."

After nearly half of the gallery stepped outside, Investigator Nichols began to play back the Whitts' interrogations. Volume was kept low to prevent any offensive words from escaping the chamber.[14] Outside the courtroom, women squeezed against the two windowed doors, straining to grasp the forbidden fruit.[15]

The following are excerpts from the recording:

Mr. Nichols: Windol, we have talked to Malcolm a good bit more than you, and we would like for you, if you will, to get clear in our minds just exactly what happened over at that house, Thomas's house, the night of the shooting.

Windol: We went there, like he said, and him and Malcolm—that is Leon and Malcolm—went to the corner of the porch and taken a piss . . . and I was there at the back and I heard a glass cracking, breaking at the door. I heard that, and I heard him moving around in there and I couldn't hear no talking. There was two or three rooms between the front door and where I was pissing, and I come back at the end of the house, and just as I got back at the end of the house, Malcolm was walking in the path—

Rodgers: Now, wait a minute. You shot that gun, didn't you?

Windol: Yes sir, I shot the shotgun. That was when I seen Malcolm was going back down the road. We met, I was a little back behind him, I was behind him, then I looked back and that was when I seen Leon.

Rodgers: What was the matter, didn't you hear that shooting going on?

Windol: No, sir, I didn't hear the shooting until—I did hear something pop, I couldn't say it was a shot. When I looked back, Leon was coming out the door and down the steps. We was almost in the road by then. That was when he commenced telling us—

Nichols: Tell us just what he said, the exact words that you remember.

Windol: He said, "Goddamn, I killed every one of them," just like that.

Now the lawmen on the playback began probing Malcolm for information:

Rodgers: Malcolm, you spell your name M-a- . . . You have a 6th grade education, haven't you?

Malcolm: Yes sir.

Rodgers: Then spell it.

Malcolm: M-a-l-c-u-m.

Rodgers: You told me now, Malcum, that when you heard this thing happen, you turned and went back down the road.

Malcum: When I found out what was gonna happen.

Rodgers: Well, how come (sic) you to find out so as to know to leave there?

Malcum: When we come to the house there, I didn't know it was the house we were going to when we left. When we got up to the house, I recognized it. I asked Leon what he was going to do and he told me just like I told you, he said he was going to fuck them or kill every one of them.

Rodgers: He said he was going to fuck or kill the whole damn passel.

Malcum: I just got up on the edge of the porch. I recognized the place and asked him what he was here for and that was when he told me. When he told me that, I told him to come on, let's not go in and not to do nothing like that. I taken him by the right arm and told him to come on and let's go, and he said, "Hell, no. I'm going to do it." When he done that, I turned and walked back towards the road. I was down the road when Leon caught up with me.

Rodgers: Caught up with you? He said what to you, now?

Malcum: He said he killed the whole damn bunch.

*Rodgers: He killed the whole damn bunch. Where was your
little brother at that time?*
Malcum: He was with me.

When the recorded discussion turned away from the
events of the alleged shooting, Judge Coleman stopped the
playback.

Officer Nichols and his machine were situated directly in
front of the press, allowing the reporters to hear every word.
While listening for the crime-related discussion, the journalists picked up another vital bit of information. In writing
stories about the murders, reporters had struggled with the
spelling of the older Whitt brother's name. They had used
such variations as "Malcolm," "Malcom," "Malcolme," and
"Malcomb." Before the trial, newsmen had agreed to spell
the name "Malcolm." After hearing Malcolm spell it on the
playback, one reporter wrote: "When . . . the district attorney asked [Malcolm] how to spell his first name, the gentlemen of the press listened carefully in the hope that the right
spelling would be established, finally, once and for all. When
Malcolm spelled it M-a-l-c-u-m, the only spelling they had
not heard, the reporters looked at each other in consternation,
shrugged their shoulders and continued to write it Malcolm,
and Malcolm it stays."[16]

The prosecution and the defense each rested its case
shortly after 11:00 a.m., and Judge Coleman went directly to
jury instructions.

The first order of business for the twelve men was to determine if the accused was guilty or innocent of the murder of
Ruby Nell Harris. Mississippi law specified that anyone aiding or abetting the crime could be considered just as guilty

as the person pulling the trigger, Coleman lectured. A vote of guilty had to be unanimous.[17] Should the jury find Whitt guilty, they would immediately decide his penalty.

In all, there were four possible verdicts: 1) Guilty as charged, with a punishment of death in the electric chair—a choice that also required a unanimous jury decision; 2) Guilty with recommendation of life imprisonment; 3) Guilty, but disagreement among the jury as to the penalty, in which case the defendant would automatically receive life imprisonment; or 4) Not guilty.[18]

After Judge Coleman's legal instructions, each lawyer presented final arguments. District Attorney Henry Lee Rodgers went first. A family of human beings had suffered grievously because of Windol Whitt, he pronounced. A little girl had been killed because of him: "The law says the crime is killing a human being and it doesn't say what color. Oh, yes, they're just Negroes, but, gentlemen, this family was in its home; and no matter how humble, a man has no right to be safe if not in his home."[19]

Turning to the empty witness chair and questioning it as if the defendant were sitting there, Rodgers addressed the fact that Windol had not personally shot anyone. "You took no part in the shooting, Mr. Whitt? Did you go for a doctor to save those wounded people, Mr. Whitt?" He came back to the jury. "Armed with a shotgun," he said, "Whitt refused to let the frightened Negroes run out the back door and thus is just as guilty" as the man who fired the fatal shots. "Had they been allowed to flee the house, the killing of Ruby Nell Harris never would have occurred."[20]

Rodgers moved relentlessly toward his summation. "Why, gentlemen, Windol Whitt's the man who drove Ruby Nell to death under the blaze of Leon Turner."[21] Asking the jurors to find Windol Whitt guilty of murder and sentence him to death, Rodgers reminded them of the nationwide attention focused on this case. "Mississippi is coming out of the dark shadow of yesteryear and into the bright sun of the future," he declared. "Let's build a bridge from the past to the future."[22] He concluded with the charge: "Do your duty as Mississippians."[23]

Mayor Alton Massey began his closing argument by reminding voters why he was speaking for Windol Whitt. "It is my very unfortunate lot by order of the court to represent him."[24] But, he emphasized, his duty was to defend Whitt as best he possibly could.

"This man, this *pauper*," Massey said, "is charged with murder. Now I ask you if this man Windol Whitt has killed anyone. If he were interested in killing the Harris children and if he had a gun at the back door, as the state charges, could he not with little difficulty have perpetrated that crime? If he had murder in mind, couldn't he have shot Verlene Harris into a dozen pieces when she came to the back door? And yet the state says he unlawfully, maliciously, and with malice aforethought killed Ruby Nell Harris. Why, he didn't even see Ruby Nell Harris that night, and I doubt if he ever saw her in his life."[25]

He reviewed Whitt's honorable military career, picturing him as a man who did his duty to defend his country at war. "He's not the type who would go around with a man like Leon Turner."[26]

From quoting the Golden Rule to asking the jury to suppose Windol "as your son," Mayor Massey pleaded with the jury to find his client innocent. His emotional pitch was reminiscent of his finest campaign speeches.

Jury deliberations began at 2:38 p.m. One hour and twenty-seven minutes later, the jury signaled they had reached a decision.[27] Before sending for them, however, Judge Coleman issued a warning to the gallery. He would not tolerate any form of demonstration; there would be "no cheers, no jeers."[28] To demonstrate that he would accept nothing less than full compliance, Coleman posted lawmen at the corners of the room to arrest anyone causing a disturbance.

Twelve serious men then entered the courtroom in single file and sat in the jury seats they had occupied for two days.

"Gentlemen of the jury, have you reached a verdict?" questioned Judge Coleman.

Jury foreman Neal C. Duncan, a Kosciusko hardware store clerk, stood and answered, "We have, Your Honor."

The judge ordered Alton Massey and his client to rise. Windol Whitt stopped chewing gum and stood open-mouthed.[29]

"We the jury find the defendant guilty as charged in the indictment but disagree as to the punishment and ask the mercy of the court."[30]

Judge Coleman immediately called Windol and his lawyer to the bench. Windol's always stooped shoulders slumped even more as he stood before the judge to receive sentence.

"Have you anything to say why the sentence of the law should not be pronounced?" asked J. P. Coleman.

In a weak voice, Whitt said, "Well, the jury reached the verdict, but I'm not guilty."

"Then I remand you to custody of the sheriff to be transported to the state penitentiary, there to spend the balance of your natural life at hard labor. That is the sentence of the court."[31]

Windol turned to his attorney and said something. Then Sheriff Braswell came to his side and escorted him out of the courtroom.[32]

As the court chamber emptied, Braswell allowed Windol to say goodbye to his family in the witness room. The sheriff knew this would probably not be a permanent parting, for the twenty-five-year-old would be eligible for parole in ten years under Mississippi law.

The last moments that Windol shared with his loved ones were not particularly private, for Sheriff Braswell permitted reporters and photographers to witness the farewell. Helen Whitt quietly sat on a bench next to her husband, joggling three-year-old Mary Louise on her knee. Beside her mother, Mary Elizabeth, age two, sucked on a comb. Nearby, Birdie Bell Baldridge looked on quietly.

Windol, meanwhile, was occupied with an interview.

"Did you get a fair trial?" a reporter asked.

"No sir. I didn't get no fair trial," Windol complained. "Anyone who heard it could say that. I don't think it's justice, but I don't know too much about the law."[33]

Helen was physically beside her husband, but she may as well have been alone. Other than a few perfunctory words about the children, the two did not speak. Even when a photographer asked Windol to turn and talk to his wife, the convicted murderer dourly responded, "I ain't much in a talking mood."[34]

And with that sad ending, Windol Whitt left for prison.

Windol Whitt (right) confers with Alton Massey.

Chapter 19

Mississippi on Trial

One newspaper called the upcoming trial of Leon Turner the "second act of Attala County's three-act court room 'Revenge Massacre' drama."[1] The first act, having demonstrated that Mississippi could fairly conduct a racially charged trial, had concluded with generally favorable national reviews. The verdict and the sentence had been satisfactory to all but the unsatisfiable. Justice had been served.

The second act, however, would be examined far more critically, for it would lay bare the beating heart of Mississippi. Leon Turner would not be the only soul under judgment in that Attala County courtroom—Mississippi herself would be in the defendant's seat.

Jury selection began at nine o'clock the morning of Monday, March 20, 1950.[2] Whereas last week's voir dire used an unusually large panel of 100 white male Attala County citizens, the Turner empanelling required 150.[3] Commendably, every man who received the jury summons showed up.

Jury selection was long and tedious. By 1:30 p.m., the original group had been whittled down to fifty men. Questioning continued nonstop as snacks of Bit-O-Honey and Hershey's Almond candy bars were passed among the remaining panel in lieu of lunch.

By 4:00 p.m., a dozen jurors had been selected to hear the case—twelve men who would shoulder the state's reputation. Eight were farmers: Archie Burchfield, Charles E. Burns, and G. T. Summerhill of Ethel; Z. D. Bingham and

O. O. Montague of West; J. O. Gibson and Arlis Steen of Vaiden; and J. E. Hubbert of French Camp. Two were merchants: A. R. Bowie and W. F. Kimbrough of McCool. Rounding out the dozen were service station operator Clyde R. Doty of Ethel, and the only Kosciusko resident, machine shop owner Irving Pylate.[4]

Judge Coleman declared a thirty-minute break, and the side doors were opened. It quickly became apparent that this crowd would exceed that for the Whitt trial. The bench seats filled within minutes. People began standing along the walls and up the two stairwells.[5] Nearly twenty visitors sat inside the bar.

Clustered at the front left of the courtroom, a large collection of Leon's relatives talked quietly among themselves. One young mother nursed her infant.[6] Howard Turner was there; but Leon's grandmother and siblings were absent.

With an audience estimated at eight hundred, the bailiff closed the courtroom doors. Hundreds more would-be spectators filled the courthouse hallways and spilled out onto the lawn.[7]

Another packed area was the press box. Without question, the captioned pictures accompanying the Windol Whitt trial stories were a rousing success. Judge Coleman's gutsy decision to allow courtroom photography had proven wise. Several more journalists were now here for the Turner trial, in addition to the ten "charter members."[8] Despite their cramped conditions, some media representatives were disappointed that it wasn't more so, for a rumor had surfaced that a representative from the *Daily Worker*, a Communist-leaning publication, would attend.[9] Reporters covering the trial had looked forward to discussing freedom of the press ideology with their Bolshevik comrade. Sadly for them, he failed to show.

By four thirty, hundreds of chattering voices combined to make one incomprehensible buzz inside the Attala County Circuit Court chamber. Dozens of hats hung from nails regularly spaced along the front wall. Cigarette smoke colored the room with a thick, murky haze that glowed around the fluorescent ceiling lights.

The volume level dropped noticeably when the door at the front right of the room opened. Into the charged atmosphere advanced the jury. Surprised voices and pointing fingers abounded as people in the gallery recognized friends and family among the panel.

Moments later, the room fell completely silent as the defendant was led into the courtroom by Sheriff Roy Braswell and Constable Hugh Bailey. Leon Turner was barely recognizable. Usually unshaven and shaggy-haired, wearing ragged, filthy clothes, the man who entered the room resembled a clothing model in a Sears Roebuck catalog: cleanly shaven face, neatly trimmed hair, and fashionable new outfit. Leon's tan vested suit—bought by relatives and probably the first one he had ever owned—was a little oversized, but natty just the same. He sported new brown shoes, a lavender-blue shirt, and a bright blue tie. One reporter who spotted him wrote, "Tall and hefty, he bears a close resemblance to movie star Dick Foran."[10] Another said he "looks a bit like Nelson Eddy."[11]

Leon smiled broadly at the audience while Braswell removed his handcuffs. It was his first time around a large group of nonconvicts since January, and he relished the attention. He whistled when he saw his father. Howard Turner, too, was spruced up in a buttoned double-breasted navy sport coat over an open-necked shirt. For the first time in recent memory, he was clean-cut and freshly barbered.

Judge Coleman emerged through the door behind his desk and assumed the bench. Forgoing the overly warm black robe, he wore a well-fitting suit. Getting straight to business, he removed an unlit cigar from his mouth and stated the rules of his court. There was a slight modification from last week: because of the crowd size, visitors could remain within the bar. It so happened that sitting in this area was his distinguished predecessor, Judge John F. Allen of Newport, also mouthing a cigar.

Finished with the preliminaries, Coleman visually scanned the room. He ended his sweep by staring at the district attorney and stating, "The State may begin."

Henry Lee Rodgers stood and announced, "The State of Mississippi calls Mary Ella Harris." From the witness room stepped Mary Ella dressed in a red coat and green scarf, clutching a black pocketbook.[12] She walked slowly to the witness chair, her pace deliberate and steady, even as she passed directly in front of the man who had murdered her children. Leon sat with crossed legs, one arm draped over the balustrade, eyes fixed straight ahead. Likewise, Mary Ella did not glance at him.

Once she had settled into the elevated witness chair, Rodgers asked her to describe the events of that night. Mary Ella sighed deeply and launched into her painful story for the second time in a week.

"After I was in the bed, I heard footsteps," she spoke mechanically, almost in a monotone. "They walked up to the door and someone knocked on my bedroom door. Then I heard some mumbling outside and someone knocked out the window by the side of my bed."

"Then what?" Rodgers prompted.

"I jumped out of the bed and picked James Edward up and Ruby Nell and went to the kitchen; I went on through the kitchen and into the other back room, where the door was half open. I heard someone say from outside, 'Don't come out that door or you'll get shot.' So I ran back to the other front room, where my husband had been sleeping."

"Did you still have Ruby Nell and James Edward?"

"I had James Edward in my arms and Ruby Nell by the hand."

"What did you see?"

"I saw Mr. Leon Turner."

"What was he doing?"

"He scared me so bad I couldn't just tell. When I got there and he was there, I broke out the door."

"Where was Ruby Nell?"

Having been through this sad memory only days ago, the answer was easier this time. "I turned her loose in the room."

Mary Ella described running with her baby son out into the yard, being stopped and ordered back to the house by "someone with a gun," and seeing Frankie shot.

Rodgers looked at Leon Turner and shook his head. Then he asked Mary Ella a last question: "When you left your little girl, was she in good health? Tell the jury."

With a life-changed sadness in her eyes, she looked toward the jury box. "Yes, sir, she was in the best of health."[13]

As the prosecutor finished and strode to his seat, defense attorney Claude Woodward stood. Woodward was a young lion eager to take on the biggest battle of his brief legal career. Though he had begun law school in 1941, he paused his education because of Pearl Harbor and enlisted in the U.S.

Navy.[14] He completed law school after the war and moved back to his hometown of Kosciusko, where he had acquired two whole years of experience before being appointed to defend Leon Turner.[15]

Woodward had consulted with his client several times in the previous two months. Leon had not talked effusively about the case, but he had been friendly and nonthreatening, answering every question his attorney asked. Claude sincerely believed that his client had not killed the children intentionally, nor had his actions been racially motivated. He felt the murders had been committed solely in an uncontrollable fit of drunken rage.[16]

His strategy was to dig meticulously into each witness's testimony and find inconsistencies; to plant a shadow of doubt in jurors' minds; and mainly, to avoid the death penalty. He would consider it a victory if Leon only received a life sentence.[17]

Claude began questioning Mary Ella and quickly showed that he was not going to be gentle. She was a threat to the life of his client rather than the grieving mother of murdered children. He interrogated Mary Ella at great length, peppering her with questions about every detail of her actions that night: "How many steps did you take then?" "How far was the man from you?" "Were you directly south from the front step or at an angle?" "Was there a fire in the fireplace?"[18]

Spectators coughed and grew restless as Woodward relentlessly examined even the most trivial element of Mary Ella's testimony. At one point, Judge Coleman commented, "The district attorney is not objecting, but I think when you've covered it sufficiently we ought to travel on."[19]

Despite his exhaustive probing, Woodward found no meaningful contradictions in Mary Ella's story. When his first cross-examination of the trial was complete, Woodward had used major time to make minor headway.

Thomas Harris was summoned next to the stand. Wheeled in on an ambulance stretcher by Dr. Frank Lacey, his appearance drew stares of shock from those who had seen him during Windol Whitt's trial. He looked significantly worse. Hollow, bloodshot eyes, gaunt face, and gray-tinted skin practically shouted "Death!" Despite his severe condition, Thomas nodded and spoke to Leon as he was rolled past.[20] His gurney was stopped directly in front of the jury.

District Attorney Rodgers stood at Thomas's head, facing the gallery, and slowly led his ailing witness through the events of that murderous night. In a voice barely above a whisper, Thomas told of running through the house and trying to escape out the back, but someone holding a gun blocked the exit. Thomas was hard to hear; no one in the courtroom made a sound lest a key description be missed.

Rodgers asked Thomas to describe how he was shot.

"Mr. Leon Turner throwed his pistol on me and marched me back into the kitchen and had the pistol on me, and I went on. And when I got to the dining room door, he shot me and I fell, and that's all."

"You were shot and fell. Did you hear anything else?"

"No sooner than he shot me, he turned and walked back in the house and went to shooting, and I heard the children hollering."

"Can you tell me how many times he shot in the house?"

"No sir, but he shot a good many times. Sure did. I heard loud shooting out there on the porch."

"You were at that time in the dining room?"

"Yes sir, laying there. I laid there until daylight."

"Could you get up to see about the children?

"No sir, I couldn't get up. My little girl called me to give her some water, but I couldn't get up to give her some water."[21]

Rodgers held out Leon's .38 automatic and asked if Thomas recognized it. "That favors the one that Mr. Leon had," Harris slurred breathlessly.[22] His eyes fluttered; he was near fainting.

It was 6:00 p.m. Deciding that Thomas Harris needed a break to regain his strength, Judge Coleman declared a recess until 7:45 p.m.[23]

During the break, Billy McMillan led many of the visiting press reporters and photographers to the Star-Herald Building to type their stories, telephone their home offices, and take a breather. McMillan's wife brought in fried ham sandwiches, dill pickles, and two pitchers of sweetened iced tea.

As the grateful visitors wolfed down supper, they spoke of their convenient front-row location in the courtroom. Photographers marveled at the dramatic profile shots they were getting of the defendant and witnesses. Reporters similarly enjoyed being close to the action, but they also mentioned a negative. With her back to them, Mary Ella Harris had been difficult to hear. In fact, the only witness of the two trials whose face could be fully seen and whose voice could be plainly heard—despite his whispering—was Thomas Harris. One scribe joked that all future witnesses should be required to lie on a cot while testifying.[24]

Even with the relatively late hour, the courtroom was full at the announced time to restart the proceedings. Surprisingly, the always punctual judge failed to appear. The minutes ticked by as several in the audience checked their watches. Finally, ten minutes late, J. P. Coleman emerged from his chambers and announced that Thomas Harris had suffered a nervous rigor and developed high fever. "We are recessed until such time as the witness can return to the stand for cross-examination."[25]

Court was declared back in session after forty-five minutes. Thomas was again positioned in front of the jury, and Judge Coleman directed the defense to begin cross-examination.

As Claude Woodward had given no quarter when questioning Mary Ella Harris, he likewise showed no mercy to her husband. He aggressively grilled Thomas on all aspects of the case. Harris gestured weakly as he struggled to answer the bombardment of questions. His arms, which had once carried the thick muscles of a hardworking farmer, now revealed the frailty of a long-term patient.

Woodward probed the social and business relationships between Thomas and the defendant. Harris admitted that he had gotten drunk with Leon and had even sold some of his homemade whiskey. What's more, Thomas had played crap games with Turner and had borrowed money from him.[26]

Then Woodward attacked the perception that Thomas was totally defenseless on the night of the murders. "Tom, wasn't there any object lying beside the back door when you tried to get out?"

Thomas hesitated. Closing his sunken eyes, he remembered. "Yes sir, there was a shotgun there."

"Was the shotgun loaded?" Woodward continued.

"Yes sir."

"Was it fired?"

"To be honest with you, I don't know nothing about it."[27]

Woodward stayed on the offensive, exploring the possibility that someone besides Leon had actually shot Thomas. "Were you looking over your shoulder when you were shot?" he questioned.

"No sir," Thomas admitted.

"You did not see him?"

"No sir."[28]

Thomas's head and neck were soaked in sweat. He had been answering questions nonstop for an hour. When Woodward paused around 9:30 p.m. to thumb through his notes, Harris lost consciousness. Coleman recessed the proceedings while Thomas was wheeled into an adjoining room for treatment.

During the delay, Claude Woodward motioned for a mistrial based on the inability of Thomas Harris to testify. Judge Coleman shook his head and icily overruled the motion.[29] Seldom one to comment during a trial on an attorney's conduct, he now spoke on the record about Woodward's grueling technique: "Never in my entire career have I seen such a tedious and rigid cross-examination. It would be bad enough on a well person, much less this sick Negro."[30]

After fifteen long minutes, the witness room door opened and Thomas Harris again came rolling in. Dr. Lacey informed the judge that Thomas had revived enough to continue, but he could probably only go another fifteen minutes or so under light questioning.

Ignoring the doctor's last comment, Leon's attorney accused Thomas of scuffling with Leon and trying to grab his gun. Harris denied it, but Woodward kept hammering away at the charge. Only when Thomas began to physically wither did Woodward stop.

Court was adjourned for the evening at 10:05 p.m.[31]

The steep, railed stairs at the right of the courtroom led upward to the courthouse attic. Owning the dry, musty smell of decades under the Southern sun, the attic was a mishmash of disintegrating boxes, forgotten ledgers, and unused courthouse equipment scattered about a jungle of countless bare wooden beams at different angles.

The only room in the attic took up a quarter of its space. Located at the top of the courtroom stairs, the sleeping quarters for sequestered jurors was furnished with twelve cots, three four-drawer wooden dressers, and two small tables holding dusty lamps with cheap lampshades.

The twelve men of the Leon Turner jury had been as surprised as the Windol Whitt trial jurors when a bailiff escorted them up the stairs and explained they would spend the night in this jury dormitory. They had not left home that morning prepared for an overnight stay.[32] But despite the Spartan conditions of the room and the inability to clean up or brush their teeth, the jurors did not grumble. They were exhausted.

Before long, a chorus of snoring filled the pitch-dark room as a lawman stood watch at the bottom of the stair.[33]

Well before proceedings began the next morning, the courtroom was packed—even more so than on the opening day of the trial. Many teenagers were present, obviously playing hooky from school. Kosciusko High School band director W. G. Skipworth showed up and announced, "All Kosciusko students rise and follow me." A small contingent of disappointed young people walked out as Skipworth gave them the eye.[34]

Similarly, Ethyl High School principal Clay Stone spotted some of his students. "What you boys doing?" he asked.

One youth said, "Well, we wanted to see it, thought it would be a good education." The principal merely smiled and shooed the kids back to school.[35]

It was amazing that so many people returned, considering their inability to hear well the previous day's proceedings. Spectators had generally heard the lawyers' questions, but understanding answers from the forward-facing witnesses had been difficult. As one observer noted, "It was, in a way, like following a telephone conversation by hearing one end of the discussion only."[36]

When court resumed at 9:00 a.m., jurors were in their same clothes.[37] Leon Turner again wore his one suit, but with a different tie.

Verlene Thurman, the first witness of the day, told of seeing a white man with a gun in her house. Asked by Henry Rodgers to identify the man, Verlene pointed to Leon Turner. He was the one, she said, who had been in her and Ruby Nell's bedroom.[38] Leon bowed his head as Verlene detailed how he stood on the porch and shot her.

Verlene remained cool and calm while recounting her experiences. Only when she described going back into the house after being shot did emotions surface.

"When Mr. Leon shot me, he stood up on the porch and says, 'I'll kill every one of you,' and the little Whitt boy called him and told him 'Let's go,' and they left, and after they left I went in the house and went into the room where the window was broken."

"Who did you see in that room when you went in there?" the DA asked.

"I saw Ruby Nell," Verlene responded.

"Where was Ruby Nell Harris?"

"She was in the bed."

"What was wrong with her?"

"She was shot." Tears filled Verlene's eyes.

"Now where was Mary C. Burnside?"

"She was on the bed where me and her slept."

"Anything wrong with her?"

"Yes, sir, she was shot. She was dead then."

"Now where was Frankie C. Thurman?"

"He was laying over against the wall."

"What was wrong with him?"

"He was shot," Verlene said weakly. "He was dead." A teardrop slid down her cheek.

Henry Rodgers handed her a handkerchief from his suit pocket and asked, "Did your little sister, Ruby Nell Harris, say anything to you?"

"She just told me that the man hit her in the stomach."[39]

A rumble spread through the audience. Judge Coleman rapped a gavel on his desk.

On cross-examination, Claude Woodward picked apart each word of Verlene's testimony. He had the girl go over every step, every position, every distance mentioned in her statement. Once everything had been covered, he repeated the process, making Verlene again tell her complete account of the night while Woodward dissected it. The procedure was tiresome and slow, but the prosecutor and the judge patiently endured the questioning.

Patience, though, has a limit. Henry Lee Rodgers's was reached when Verlene finished her second run-through and Woodward said, "All right, let's go over the whole thing again."[40]

Not attempting to hide his exasperation, Rodgers proclaimed, "I object!"

Woodward responded, "Your Honor, we intend to show the witness has memorized her story and can repeat it indefinitely."[41]

"You've had her cover her story twice," Judge Coleman pointed out. "If I allow you to go on a third time, by the same rule you could go over a fourth, fifth, and sixth time, and on indefinitely. Objection sustained."[42]

The prosecution next called Sheriff Braswell to the stand. Roy told of finding empty bullet shells in and around the Harris home.[43] Rodgers retrieved a small box from his tabletop and pulled out two brass objects found at the home. Braswell identified them as .38 caliber automatic cartridge shells.

Finding little to contest in his good friend's testimony, Woodward kept his cross-examination brief. To the relief of everyone in the chamber, he did not subject the sheriff to the same needling he gave the others.

Despite sluggish periods, the morning session proceeded briskly. Judge Coleman kept the trial moving along without a break through several more witnesses. Roosevelt Whitcomb revealed that he had overheard Leon tell Howard Turner that he "had did murder down on judge's place." Dr. Frank Lacey described Thomas's paralyzing wound. Pat Smithson testified that Ruby Nell had been "shot in the belly" and was still alive when he got to the Harris house around 2 a.m. Caesar Young also told his story.[44]

Claude Woodward pushed the judge's tolerance all morning. Having questioned events in excruciating detail during his own cross-examinations, he also began raising frequent objections during the DA's presentation. Some challenges were legitimate; but others were frivolous, such as when he objected to law officers sitting too close to the witness stand while Sheriff Braswell was testifying; or when he complained about the prosecutor "going over the same thing over and over" when Rodgers asked a witness once to repeat a statement louder.[45]

The State of Mississippi rested its case against Leon Turner at 11:20 a.m. Well on track for the day, Judge Coleman ordered a lunch recess.

A lively crowd stuffed the courtroom after the break. Based on a rumor that the defendant might testify on his own behalf, even more onlookers than in the morning showed up for the afternoon session. Since the audience had thus far been very well behaved, Judge Coleman permitted the extra viewers.[46]

The press had also conducted themselves well, demonstrating during both trials that they could operate with dignity and minimal disruptions. To show appreciation to the media and to allow more interesting shots of trial participants, including himself, Coleman passed word that the photographers could discretely move about the courtroom.

At 1:00 p.m., Judge Coleman gaveled court back into session. Claude Woodward slicked back the shortly trimmed hair on his retreating hairline, stood, and spoke in a confident voice: "Your Honor, the defense calls Leon Turner to the stand."

Over 1,600 eyes watched the tall defendant step to the witness stand. Leon sat in the witness chair and rocked it back and forth. Each rock was accompanied by a loud squeak.[47]

Instead of walking his client through a meticulous set of questions, Claude Woodward merely asked Turner to tell the jury what happened that night.

Leon crossed his legs. "We went to Thomas Harris's house that night to sell whiskey to him," he explained.

> When we got near the house, I told the Whitts to wait, that I'd go up to the house since they didn't know Tom.
>
> I knocked on the door. Someone turned the light on inside and I pushed the door open. Tom was standing across the room in the door to the back room.
>
> I started to tell him we had brought some whiskey for him. But he came at me and went for my gun. We tussled for it and then the gun fired. It fired real fast.

"Would it automatically cock itself?" Woodward asked. "Yes."

"Were you looking where it was going?"

"No," Leon shook his head. He stopped rocking and gazed over his left shoulder at his father. Then he looked again at Claude Woodward. The squeaking resumed.

"I saw Tom fall," Leon continued. "I asked him if he was hit. He said 'Yes' and I turned and ran out of the house."[48]

Leon then testified how he and the Whitt brothers fled to the Delta but later turned back to Newport. The first he knew that any children had been killed was when his grandmother told him after his return.[49]

Switching the line of questioning, Woodward asked why Leon and the Whitts needed guns while hiding out after the jailbreak. Leon replied they used the weapons to shoot "squirrels and rabbits and things like that."[50]

Leon finished soon after. All told, he spent less than ten minutes giving his version of the story.[51]

Henry Lee Rodgers was already speaking as he rose. Expressing amazement at Leon's shooting skills, he remarked that everyone knew Leon was good, but it took an exceptional marksman to hunt rabbits with a pistol.

"And you were going to Harris's house to sell whiskey?" Rodgers asked. "Why didn't you go in the daylight?"

"We were afraid we'd get caught," Leon replied.

"Who suggested going to Harris's house?"

"I knew Harris wanted three gallons of whiskey, so I told the boys we could get him to sell it for us."

"Well, if you went there to sell some whiskey, why didn't you take any whiskey with you?"

"We left it within hollering distance in a ditch up the road. We didn't want to take chances. A fellow never knows who might be in the house."[52]

Rodgers pressed harder, addressing Leon's prior statement that his .38 had gone off as he wrestled with Thomas Harris. "Where was the gun?" asked the district attorney.

Leon touched his waist, "On the right side of my belt."

"Didn't you pull that gun on him?"

"No, he tried to take it away from me."

"What happened when you got to tussling?"

"I pulled the gun out of the holster; and while we were scuffling, I pulled the trigger.

"You have to cock that automatic, don't you? You can't fire it just by pulling the trigger. I mean you can't fire it accidentally. The first time, you have to cock it?"

"Yes sir."

Men in the press box noticed Leon's right hand shaking.[53] Rodgers saw it too.

"Did you cock it?"

"I cocked it and shot trying to get loose. I shot it down by him trying to get loose."

"Well, why did you cock it?"

"I was scared."

The DA glanced toward the jury and raised his eyebrows. Leon looked to be half again the weight of Thomas Harris.

"Oh, so you went down to Thomas Harris's house that night to sell him whiskey and you were scared of him."

"Yes."

Rodgers turned away from the witness. Over his shoulder he queried, "Was he backing up to you?"

"What?" Leon asked.

"You shot him in the back."

"The last time the gun fired, he fell," Leon replied quickly.

Rodgers faced Leon and stepped closer. "Did you see Ruby Nell?"

"No."

"Did you see Mary C. Burnside?"

"No."

"Did you see Frankie C. Thurman?"

"No."

"You say you didn't see any of them—yet you hit every one of them when you started shooting."[54]

Leon Turner did not respond. He merely looked to the left and rocked his chair back and forth. The squeaks only magnified his silence.

Rodgers was done.

And so was the defense. After his only witness had been on the stand forty minutes, Claude Woodward rested his case.

The two lawyers now began their final arguments. District Attorney Rodgers addressed the jury first.

"This is one of the foulest murders your county has ever known," he declared.[55] Emphasizing the brutality of the shootings, he insisted that Leon Turner had killed intentionally.

"He didn't miss the boy. He didn't miss the two little girls. He didn't miss Thomas Harris and he didn't miss Verlene Thurman. Leon said the shooting was accidental. If that's accidental shooting, it's the best accidental shooting I've ever seen in my life. He killed a human being with every shot."[56]

Positioning the empty pistol cartridges on a table to illustrate placement of the victims, Rodgers explained how this "mad dog" had purposefully fired on each one. "Every pop he made, he hit a human being."

Warming to his summation, Rodgers faced the jurors. "Was Leon Turner hunting squirrels or killing rabbits that night? No. He was killing babies."[57]

Rodgers concluded his fiery monologue by telling the jury that the evidence was plain; they had no choice other than to find Leon Turner guilty of murder. And with a guilty verdict, "the State of Mississippi insists on the death penalty."[58]

At these dramatic words, several jurors looked at the defendant. His face was ashen.[59]

Upon opening his final argument, Claude Woodward surprised the jury by admitting that he wasn't concerned about their guilty verdict. His intent was to show that the evidence presented in the trial had been insufficient to impose the death penalty.[60]

Reviewing the testimony of each witness, he emphasized that no one had actually observed Leon Turner shoot the children. Even Thomas Harris had not seen the person who shot him. Verlene was the only witness to positively identify Leon firing a pistol, but he had only wounded, not killed, her; and he certainly had the opportunity to finish her off. Leon had not intended to kill anyone, Woodward preached. The children's deaths had been a tragic accident resulting from the accidental discharge of a pistol during the struggle to protect himself from Thomas Harris.

The killings were not the one-sided slaughter that everyone had heard, Woodward claimed. Leon Turner was not the monster that newspapers had described. "You have found," he said, "that the case the Yankees were so interested in wasn't the same case heard in this courtroom."[61]

In closing, the defense counsel urged the jury to spare the life of Leon Turner. Woodward pleaded that Leon had spoken truthfully when he said he didn't knowingly shoot Ruby Nell Harris. "Give the defendant the benefit of the doubt."[62]

The case entered the hands of the jury at 5:25 p.m.

Before the trial started, jurors had elected Z. D. Bingham as foreman. A no-nonsense farmer, Bingham wanted to get this civic duty over with and get back to his fields. The twelve men had barely settled around the well-used rectangular table in the jury room when he called for a vote. To no one's surprise and everyone's relief, each man raised his hand when Bingham asked for those who believed Turner was guilty of murdering the little girl.

Now came the determination of punishment. Like the choices in the Whitt trial, the jury could impose a sentence of either life in prison or death. The death decision had to be unanimous, or else a life sentence was automatic.

Jurors calmly discussed the case, and misconceptions and disagreements over aspects of the testimony surfaced. It seemed that neither choice of punishment would obtain unanimity. A quick count was taken: nine men were for death, three for life.

Again the jurors dove into details of the evidence and the witnesses' stories. Half an hour later, Foreman Bingham conducted another poll. J. E. Hubbert's vote swung to the side favoring the death penalty, but J. O. Gibson and O. O. Montague did not switch. They voted life in prison for Leon Turner.

Ten to two.

Arguing began. The main holdout, O. O. Montague, an over-fifty, black-haired farmer, insisted that the State had failed to show that anyone actually saw Turner shoot the little girl. Clyde Doty of Ethyl tried hard to convince him that the shooter couldn't have been anyone but Leon. Doty's nephew, Charles Burns, at twenty-four the youngest man on the jury, also attempted to reason with Montague; but the mulish farmer wouldn't budge.[63] J. O. Gibson merely said that he agreed with Montague, but otherwise did not participate in the debate.

An hour and a half after deliberations began, Judge Coleman allowed the jury to briefly break for supper at Vicker's Café, an eatery on the town square.[64] But full stomachs did nothing to sway opinions, as another 10–2 vote taken shortly after 8:00 p.m. revealed.

The jurors were tired. No one wanted to spend another night in the attic dorm. Discussions grew louder and faces grew redder, but Montague stubbornly refused to consider alternatives to his thinking.

Clyde Doty later described the jury room atmosphere: "We lectured him. We told him the whole United States was watching this trial to see how the State of Mississippi would show up. . . . There was pretty rough talk inside that room."[65] But Montague "insisted that his mind was made up and it would stay made up if we deliberated in there a month."[66] Gibson seemed about to change his mind at times; but when it mattered, he remained on Montague's side.[67]

Some in the majority suspected the two holdouts could not emotionally understand what it would be like to have a child murdered. Gibson was in his forties and single; Montague was married but had no children.[68]

Any racial considerations in the minds of the holdout jurors were not revealed. Montague never brought up that a white man should not die for killing a Negro. He maintained that his position was based solely on the fact that no one actually saw Turner shoot Ruby Nell.[69] Because of that uncertainty, he could not send Leon Turner to the electric chair.

While the jury deliberated, Leon Turner remained seated in the courtroom, smoking, seemingly calm and relaxed. He smiled while listening to the jokes and conversation of Roy Braswell and others nearby. Ever the publicity hound, he readily posed for photographs with his father and other relatives.[70]

As the grays of twilight faded and the sky turned black, Circuit Clerk C. H. McWhorter began paying witnesses a small fee for their time.[71] Some spectators went home, but most remained.

At 8:25 p.m., a knock from inside the jurors' chamber caused the crowd to scurry back to their seats. It turned out to be a false alarm; the jury was simply complaining about a distracting conversation in an adjoining room. Judge Coleman personally visited the room, kicked out the offenders, and urged the jurors to proceed.[72]

Inside the jury room, it was becoming plain that the death-sentence proponents were not going to win over jurors Montague and Gibson. Though both had sworn during voir dire that they were not opposed to capital punishment, they now flatly refused to impose that sentence.

A final tally was taken. The vote remained ten for death, two for life in prison.

Another rap on the door from within the jury room brought the milling spectators scrambling back into the courtroom. This time it was real; a decision had been reached. The time was 9:18 p.m., nearly four hours since the jury was handed the case.

Five minutes later, twelve worn-out and somber men entered the courtroom and sat in the jury box. Coleman asked Leon Turner to rise. Leon stood rubbing nicotine-stained fingers nervously across his forehead. Two deputies moved to his side.[73]

"Gentlemen of the jury, have you reached a verdict?" asked Judge J. P. Coleman.

Z. D. Bingham rose to his feet and replied, "We have, Your Honor."

"What is your verdict?"

As one, the crowd held its breath. Not a single noise was made as Bingham announced the long-awaited words.

"We the jury find the defendant guilty as charged. . . ." The foreman paused briefly, "but disagree as to punishment."[74]

Leon Turner looked at the floor and took a drag off his cigarette. He showed no reaction.[75] Judge Coleman asked him if he had anything to say before a sentence was imposed. With his left hand buried deep in his trousers pocket, Turner flipped ashes from his cigarette with his right and shook his head. Seeing the negative response, Coleman announced that Leon was to be transported to the state penitentiary to "spend the balance of your natural life at hard labor."[76]

No shouts of either joy or protest arose from the gallery. The crowd remained orderly and quiet. As *Life* magazine put it, "There was no racial rabble rousing . . . although it was black vs. white in the heart of Mississippi."[77]

District Attorney Rodgers was deeply disappointed with the verdict. He knew that the life sentence meant Turner could be eligible for release on parole in ten years—an event, should it occur, that would cause incalculable damage to Mississippi's reputation. Rodgers approached the bench and spoke quietly with Judge Coleman and Claude Woodward. Afterward, Coleman announced that court would resume in the morning at 9:00 a.m. A decision on whether or not Leon Turner would face trial on the two other murder indictments would be made at that time.

After Judge Coleman adjourned the proceedings, reporters approached Leon as he was being shackled. The mood of the now convicted murderer was understandably low. "I ain't talking. I got nothing to say," he growled. But the press persisted. When photographers surrounded him with cameras at the ready, Leon asked them to wait while he put his hat on. As the shutters began clicking, he answered a few questions.

What did he think about the indictments against him for the other children's murders?

"I don't know nothing about them there other indictments."[78]

Did he feel his lawyer did a good job?

"I want to thank Woodward for what he done."[79]

Standing nearby, Claude Woodward was satisfied. He had avoided the death penalty for his client.[80] "You know how I feel," he said as a photographer snapped a picture of him and Leon Turner shaking hands and grinning.[81]

The next morning, Turner and Woodward returned to a half-full courtroom gallery.[82] The crowd wasn't sure what to expect. The tough Newport native had a reputation of never backing down from a fight, but going through yet another child murder trial was a battle that he would surely lose. And the loss may cost his life if the DA finally got his wish.

The spectators did not have to wait long for the answer. Once court convened, Claude Woodward declared that his client had decided to plead guilty to the murders of both Frankie Thurman and Mary Burnside.

This was unacceptable to District Attorney Rodgers, who immediately petitioned that the plea be rejected and a new trial be held. "The state feels it must ask for the death penalty," he appealed, "because a generation is on trial here in addition to the fact that this man committed cold-blooded murder."[83]

Judge Coleman faced a difficult decision. Taking the lives of three of society's most innocent members had been a heinous act, one that called for the ultimate punishment. Turner surely deserved death, and the clamor from the nation was to give him what he deserved. But this court's jurisdiction was not national; it represented the people of Mississippi and reflected their views.

"The court thinks the State of Mississippi did its dead-level best in the trial this week," the judge responded. "The court fails to see where the State could improve on what it has already done."[84]

Emphasizing that the punishment for murder was up to a jury and not the court, Coleman explained that the Turner trial jury had been "legally empanelled from a special venire of 150 men and accepted by both sides. This jury was not willing, for reasons satisfactory to it, and whether I agree or not, to inflict the death penalty."[85]

Calming any fear of Turner being paroled in ten years, Coleman revealed, "It is the law of Mississippi that a man convicted three times of a felony is ineligible of parole."

And so, he ended the affair. "It is my duty as judge of this court to close the matter by accepting the defendant's pleas of guilty on the other two indictments and removing him from society for the rest of his life without hope of parole."[86]

Mary Ella Harris was present for this final judgment along with Verlene, her only living daughter.[87] As was her way, Mary Ella remained quiet and showed no emotion when her tormentor was put away for life. She saw Leon Turner for the last time when Sheriff Roy Braswell escorted him out of the courtroom. Leon caught her eye, and they looked at each other for a moment. Then he was gone.

Crowd outside the Attala County
courthouse during a break in the trial.

Leon (left) and Howard Turner cleaned up for the trial.

The courtroom. The jury (back left) listens to Caesar Young testifying. Leon Turner (right of Caesar in light suit). Billy McMillan in press box has his arm resting on railing next to Leon.

Leon Turner (foreground) listens as
Mary Ella Harris testifies in front of jury.

Press photographers focus on Leon Turner.

Henry Lee Rodgers (far left) listens to Leon Turner
testimony. Jury in background. Note murder weapon on table.

Thomas Harris, on gurney, being questioned by Claude Woodward
(right of Thomas with parted hair and back to camera).
Henry Lee Rodgers observes from witness chair.
Leon Turner second to right of Rodgers.

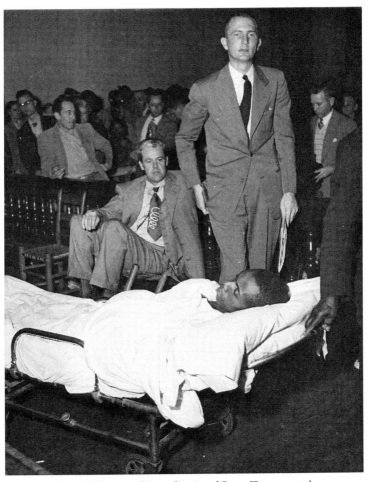

Claude Woodward (standing) and Leon Turner watch
Thomas Harris being wheeled out of the courtroom.

Chapter 20

Aftermath

Although Leon Turner's role in the Attala County "revenge murder" story ended when he walked out of that court-room, Mary Ella Harris had one more act remaining.

With Turner's sentencing concluded, the March 22 Circuit Court session moved to its next order of business: trying the third man charged in the death of Ruby Nell Harris. Malcolm Whitt and his lawyer, David Crawley, stood before Judge Coleman. In a business-like scene vastly more subdued than the recent high drama, Coleman calmly asked for Malcolm's plea to the charge of murdering Ruby Nell.

"Not guilty," came the reply, and with it, the identification that another trial would be necessary.

Two physically and emotionally exhausting trials in as many weeks had pushed the Attala County court system and its judge to their limits. Another week would exceed those limits. Accordingly, Judge Coleman decided to skip a week "in order to give everybody a much-needed rest." The trial of Malcolm Whitt would start Monday, April 3.[1]

Sitting with Verlene in the courtroom, Mary Ella Harris closed her eyes at the announcement. The delay meant one more week waiting for her agonizing odyssey to be over; one more week dreading yet another trial where she would relive that most horrible night of her life.

During the week delay, opinions about the Turner trial results began to surface. As newspapers and radio spread news of the outcome, an outpouring of views erupted. About the guilty verdict, there was approval and satisfaction. About the imposed punishment, there was condemnation and discontent.

"Disappointed" would woefully understate Mississippians' reaction to the life sentence doled out to Leon Turner. "Furious" would be a more appropriate adjective. Citizens blasted the fact that Turner had not received the death penalty, and they placed blame squarely on the two jurors who failed to vote for the electric chair.

With a headline proclaiming "Justice Went Awry," a Jackson newspaper editorial colorfully complained that even though the prosecution of the "big, blustering, cowardly killer was ably handled by the district attorney," the "cowardly slayer of three Negroes . . . escaped the gallows because some chicken-hearted jurors wouldn't vote the death sentence although they had previously raised their hands to God and swore that they were not opposed to the imposition of the death sentence."

"Turner should have been sentenced to death," the piece concluded. "In fact, it is too bad that a criminal of his type can't undergo the death penalty more than once."[2]

Another blistering rebuke came from Mississippi's famous author William Faulkner. A social moderate, Faulkner dearly loved his home state and often defended it publicly, a stance that typically injured the liberal side of his reputation.

Concerned about this latest threat to Mississippi's dubious standing among the national family of states, Faulkner closely followed the trial of Leon Turner. When a mere life sentence was handed down by the jury, he was deeply disappointed. He aired his feelings in a letter to a Memphis newspaper that was published four days after the sentencing.

To The Commercial Appeal,

All native Mississippians will join in commending Attala County. But along with the pride and the hope we had better feel concern and grief and shame too; not grief for the dead children, but concern and grief because what we did was not enough; it was in effect only a little better than nothing, not for justice nor even punishment, just as you don't mete out justice or punishment to the mad dog or the rattlesnake; grief and shame because we have gone on record with the outland people who are so quick to show us our faults and tell us how to remedy them, as having put the price of murdering three children as the same as robbing three banks or stealing three automobiles.

And those of us who were born in Mississippi and have lived all our lives in it, who have continued to live in it forty and fifty and sixty years at some cost and sacrifice simply because we love Mississippi and its ways and customs and soil and people; who because of that love have been ready and willing at all times to defend our ways and habits and customs from attack by the outlanders whom we believed did not understand them, we had better be afraid too,—afraid that we have been wrong; that what we had loved and defended not only didn't want the defense and the love, but was not worthy of the one and indefensible to the other.

Which fear, at least, it is to be hoped that the two members of the jury who saved the murderer, will not share.

It is to be hoped that whatever reasons they may have had for saving him, will be enough so that they can sleep at night free of nightmares about the ten or fifteen or so years from now when the murderer will be paroled or pardoned or freed again, and will of course murder another child, who it is to be hoped— and with grief and despair one says it—will this time at least be of his own color.

WILLIAM FAULKNER
Oxford, Miss.[3]

As is often the case when those of notoriety jump into the fray of a social cause, Faulkner's letter became the focus of much criticism and debate.[4] Intentionally or not, the author thus deflected some of the controversy away from his beloved state and toward himself.[5]

Reactions to the Mississippi verdict by major national publications—written by those labeled by Faulkner as "outlanders"—were actually rather neutral. The April 3, 1950, issue of *Life* magazine carried a factual, almost complimentary two-page, five-photograph spread on the Turner trial. Giving the South credit, the article noted that "Other Southern juries have in the past month stood up to the problem of justice for the Negro." About the coverage, the *Kosciusko Star-Herald* commented, "All in all, LIFE was extremely fair. Also fair in what it had to say was NEWSWEEK."[6]

Of more concern to Attala County residents was *Time* magazine, which had been so critical of the methods used to capture Leon Turner. But Attalans dodged a journalistic bullet, for as the *Star-Herald* put it, "TIME, thank goodness, had nothing whatever to say."[7]

As controversy swirled about Leon Turner's punishment, Malcolm Whitt's attorney was negotiating a deal for his client. David Crawley had seen all of the prosecution's evidence at the two preceding trials and knew that the case against Malcolm was weak. The only damning evidence of Malcolm's role in the killings was the nebulous statement by Mary Ella Harris that someone "who looked like the largest Whitt boy" pointed a rifle at her in the front yard and tried to force her back toward the house. Crawley approached Judge Coleman and District Attorney Rodgers and offered to change his client's plea from "not guilty" of murder to "guilty" of manslaughter if, in return, the court would sentence Whitt to no more than ten years in prison.[8]

Only fifty spectators were in attendance when Circuit Court convened at 9:00 a.m. on April 3. As anticipated, Crawley changed Malcolm Whitt's plea to an admission of guilt on the charge of manslaughter. Judge Coleman immediately accepted the change and sentenced the twenty-seven-year-old Alabama bricklayer to ten years in Parchman Penitentiary. The ruling meant that Malcolm would be eligible for parole in three years and four months.[9]

Mary Ella missed Malcolm's court appearance. She was instead caring for her injured daughter and infant son at her brother's home, where the three had moved after the murders. They would never again live in their Newport home.[10]

Unfortunately for Mary Ella, her avoidance of the court proceeding would not end her agony. The effects of Leon Turner's rampage would continue; for even as Judge Coleman gaveled the proceedings closed, fate's last cruel blow would hit the Harris family eight days later.

Three weeks after the conviction of his shooter, the suffering of Thomas Harris came to an end. Months in a hospital had steadily dissipated the stamina of the once hardy farmer. Strenuous testifying at two trials in succession had sapped the remainder of his energy. At 10:50 on the evening of Tuesday, April 11, 1950, the young man's heart finally stopped beating.

Thomas was buried the next day beside his three murdered children. No special funeral services were held. For Mary Ella, it was one more wrenching emotional trauma, one that she could not publicly handle. As she did not attend the funerals of her children, neither was she at the burial of her husband.[11]

Epilogue

Mary Ella Harris

Mary Ella never again resided in Newport, Mississippi. She moved to Kosciusko, where she worked for years as a maid. Eventually, she remarried and moved to Durant, where she lives today. She had no more children.[1]

Verlene Thurman

Verlene recovered fully from her wounds. She and Buck Roby married, and their daughter, Minnie Joyce Roby, was born August 28, 1950. The marriage did not last. For a while, Verlene worked as a hairdresser in Kosciusko. Eventually, she moved to Milwaukee and made a career as a nurse's aide.[2] She died in 1990.[3]

James Harris

James grew up in Kosciusko and Durant and eventually obtained two college degrees. He worked in New Jersey as a computer programmer before taking a similar job in Mississippi. He now lives with his mother in Durant, taking care of her in the twilight of her life. James never married.

Leon Turner

Leon became a model prisoner at the Parchman Penitentiary. He helped with the dogs for a while and was even sent out with them on a manhunt. The public raised such an uproar that the prison never released him again.[4]

He was found dead of an apparent heart attack in his prison cell bed on February 12, 1968, after serving almost eighteen years, and was buried in the East Salem Cemetery south of Newport.[5] The grave lay unmarked until 2005, when Bailey Hutchinson of Newport installed a marker.

Sheriff Roy Braswell

Roy finished his first term as sheriff in 1952 and, after waiting the four years mandated by law, served a second term from 1956 to 1960. Afterward, he worked in various state government jobs. Roy died on December 23, 1987.[6] His widow, Inez, lives today in Kosciusko.

Malcolm Whitt

Malcolm was paroled from Parchman in 1954, after which he moved to Cincinnati and then Chicago. He and his first wife divorced. Imprisoned in 1956 on a suspicion of rape, he was cleared and discharged two years later.[7] After this release from prison, he returned to the masonry trade and lived in Greenville, Mississippi, where he remarried and raised five children. Malcolm died on October 11, 1996.[8]

Windol Whitt

Windol Whitt appealed his conviction, and the case went to the Mississippi Supreme Court.[9] While waiting to appear before the Supreme Court, he was released on $5,000 bond on November 18, 1950. Ordering his release was the new judge of the Mississippi Fifth Circuit Court, former district attorney Henry Lee Rodgers, who had followed Judge Coleman to the bench.

The sentence was upheld by the Mississippi Supreme Court on February 12, 1951, and Windol was sent to Parchman.[10] He went through several parole/incarceration cycles at Parchman, with his final release coming in 1984 at age sixty. [11] He and his wife divorced, and Windol never remarried.[12] He died in 1992.[13]

"Hogjaw Mullen"

Clarence Grammer, aka Hogjaw Mullen, was rewarded for capturing Leon Turner and Windol Whitt with a four-day vacation from Parchman after the trials. The warden's words that the convict "can't seem to stay out of trouble on the outside," were proved true.[14] Hogjaw was paroled in 1952, but returned to prison in 1954; paroled in 1556, returned in 1957; paroled in 1959, returned in 1962; and again paroled and returned in 1963.[15] Finally, in May 1966, he was paroled for good. He lived out the rest of his days under the name Hogjaw Mullen in Greenwood, Mississippi, where he died in the 1970s.[16]

His assumed name captured Hollywood's fancy. Months after his heroic exploits during the Turner capture made national news, an episode of *The Lone Ranger* television series ("Pardon for Curly," first aired on June 22, 1950) contained a character named Hogjaw Mullins.[17]

Others

Elvira Turner lived one more year after her oldest grandson was sentenced to life in prison. She died April 1, 1951, and was buried in East Salem Cemetery. For years afterward, her son, Howard, walked the roads of Newport and Kosciusko with his children by Hattie Levy. Howard died on February 6, 1974, and was buried next to his son Leon in the same cemetery as his mother.

Billy McMillan became editor/publisher of the Star-Herald after the death of his father-in-law. In the late 1960's, he sold the newspaper and took up other endeavors. He died in 1983.

Claude Woodward practiced law in Kosciusko until well into his 80's. He died in 2009 at age 92.

Judge J. P. Coleman's star rose rapidly after the Harris murder trials. Just five months later, he was appointed by Governor Fielding Wright to serve on the Mississippi Supreme Court. Coleman was subsequently elected as the state's attorney general, a position he held until 1956, when he was voted to be governor of Mississippi at age forty-two. Defeated after one four-year term, he eventually served in the Mississippi House of Representatives, thus becoming the only politician in Mississippi history to be elected to all three branches of state government. In 1965 President Lyndon Johnson nominated him to the U.S. Court of Appeals for the Fifth Circuit, where he remained until 1984. Coleman died in 1991 and was laid to rest in his hometown of Ackerman.[18]

Notes

Prologue

1. Attala County Historical Society, *Kosciusko—Attala History* (Marceline, Mo.: Walsworth Publishing Company), 4. *Attala* is pronounced uh-TA-luh.

2. Francois Rene Chateaubriand, *Atala, ou les amours de deus sauvages dans le desert* (Atala; or, The Romance of a Primitive Couple in the Wilderness), published in 1818.

3. 1950 U.S. Census. *Kosciusko* is pronounced kah-zee-ES-koh.

Chapter 1

1. Letter from Velma Crawford Fly, April 1978, Genealogy Department of Attala County Library, Kosciusko, Miss.

2. The Natchez Trace is now a federal parkway. Under the jurisdiction of the National Park Service, it is a well-maintained two-lane road that parallels the route of the original Indian trail. For 450 miles, it runs with no stop signs through Tennessee, Alabama, and Mississippi on an unhurried, scenic journey from Nashville to Natchez.

3. Attala County Historical Society, *Kosciusko—Attala History*, 17

4. "Murder in Mississippi," *St. Louis Post-Dispatch*, January 29, 1950, pt. 7, 1.

5. Interview with Pat Smithson, December 2, 2002; *St. Louis Post-Dispatch*, April 2, 1950, Pictures sec., p. 6.

6. Attala County World War I Draft Registration, card 3777.

7. Interview with Thurman Lacey, Elvira Turner's nephew, October 22, 2002.

8. Samuel and Elvira's divorce became official July 14, 1893. Attala County Chancery Clerk divorce record 1350.

9. "Murder in Mississippi."

10. Handwritten note attached to Attala County Circuit Clerk marriage records.

11. Attala County Circuit Clerk marriage record K167.

[12] Leon Turner, prison records, Mississippi State Penitentiary, Parchman, Miss.

[13] Telephone interview with Bug Levy, December 16, 2002.

[14] The same social stigma was not attached to relations between the early white pioneers and the indigent Indian population. Choctaw Indian women were known for their beauty, and the tribe had no problem with their women marrying white men. This racial intermingling, and the acceptance of their offspring into white society and business, proved to be a major factor in the Choctaw's ultimate demise.

[15] Don H. Doyle, *Faulkner's County: The Historical Roots of Yoknapatawpha* (Chapel Hill: University of North Carolina Press, 2001), 148.

[16] The word *miscegenation*, referring to the interbreeding of persons of different races, was invented during the presidential campaign of 1864. The Northern Democratic Party coined the term (from the Latin *miscere*, "to mix," and *genus*, "race") in asserting that Abraham Lincoln's Republican Party advocated sex and marriage across racial lines. Martha Hodes, *White Women, Black Men: Illicit Sex in the 19th-Century South* (New Haven: Yale University Press, 1997), 144.

[17] Neil R. McMillen, *Dark Journey: Black Mississippians in the Age of Jim Crow* (Urbana: University of Illinois Press, 1990), 17.

[18] Sexual relationships between Southern white women and Negro men were not socially accepted. White men tended to assert that a white woman would never willingly have sex with a black man, thus such occurrences were assumed to be cases of rape. Such prejudice frequently resulted in horrible consequences, typically lynching, for the black man.

[19] 1930 U.S. Census.

[20] "Murder in Mississippi."

[21] This custom may have derived from the days of slavery when Southern laws decreed that a racially mixed child's status as slave or free followed the mother. From Hodes, *White Women, Black Men*, 121.

[22] Prison records, Mississippi State Penitentiary, Parchman.

[23] E. R. Hutchinson; *Yesterday: The Descendants of John Hutchinson and Elizabeth Frazier of Attala County, Miss.* (Jackson, Miss.: North Point Publishing), 71.

[24] Ibid.

[25] Interviews with Bug Levy and Annie Mae Levy Johnson.

[26] Interview with Archie "Bug" Levy, October 20, 2002.

[27] Howard became a big lover of Bush's Pork & Beans when the brand came out in the early 1950s. To him the ideal picnic was to relax next to a

spring while dining on Bush's Pork & Beans and crackers. Interview with Bobby Hugh McDaniel, July 11, 2002.

28. Telephone interview with Bug Levy, December 16, 2002.

29. Howard was similarly afflicted when he was older. He developed a large, oozing sore on the back of his neck, which he treated by pouring a liberal dosage of iodine from the bottle straight on the sore. This left a large purple stain on the back of his unwashed shirt.

30. Interview with Chatwin Jackson, April 17, 2002.

31. Telephone interview with Bug Levy, December 16, 2002.

32. Interviews with Bug Levy and Annie Mae Levy Johnson.

Chapter 2

1. Interviews with John Owen Edwards and Bailey Hutchinson, July 10, 2002.

2. Interview with Roosevelt Whitcomb, October 23, 2002.

3. Interview with Rick McDaniel, April 15, 2002, describing the scene as told by his father, Clyde, who was a frequent musician at the dances.

4. Attala County Circuit Clerk record Q396.

5. Hutchinson; *Yesterday*.

6. Interviews with John Owen Edwards, July 10, 2002; Bailey Hutchinson, August 9, 2002; Billie McCrory Nance, October 21, 2002, and Patty Branch Wigginton, May 30, 2003.

7. See http://www.deltablues.net/books.html.

8. Rick McDaniel, e-mail to author, April 10, 2003.

9. Interviews with John Owen Edwards and Bailey Hutchinson, July 10, 2002; and Dave Ballard Jr., August 11, 2002.

10. Interview with Bailey Hutchinson, July 10, 2002.

11. Attala County Historical Society, *Kosciusko—Attala History*, 232.

12. Interview with Pat Smithson Jr., December 2, 2002.

13. The car probably belonged to Parvee Rutherford. Leon never owned an automobile.

14. Interview with Mary Ella Harris Carson, July 11, 2002.

15. Interview with Annie Mae Levy Johnson, January 5, 2003.

16. Interviews with John Owen Edwards and Bailey Hutchinson, July 10, 2002; and Billie McCrory Nance, October 21, 2002.

17. Record of Fifth Circuit Court of Mississippi, cause number 4934, *State of Miss. v. Leon Turner*, September 12, 1940.

18. Newsweek, January 23, 1950, 26.

19. "Freedom for Grandson Won by 74 -Year-Old Woman after 20-Mile Walk to See Governor," *Jackson Clarion-Ledger*, April 15, 1943, 6.

20. Ibid.

21. "Attala County Grandmother, 74, Gets 'Boy' Freed," *Kosciusko Star-Herald*, April 22, 1943, 1.

22. "Freedom for Grandson," *Jackson Clarion-Ledger*, April 15, 1943.

23. Letter of sentence suspension, Mississippi Department of Archives and History. Its justification for release stated, "Leon Turner is the sole support of his grandmother, who is 74 years of age. She is poverty stricken, lives alone, and is unable to earn a livelihood. Numerous citizens have signed a petition stating that they believe this convict has been sufficiently punished and endorse his release. He has a good penitentiary record."

24. Interview with Eva D. Jones.

25. Interview with Suzie Lee Brewer, August 3, 2002.

26. Interview with John Owen Edwards, July 10, 2002.

27. Revocation of Suspension, Mississippi Department of Archives and History.

28. Alma Reed married a man named Vester Moore in the early 1950s, and he legally adopted Suzie. Suzie grew up with Vester as the only father she knew. Only when Alma Reed Moore was on her deathbed in the late 1960s did she tell Suzie that Leon Turner was her father. Suzie then contacted her biological father and visited him in prison. Interview with Suzie Lee Reed Brewer, October 21, 2002.

29. Prison records, Parchman.

30. Interviews with Bailey Hutchinson, July 10, 2002; and Bug Levy, October 20, 2002. Parvee died from this injury on March 4, 1952, at age forty-three.

31. Interview with Sidney Bishop, July 9, 2002.

Chapter 3
The many personal stories about Mary Ella Harris and her family were revealed during multiple interviews with Mary Ella Harris Carson and James Harris, her youngest child, from 2002 to 2007.

1. Attala County Bill for Divorce No. 8730, Eli Thurman v. Mary Ella Thurman, December 1943; Attala County Chancery Court records.

2. William was born September 10, 1933. James Harris, e-mail to author, February 17, 2004.

3. Ibid.

4. Frankie was born April 14, 1937. The initial C. did not stand for anything; Mary Ella simply liked the way it sounded. Ibid.

5. Like Frankie's, Mary's initial C. stood for no name. Ibid.

6. Bill for Divorce No. 8730, Attala County Chancery Court records.

7. Decree Granting Divorce No. 8730, Eli Thurman v. Mary Ella Thurman, December 1943; Attala County Chancery Court records.

8. Interview with Mary Ella Harris Carson, February 22, 2004.

9. Nell was born January 2, 1946. James Harris, e-mail to author, February 17, 2004.

10. Interview with Dr. Beverly McMillan, February 14, 2003.

11. Old seafarers had a modified version of this superstition, whereby any mariner born under the veil would never drown. A sailor whose infant son was so born typically saved the amnion, so the future sailor could carry it with him for good luck. Other seamen wanted to be on the fortunate one's ship.

12. James Harris, e-mail to author, February 17, 2004.

Chapter 4

The many personal stories about Roy Braswell and his wife, Inez, were revealed during multiple interviews with Inez Braswell during 2002 and 2003.

1. "Does Attala County Need a New Jail?" *Kosciusko Star-Herald*, May 11, 1950, 1.

2. This law was not changed until 1972, when the office of Sheriff and Tax Collector was split into separate offices. Now divorced from having responsibility for the county's income, the sheriff was allowed to run for reelection. In 1980, nearly 150 years after Attala County was formed in 1833, Marvin "Pop" Lawrence became its first sheriff to serve more than four years in a row. He was in office for twelve straight years.

3. Although the sheriff can be a man or a woman, no female has yet worn the sheriff's badge in Attala County.

4. Attala County Historical Society, *Kosciusko—Attala History*, 114, 213.

5. Interview with Inez Braswell, July 20, 2003.

6. Marriage records, October 6, 1937, Attala County Chancery Court records.

7. Interview with Jeweldene Morgan, July 9, 2002.

8. Telephone interview with Roy Braswell Jr., August 11, 2003.

9. Ibid.

[10.] Interview with Inez Braswell, April 16, 2002.

[11.] Ann Breedlove, e-mail to author, September 5, 2003, telling of events witnessed by her father.

[12.] "Apparently Crazed Vet Shot Fatally by Police Officer," *Kosciusko Star-Herald*, November 22, 1945.

[13.] Usually in such matters, a gentleman's agreement sufficed to cement the deal. In this case, however, Braswell had a lawyer draft a written contract solidifying their agreement—evidence that he distrusted Hall.

[14.] Minutes of the Supervisor's Court of Attala County, March 10, 1949.

[15.] "Roy Braswell Elected Sheriff in Special Election Tuesday," *Kosciusko Star-Herald*, May 12, 1949, 1.

Chapter 5

[1.] "Former Boxer Serving Time May Get Pardon for Capture of Attala Pair," *Greenville (Miss.) Delta Democrat-Times*, January 12, 1950, 14.

[2.] "Jackson Point Fisherman Is Murder Victim," *Natchez (Miss.) Democrat*, October 31, 1940, 1.

[3.] Clarence Grammer, No. 14497, prison records, Mississippi State Penitentiary, Parchman.

[4.] Ibid.

[5.] "Indict Grammar for Murder of Aged Fisherman," *Natchez Democrat*, November 13, 1940, 8.

[6.] "'Hog Jaw' Mullen Was Sent Up for Weird Killing on River," *Memphis Commercial Appeal*, January 12, 1950, 25.

[7.] "Jackson Point Fisherman Is Murder Victim."

[8.] "Three Suspects in Leche Murder Now Lodged in County Jail, Sheriff Says," *Natchez Democrat*, November 3, 1940, 1.

[9.] Ibid.

[10.] "'Hog Jaw' Mullen Was Sent Up."

[11.] Clarence Grammer, prison records, Parchman.

[12.] William Banks Taylor, *Down on Parchman Farm: The Great Prison in the Mississippi Delta* (Columbus: Ohio State University Press, 1999), ix.

[13.] Ibid., viii.

[14.] Ibid., 42.

[15.] Columbus B. Hopper, *Sex in Prison: The Mississippi Experiment with Conjugal Visiting* (Baton Rouge: Louisiana State University Press, 1969), 43.

[16.] Taylor, *Down on Parchman Farm*, 51.

[17.] David M. Oshinsky, *Worse than Slavery: Parchman Farm and the Ordeal of Jim Crow Justice* (New York: Free Press, 1996), 140.

[18.] "Mixup over Nickname 'Hog Jaw' May Be Cleared Up by Texas Ring Man," *Greenville Delta Democrat-Times*, January 13, 1950, 1.

[19.] Oshinsky, *Worse than Slavery*, 166.

[20.] Ibid., 196.

[21.] Ibid., 140.

[22.] Grammer's brother, however, a Parchman inmate called "Pork Chop," was considered highly untrustworthy, even among criminals. He never attained the lofty trusty status that Hogjaw did. Interview with former patrolman and sheriff Tom Sadler, August 15, 2004.

[23.] Taylor, *Down on Parchman Farm*, 122.

[24.] "Hogjaw Likes to Tell Tall Tales, Columbus Folks Say," *Jackson Clarion-Ledger*, January 16, 1950, 1.

[25.] Oshinsky, *Worse than Slavery*, 166.

[26.] "Former Boxer Serving Time May Get Pardon."

[27.] "Hogjaw Likes to Tell Tall Tales."

[28.] Ibid.

[29.] Ibid.

[30.] Oshinsky, *Worse than Slavery*, 153.

[31.] Taylor, *Down on Parchman Farm*, 99.

[32.] Ibid., 59.

[33.] So reads Leadbelly's tombstone at the Shiloh Baptist Church outside Mooringsport, Louisiana; see http://www.deltablues.net.

[34.] Other famous blues artists who sang about the time they served at Parchman include Eddie "Son" House, McKinley Morganfied (aka Muddy Waters), and Washington "Bukka" White. Taylor, *Down on Parchman Farm*, 113.

[35.] "Hogjaw Likes to Tell Tall Tales."

[36.] Kennie wasn't recaptured until 1956. Taylor, *Down on Parchman Farm*, 101.

[37.] "The Real 'Hogjaw' Is Living in Texas," *Memphis Press-Scimitar*, January 14, 1950; picture caption.

[38.] The prison's hounds got to practice their skill fairly often, going from an annual average of seventy-three escape attempts during the early 1940s to sixteen at the end of the decade. The decline in escape attempts was due to both improved conditions at the prison and increased security. Taylor, *Down on Parchman Farm*, 107.

[39] "'Hogjaw' Mullen Eating High on Hog at Parchman after Subduing Fugitives," *Memphis Press-Scimitar*, January 12, 1950.

Chapter 6
[1] Hutchinson; *Yesterday*.
[2] Interview with Pat Smithson, October 20, 2002.
[3] Hutchinson; *Yesterday*; Windol Whitt, prison records, Mississippi State Penitentiary, Parchman.
[4] Don Whitt, e-mail to author, November 6, 2003. Don is first cousin of Malcolm and Windol Whitt.
[5] Interview with Malcom Whitt Jr., July 12, 2002.
[6] Trial transcript of Circuit Court of Attala County, Mississippi, March 1950, *State of Mississippi v. Windol Whitt* (hereafter cited as *Mississippi v. Whitt*), 150.
[7] See http://www.redstone.army.mil/history.
[8] Interview with Malcom Whitt Jr., July 12, 2002.
[9] National Personnel Records Center record on Private Malcum Whitt, Serial number 34394471.
[10] Interview with John Owen Edwards, July 10, 2002.
[11] Hutchinson; *Yesterday*.
[12] John Owen Edwards Interview, July 10, 2002.
[13] Interview with Malcom Whitt Jr., July 12, 2002.
[14] Letter from National Personnel Records Center dated September 23, 2002; *Mississippi v. Whitt*, 147.
[15] "Windol Whitt, Trial Nearing, Hopes 'Turner Tells the Truth,'" *Memphis Commercial Appeal*, March 13, 1950.
[16] Doctors used screws to reassemble Windol's elbow. Later in life, Windol would entertain his nieces and nephews by holding his right elbow up to a car radio antenna. The metal in his elbow caused the radio to release a stream of static. Interview with Malcom Whitt Jr., July 12, 2002.
[17] *Mississippi v. Whitt*, 151.
[18] Interview with Malcom Whitt Jr., July 12, 2002.
[19] Madison County, Alabama, Circuit Court record 9980.
[20] Madison County, Alabama, Circuit Court record 10048.
[21] "2 Whitt Brothers Have Lived Here," *Huntsville (Ala.) Times*, January 12, 1951, 1; Don Whitt, e-mail to author, November 6, 2003.
[22] "Killers Captured," *Belzoni (Miss.) Banner*, January 12, 1950, 1.
[23] At this point, the true spelling of their first names became confused in the public records. Court-related documents list Windol as "Wendell,"

"Wendall," and "Wendle," while Malcolm is often recorded as "Malcom." These and other variations would continue.

24. "Windol Whitt Given Life Term in Prison in 'Massacre' Trial," *Memphis Commercial Appeal*, March 17, 1950, 1.

Chapter 7

1. Martha was Thomas Harris's niece. Her sister, Bessie May Harris, had married Howard's son, "Kook" Levy. Bessie and Kook were often at Howard's house on Saturday afternoons. Telephone interview with Bug Levy, December 16, 2002.

2. The owner of the car was James Roundtree, brother of Edward Roundtree, who was Leon Turner's barber. Interview with Mary Ella Harris Carson, July 11, 2002.

3. Interview with Annie Bell Harvey, January 11, 2004.

4. Interview with Helen Roby Ward, November 24, 2004. Willie Latiker told her this story soon after it happened.

5. Interview with Mary Ella Harris Carson, February 22, 2004.

6. Interview with Mary Ella Harris Carson, October 23, 2002.

7. Interview with Pat Smithson, October 20, 2002.

Chapter 8

1. Interview with John Owen Edwards, July 10, 2002.

2. Rick McDaniel, e-mail to author, February 2, 2005.

3. *Mississippi v. Whitt*, testimony of Malcolm Whitt.

4. Ibid.

5. Interview with Mary Ella Harris Carson, October 23, 2002.

6. Interview with Annie Bell Harvey, January 11, 2004. A granddaughter of Sally Ward, she was in the house during Leon Turner's visit.

7. Interview with Cassell Ward, son of Sallie Ward, July 12, 2002.

8. Interview with Flowery Levy, November 16, 2004.

9. Annie Bell Harvey Interview.

10. "Attala Killers May Have Fled," *Jackson Clarion-Ledger*, January 11, 1950, 1.

11. "Armed Desperadoes Rushed to Hinds Jail after Capture Upstate," *Jackson Daily News*, January 11, 1950, 1.

12. Interview with Flowery Levy, November 16, 2004.

13. 1900 U.S. Census.

14. Interview with Mary Ella Harris Carson, July 11, 2002.

[15] Interview with Helen Roby Ward, July 12, 2002. The sister of Ike Roby, she was in the house when Mary Katherine Ward came.

[16] Ibid.

[17] As in this case, not all harassment of blacks in the South involved the Ku Klux Klan. Sometimes, groups of white men without the KKK regalia would barge into a Negro home, brandish their guns, order the wife to cook for them, shatter a few pieces of furniture, and sexually molest the women. When finished with their "fun," the unwelcome visitors left with a warning to the family to keep their mouths shut or risk death. This form of lawlessness was called "whitecapping," a reference to a similar and often more violent practice by the Klan, whose members wore white hooded caps and robes. From Doyle, *Faulkner's County*, 314.

Chapter 9

[1] Interview with Mary Ella Harris Carson, July 11, 2002.

[2] "Murder in Mississippi."

[3] *Mississippi v. Whitt*, testimony of Verlene Thurman.

[4] Interview with Mary Ella Harris Carson, February 22, 2004.

[5] Interview with Mary Ella Harris Carson, April 17, 2002.

[6] *Mississippi v. Whitt*, testimony of Malcolm Whitt.

[7] *Mississippi v. Whitt*, testimony of Windol Whitt.

[8] Interview with Mary Ella Harris Carson, April 17, 2002.

[9] Ibid.

[10] Interview with Flowery Levy, November 16, 2004.

[11] *Mississippi v. Whitt*, testimony of Malcolm Whitt.

[12] Interview with Mary Ella Harris Carson, July 11, 2002.

[13] Ibid.

[14] "Murder in Mississippi."

[15] Interview with Cassel Ward, July 12, 2002.

Chapter 10

[1] *Mississippi v. Whitt*, testimony of Malcolm and of Windol Whitt.

[2] Interview with Dallas Bailey, August, 7, 2003; "Does Attala County Need a New Jail?"

[3] Interview with Mary Ella Harris Carson, October 23, 2002.

[4] *Mississippi v. Whitt*.

[5] *Mississippi v. Whitt*, testimony of Malcolm Whitt.

[6] "Eyes of the Nation on Mississippi Trial," *Memphis Commercial Appeal*, March 12, 1950, sec. 2, p. 1.

7. Interview with Billie McCrory Nance, September 22, 2002.

8. *Mississippi v. Whitt*, testimony of Windol Whitt.

9. "Does Attala County Need a New Jail?"

10. *Memphis Press Scimitar*, March 16, 1950, sec. 2, p. 17.

11. *Mississippi v. Whitt*, testimony of Malcolm Whitt.

12. "Three Men Escape from Attala Jail," *Kosciusko Star-Herald*, January 5, 1950, 1.

13. *Mississippi v. Whitt*, testimony of Malcolm Whitt.

14. Interview with Bug Levy, October 20, 2002.

15. *Mississippi v. Whitt*, testimony of Roosevelt Whitcomb.

16. Interview with Roosevelt Whitcomb, October 23, 2002.

17. *Mississippi v. Whitt*, testimony of Roosevelt Whitcomb and of Malcomb Whitt.

18. Interview with Edward Roundtree, September 22, 2002.

19. "Negro Father Admits He Had Gun in House on Night of Slayings," *Memphis Commercial Appeal*, March 21, 1950, 1.

20. Interview with Pat Smithson Jr., October 1, 2002.

21. Interview with Mary Ella Harris Carson, October 23, 2002.

22. "Three Men Escape from Attala Jail."

23. *Mississippi v. Whitt*, testimony of Malcolm Whitt.

24. Ibid., 131.

25. *Mississippi v. Whitt*, testimony of Malcolm and of Windol Whitt.

26. *Mississippi v. Whitt*, testimony of Malcolm Whitt.

27. Interview with Mary Ella Harris Carson, October 23, 2002.

28. Ibid.

29. Ibid.

30. The *Star-Herald*, then published every Thursday, now comes out on Wednesdays.

31. "Three Men Escape from Attala Jail."

32. *Mississippi v. Whitt*, testimony of Malcolm Whitt.

33. Ibid.

Chapter 11

Unless otherwise noted, the events, conversations, and descriptions used in this chapter were taken from the testimonies of the participants as contained in the trial transcript of *Mississippi v. Whitt*.

1. "Hair of the dog" (shortened from "hair of the dog that bit you") means attempting to get rid of a hangover by drinking the same alcohol that gave it

to you in the first place. The phrase has been in use since at least the mid-1500s. See http://www.randomhouse.com/wotd/index.pperl?date=20010613.

[2.] Interview with Edward Roundtree, September 22, 2002.

[3.] Interview with Mary Ella Harris Carson, July 11, 2002.

[4.] Interview with Helen Roby Ward, July 12, 2002.

[5.] "Murder in Mississippi."

[6.] *Memphis Commercial Appeal*, March 22, 1950.

[7.] "Murder in Mississippi."

[8.] "Armed Desperadoes Rushed to Hinds Jail."

[9.] Interview with Edward Roundtree, September 22, 2002.

[10.] Interview with Helen Roby Ward, April 17, 2002.

[11.] "Armed Desperadoes Rushed to Hinds Jail."

Chapter 12
Unless otherwise noted, the events, conversations, and descriptions used in this chapter were taken from the testimonies of the participants as contained in the trial transcript of *Mississippi v. Whitt*.

[1.] Missing was the father, Isaac Roby Sr, who occasionally, and not without being noticed, spent the night with his girlfriend Sarah, Mary Ella's sister. Interview with Bailey Hutchinson, October 31, 2005.

[2.] Interview with Helen Roby Ward, July 12, 2002.

[3.] Interview with Mary Ella Harris Carson, April 17, 2002.

[4.] Interview with Helen Roby Ward, July 12, 2002.

[5.] "Murder in Mississippi."

[6.] Interview with Billie McCrory Nance, October 21, 2002.

[7.] "One of Three Captives Admits Part in Triple Murder during Questioning in Jackson Office," *Jackson Clarion-Ledger*, January 12, 1950, 1.

[8.] "Murder in Mississippi."

[9.] "One of Three Captives Admits Part in Triple Murder."

[10.] Ibid.

[11.] Interview with Roosevelt Whitcomb, October 23, 2002.

[12.] Interview with Tom Sadler, August 15, 2004.

[13.] Interview with Bailey Hutchinson, July 10, 2002.

Chapter 13
Unless otherwise noted, the events, conversations, and descriptions used in this chapter were taken from the testimonies of the participants as contained in the trial transcript of *Mississippi v. Whitt*.

1. It was a stroke of luck for Leon that Caesar Young was there with his pickup. As revealed in the Windol Whitt trial, Young was spending the night at Mr. and Mrs. Ezra Burns's house after having taken Mr. and Mrs. Willie West Nash there for reasons undisclosed.

2. "Attala Bootleggers Have Rough Month," *Kosciusko Star-Herald*, July 7, 1949, 1.

3. "One of Three Captives Admits Part in Triple Murder."

4. "Fugitives Nabbed by Armed Posse Ending 3-Day Hunt," *Yazoo City (Miss.) Herald*, January 12, 1950.

5. Lloyd Turner is of no known relation to Leon and Howard.

6. Interview with Bailey Hutchinson, July 10, 2002.

7. W. W. "Billy" McMillan is the author's father.

8. "3 Children Shot to Death by 3 Jailbreakers," *St. Louis Post-Dispatch*, January, 10, 1950, 1.

9. "Posse Hunts Killers of 3 Negro Children in 'Revenge Mistake,'" *Jackson Clarion-Ledger*, January 10, 1950, 1.

10. "Search for Child Killers Moves into Delta Today," *Greenville Delta Democrat-Times*, January 10, 1950, 1.

11. "Fugitives Are Hunted for 'Revenge Slaying' of 3 Negro Children," *Memphis Commercial Appeal*, January 10, 1950, 1.

12. "Search for Child Killers Moves into Delta Today."

13. "Attala Desperadoes Captured after Killing 3 Negro Children," *Kosciusko Star-Herald*, January 12, 1950, 1.

14. Interview with Bug Levy, October 20, 2002.

15. Ibid.

16. Interview with Helen Roby, July 12, 2002.

Chapter 14
Unless otherwise noted, the events, conversations, and descriptions used in this chapter were taken from the testimonies of the participants as contained in the trial transcript of *Mississippi v. Whitt*.

1. Vaiden.net/winona_trailway_station_postcard.jpg.

2. Ibid.

3. Interview with John (Jack) Aldridge Jr., July 8, 2002. Jack would go on to enter the University of Mississippi at age sixteen and begin medical school at nineteen. He eventually became a Jackson physician.

4. Ibid.

5. Interview with John Aldridge Sr., July 7, 2002.

[6] Ibid.

[7] Interview with Bailey Hutchinson, July 10, 2002.

[8] "3 Children Shot to Death by 3 Jailbreakers."

[9] Interview with Billie McCrory Nance, October 21, 2002.

[10] Still broadcasting, WKOZ remains the town's only radio station.

[11] "Death in the Chair Demanded after Capture of Killer Trio," *Memphis Commercial Appeal*, January 12, 1950, 1.

[12] "Wright and Senate Ask Swift Justice," *Memphis Commercial Appeal*, January 12, 1950, 1.

[13] Interview with Ellen Pettit, December 11, 2002.

[14] "Armed Desperadoes Rushed to Hinds Jail."

[15] Ibid.

[16] "Attala Killers May Have Fled."

[17] Ibid.

[18] "Negro Massacre Posse Called Off 2-Day Hunt," *Houston Post*, January 11, 1950.

[19] A fact so noted in the Great Seal of the United States. The phrase *Annuit Coeptis* ("Providence favors") hovering over the eye of Providence refers to divine assistance to the colonists in establishing the new country.

[20] Interview with Jack Aldridge, July 8, 2002.

[21] *Jackson Daily News*, January 10, 1950, 1.

[22] Interview with John Aldridge Sr., July 7, 2002.

Chapter 15

[1] "Death in the Chair Demanded after Capture of Killer Trio"; "Attala Desperadoes Captured after Killing 3 Negro Children."

[2] "Armed Desperadoes Rushed to Hinds Jail."

[3] "Two Killers of Kosciusko Massacre Trio Are Caught," *New Orleans Times-Picayune*, January 12, 1950.

[4] Ibid.

[5] Ibid.

[6] "Armed Desperadoes Rushed to Hinds Jail."

[7] Interview with Edward Roundtree, September 22, 2002.

[8] "Attala Desperadoes Captured after Killing 3 Negro Children."

[9] "Trusty Tells How He Shot Fugitive," *Jackson Clarion-Ledger*, January 12, 1950, 1.

[10] Ibid.

[11] Interview with Edward Roundtree, September 22, 2002.

[12] "Death in the Chair Demanded after Capture of Killer Trio."

13. Interview with Tom Sadler, July 11, 2006.

14. One of McMillan's photographs of the capture went on to win the prestigious National Press Photographer's Association 1950 Photograph of the Year award.

15. "Attala Desperadoes Captured after Killing 3 Negro Children."

16. "Death in the Chair Demanded after Capture of Killer Trio."

17. Interview with Tom Sadler, August 15, 2004.

18. *Mississippi v. Whitt*, testimony by Windol Whitt.

19. "Armed Desperadoes Rushed to Hinds Jail."

20. *Jackson Clarion-Ledger*, January 15, 1950, picture caption on p. 6.

21. "Trusty Tells How He Shot Fugitive."

22. "Death in the Chair Demanded after Capture of Killer Trio."

23. Ibid.

24. Ibid.

25. "Attala Desperadoes Captured after Killing 3 Negro Children."

26. Interview with Roosevelt Whitcomb, October 23, 2002.

27. Interview with Mary Ella Harris Carson, July 11, 2006.

Chapter 16

1. Interview with William Winter, former governor of Mississippi, July 10, 2006. Winter was a young legislator in the Mississippi House of Representatives in 1950.

2. Stokes Sanders is the author's maternal grandfather.

3. "Wright and Senate Ask Swift Justice."

4. "Wright Denounces Attala Killing of 3 Negro Children," *Jackson Daily News*, January 12, 1950, 4.

5. "Special Fund for Survivors," *Kosciusko Star-Herald*, January 12, 1950, 1.

6. "Indignation over Wanton Slaying of Children Turns to Aid for Family," *New Orleans Times-Picayune*, January 13, 1950.

7. "Badmen on the Loose," *Newsweek*, January 23, 1950, 26.

8. "Special Court Term Asked for Attala Slaying Suspects," *Jackson Clarion-Ledger*, January 14, 1950, 1.

9. "Windol Whitt Gets Life Term," *Jackson Clarion-Ledger*, March 17, 1950, 1.

10. Even the mechanics of disseminating photographs of the capture to the national press made good copy. The *Jackson Daily News*, which boasted of owning the only Wirephoto facility in Mississippi, wrote that it "co-operated with the Associated Press in sending the pictures to

other newspapers over the United States" using "a portable Wirephoto transmitter set up in the Daily News photographic darkroom." From "Photos of Dramatic Capture in Attala Fed to Nation via Exclusive AP Wirephoto," *Jackson Daily News*, January 11, 1950.

[11.] "Trusty Lifer May Win Parole for Capture of 2 Desperadoes," *Houston Post*, January 12, 1950, 1.

[12.] "Three Escapees Face Charges," *Jackson Clarion-Ledger*, January 13, 1950, 1.

[13.] "Revenge Killing Case Goes to Trial Today," *Memphis Commercial Appeal*, March 15, 1950.

[14.] "Three Escapees Face Charges."

[15.] "Eyes of Nation on Mississippi Trial," *Memphis Commercial Appeal*, March 12, 1950.

[16.] See, e.g., Wikipedia: http://en.wikipedia.org/wiki/Lynching_in_the_United_States.

[17.] "The People Are Angry," *Greenville Delta Democrat-Times*, January 11, 1950.

[18.] See http://www.geocities.com/Colosseum/Base/8507/NLists.htm.

[19.] "Trusty Lifer May Win Parole for Capture of 2 Desperadoes."

[20.] "The Real 'Hogjaw' Is Living in Texas."

[21.] "Shooter's Chance," *Time*, January 23, 1950, 15.

[22.] *Time*, February 20, 1950.

[23.] Ibid.

[24.] "Mayor's Criticism of Time Magazine Brings Flood of Letters," *Kosciusko Star-Herald*, February 23, 1950.

[25.] Editorial: "Those Who Would Malign Mississippi Should at Least Get Their Facts Straight," *Kosciusko Star-Herald*, January 26, 1950.

[26.] Ibid.

[27.] "Special Court Term Asked for Attala Slaying Suspects."

[28.] Interview with Mary Ella Harris Carson, October 23, 2002.

Chapter 17

[1.] *Mississippi v. Whitt*.

[2.] Ibid.

[3.] "Turner Denies Slaying Children," *Greenville Delta Democrat-Times*, January 11, 1950, 1.

[4.] Ibid.

[5.] *Mississippi v. Whitt*.

[6.] "Death in the Chair Demanded after Capture of Killer Trio."

7. Introducing the declaration was the distinguished member from Attala County, Icey W. Day. Born in 1891, Day was blind by the age of ten. Despite the disability, he obtained a law degree from Ole Miss, practiced law for several years, and won a seat in the state legislature. He eventually served Attala County for twenty-four years, easily navigating the cavernous interior of the Capitol Building without assistance. From Attala County Historical Society, *Kosciusko—Attala History*, 236; "Special Court Term Asked for Attala Slaying Suspects."

8. Ibid.

9. "Eyes of the Nation on Mississippi Trial."

10. "Death in the Chair Demanded after Capture of Killer Trio."

11. "First of Trio Goes on Trial Here for Revenge Massacre of Children," *Kosciusko Star-Herald*, March 16, 1950, 1.

12. "Accused Get Counsel in Negro Killing Case," *Memphis Commercial Appeal*, January 21, 1950, 1.

13. "Chair Requested for Windol Whitt," *Huntsville Times*, March 15, 1950, 6.

14. "Accused Get Counsel in Negro Killing Case."

15. Ibid.

16. Ibid.

17. "Preliminary Hearing Set Friday for Men Accused of Mass Killing," *Kosciusko Star-Herald*, February 2, 1950, 1.

18. "Eyes of the Nation on Mississippi Trial."

19. Ibid.

20. "Murder in Mississippi."

21. Ibid.

22. "Hearing Waived by Men Accused of Attala Killing," *Kosciusko Star-Herald*, February 9, 1950, 1.

23. "First of Trio Goes on Trial."

24. Constitutional Rights Foundation, "Bill of Rights in Action" (Fall 1993; updated July 2000), http://www.crf-usa.org/bria/bria10_1.html.

25. Claude Cookman, *A Voice Is Born: The Founding and Early Years of the National Press Photographers Association under the Leadership of Joseph Costa* (Durham: National Press Photographers Association, 1985), 154.

26. "Mississippi Joins Rest of Nation by Lifting Camera Ban in Courts," *Jackson Clarion-Ledger*, May 25, 2003, 3G.

27. "Trial of Revenge Murderers to Be in National Spotlight," *Kosciusko Star-Herald*, March 9, 1950, 1.

28. *Memphis Press-Scimitar*, March 16, 1950, sec. 2, p. 17.

[29.] Ibid.

[30.] Ibid.

[31.] Ibid.

[32.] Ibid.

[33.] "Revenge Killing Case Goes to Trial."

[34.] "Windol Whitt, Trial Nearing, Hopes 'Turner Tells the Truth,'" *Memphis Commercial Appeal*, March 13, 1950.

[35.] "Revenge Killing Case Goes to Trial."

[36.] Ibid.

[37.] Ibid.

[38.] "Eyes of the Nation on Mississippi Trial."

[39.] "Trial of Revenge Murderers to Be in National Spotlight."

[40.] "Court Refused Delay in Trial of Turner," *Memphis Commercial Appeal*, March 14, 1950, 1.

[41.] Ibid.

Chapter 18
Unless otherwise noted, the events, conversations, and descriptions used in this chapter were taken from the testimonies of the participants as contained in the trial transcript of *Mississippi v. Whitt*.

[1.] "Trial Set Wednesday in 'Revenge' Slaying," *Memphis Commercial Appeal*, March 12, 1950.

[2.] Eight jurors were farmers: Ollie Jones, David P. Boyd and Wallace B. Hunt of McCool; O. M. Miller and Donald S. Oakes of West; Grover C. Bennett of Center; and W. C. Croft Jr. and Louis Flanagan of Kosciusko. The remaining four were Alton Nowell, a barber; Neal C. Duncan, a clerk in Hammonds Hardware Store; Walter Patterson, an employee of the S. J. Peeler Lumber Co.; and Ray Shelly, who worked for the Sanders Textile Mill. From "Whitt Brothers Blame Turner for Negro 'Revenge Massacre,'" *Memphis Commercial Appeal*, March 16, 1950, 1.

[3.] Present were reporter Bill Keith and photographer Jimmy Cockrell from the *Jackson Clarion-Ledger*; reporter Ellis Moore and photographer Rudy Vettes from the *Memphis Commercial Appeal*; reporter Keith Fuller and photographer Dave Taylor from the Jackson bureau of the Associated Press; reporter Stokes Sanders Jr. and photographer Billy McMillan from the *Kosciusko Star-Herald*; and Bill Minor going solo for the *New Orleans Times-Picayune*. From "A Press Box Eyeview of the Attala Trial," *Jackson Clarion-Ledger*, March 19, 1950, 1.

This was one of the first big stories for young Keith Fuller, a former World War II POW who would become president of the Associated Press for ten years. From "AP Executive Keith Fuller Spent Early Days 'Bumming' in Miss.," *Jackson Clarion-Ledger*, June 23, 2002, 3G.

4. "A Press Box Eyeview of the Attala Trial."

5. "Swift Southern Justice," *Newsweek*, March 27, 1950.

6. "Whitt Brothers Blame Turner for Negro 'Revenge Massacre.'"

7. Interview with Bill Minor, correspondent with the *New Orleans Times-Picayune*, July 8, 2002.

8. *Memphis Press-Scimitar*, March 16, 1950, sec. 2, p. 17.

9. Ibid.

10. "A Press Box Eyeview of the Attala Trial."

11. "Windol Whitt Given Life Term in Prison in 'Massacre' Trial."

12. "A Press Box Eyeview of the Attala Trial."

13. "Windol Whitt Given Life Term in Prison in 'Massacre' Trial."

14. "A Press Box Eyeview of the Attala Trial."

15. "Windol Whitt Given Life Term in Prison in 'Massacre' Trial."

16. "A Press Box Eyeview of the Attala Trial." According to his son (who spells his own name M-a-l-c-o-m), Malcolm continued to spell his name M-a-l-c-u-m for the rest of his life. Interview with Malcom Whitt Jr., July 12, 2002.

17. "Whitt Brothers Blame Turner for Negro 'Revenge Massacre.'"

18. "White Man Convicted in Negro Massacre; Judge in Mississippi Imposes Life Sentence," *New York Times*, March 17, 1950, sec. 1.

19. "Swift Southern Justice."

20. "Windol Whitt Gets Life Term."

21. "Windol Whitt Given Life Term in Prison in 'Massacre' Trial."

22. "Windol Whitt Gets Life Term."

23. "Mississippi Jury Finds White Man Guilty in Killings," *St. Louis Post-Dispatch*, March 17, 1950, 8A.

24. "Windol Whitt Gets Life Term."

25. "Windol Whitt Given Life Term in Prison in 'Massacre' Trial."

26. "Windol Whitt Gets Life Term."

27. "White Man Convicted in Negro Massacre."

28. "Windol Whitt Given Life Term in Prison in 'Massacre' Trial."

29. "White Man Convicted in Negro Massacre."

30. "Swift Southern Justice."

31. "Windol Whitt Given Life Term in Prison in 'Massacre' Trial."

32. "Windol Whitt Gets Life Term."

[33] "Windol Whitt Given Life Term in Prison in 'Massacre' Trial."

[34] Ibid.

Chapter 19

[1] "Second Act of Kosciusko's Court Drama Opens Monday," *Jackson Clarion-Ledger*, March 20, 1950.

[2] "'DA' to Ask Death Penalty for Leon Turner in Pistol Slaying of Three Children," *Jackson Daily News*, March 20, 1950.

[3] "Attala Court Judge Overrules Mistrial Motion by Defense," *Jackson Clarion-Ledger*, March 21, 1950, 1.

[4] "Negro Father Admits He Had Gun in House on Night of Slayings."

[5] "Second Act of Kosciusko's Court Drama Opens Monday."

[6] Interview with Bill Minor, correspondent with the *New Orleans Times-Picayune*, July 8, 2002.

[7] "Attala Court Judge Overrules Mistrial Motion by Defense."

[8] Among them were Harold Foreman, a reporter for United Press International; Louis Collins, a freelance photographer from Starkville, Mississippi; and Arthur Whitman, feature photographer from the *St. Louis Post-Dispatch*. From *Kosciusko Star-Herald*, March 23, 1950, 1, caption under photo of press coverage.

[9] "A Press Box Eyeview of the Attala Trial."

[10] "Negro Father Admits He Had Gun in House on Night of Slayings."

[11] *St. Louis Post-Dispatch*, April 2, 1950, Pictures sec., p. 7.

[12] "Attala Court Judge Overrules Mistrial Motion by Defense."

[13] "Negro Father Admits He Had Gun in House on Night of Slayings."

[14] Woodward served on a yard minesweeper, the USS YMS-21, and saw action in the Mediterranean Sea off the coasts of North Africa, Sicily, Italy, and France. When YMS-21 was sunk off the coast of southern France, he was given command of the YMS-307. His ship was in harbor at San Pedro, California, being prepared to sail into the Pacific war when the Japanese surrendered. He was on the streets of Hollywood that night, "a great place to be on VJ night," he said during a July 16, 2007, interview.

[15] Interview with Claude Woodward, April 15, 2002.

[16] Ibid.

[17] Ibid.

[18] "Attala Court Judge Overrules Mistrial Motion by Defense."

[19] Ibid.

[20] "Negro Father Admits He Had Gun in House on Night of Slayings."

[21.] This dialog was taken from the *Mississippi v. Whitt* trial transcript. For purposes of this story, it is assumed the Turner trial dialog would have been similar since it involved the same participants about the same subject.

[22.] "Negro Father Admits He Had Gun in House on Night of Slayings."

[23.] "Attala Court Judge Overrules Mistrial Motion by Defense."

[24.] "A Press Box Eyeview of the Attala Trial."

[25.] "Man Collapses, Court Recessed," *New Orleans Times-Picayune*, March 21, 1950.

[26.] "Attala Court Judge Overrules Mistrial Motion by Defense."

[27.] "Negro Father Admits He Had Gun in House on Night of Slayings."

[28.] Ibid.

[29.] "Attala Court Judge Overrules Mistrial Motion by Defense."

[30.] "Negro Father Admits He Had Gun in House on Night of Slayings."

[31.] Ibid.

[32.] Interview with juror Charles Burns, July 30, 2002.

[33.] Interview with juror Irving Pylate, April 17, 2002.

[34.] Interview with former circuit clerk Sara Reese, April 15, 2002.

[35.] Interview with former student Wade Shipt of Ethyl, 2002.

[36.] "A Press Box Eyeview of the Attala Trial."

[37.] Interview with Irving Pylate, April 17, 2002.

[38.] "'That Man Hit Me in the Stomach,' 4-Year-Old Points Finger at Turner," *Jackson Daily News*, March 21, 1950.

[39.] This dialog was taken from the *Mississippi v. Whitt*, trial transcript. It is assumed the Turner trial dialog would have been similar since it involved the same participants about the same subject.

[40.] "Turner Gets Life Term," *Memphis Commercial Appeal*, March 22, 1950, 1.

[41.] *Jackson Daily News*, March 21, 1950; "'That Man Hit Me in the Stomach.'"

[42.] "Turner Gets Life Term," *Memphis Commercial Appeal*.

[43.] "'That Man Hit Me in the Stomach.'"

[44.] "Attala Murder Jury Is Still Deliberating," *Jackson Clarion-Ledger*, March 22, 1950, 1.

[45.] "Attala Murder Jury Is Still Deliberating."

[46.] Ibid.

[47.] "Turner Gets Life Term," *Memphis Commercial Appeal*.

[48.] Ibid.

[49.] Ibid.

50. "Attala Murder Jury Is Still Deliberating."

51. "Turner Gets Life Term," *Memphis Commercial Appeal*.

52. Ibid.

53. Ibid.

54. Combination of testimony quoted in "Turner Gets Life Term," *Memphis Commercial Appeal*; and "Attala Murder Jury Is Still Deliberating."

55. "Turner Gets Life Term," *Memphis Commercial Appeal*.

56. Combination of testimony quoted in "Turner Gets Life Term," *Memphis Commercial Appeal*; and "Attala Murder Jury Is Still Deliberating."

57. "Windol Whitt Gets Life Term."

58. "Turner Gets Life Term," *Memphis Commercial Appeal*.

59. Ibid.

60. Ibid.

61. Ibid.

62. "Attala Murder Jury Is Still Deliberating."

63. Interview with Charles Burns, July 30, 2002.

64. Ibid.

65. "Life for Three Deaths," *Newsweek*, April 3, 1950, 21.

66. "No Parole for Killer Turner; Juror Tells the Inside Story," *Memphis Commercial Appeal*, March 23, 1950, 1.

67. Interview with Charles Burns, July 30, 2002.

68. "No Parole for Killer Turner; Juror Tells the Inside Story."

69. Ibid.

70. "Attala Murder Jury Is Still Deliberating."

71. Ibid.

72. "Turner Guilty, Jurors Disagree on Penalty," *Jackson Clarion-Ledger*, March 22, 1950, 1.

73. "Turner Gets Life Term for Killing," *New Orleans Times-Picayune*, March 22, 1950, 1.

74. "Turner Gets Life Term," *Memphis Commercial Appeal*.

75. Ibid.

76. "Turner Guilty, Jurors Disagree on Penalty."

77. "Mississippi Justice," *Life*, April 3, 1950, 31.

78. "Life for Three Deaths."

79. "Turner Gets Life Term," *Memphis Commercial Appeal*.

80. Interview with Claude Woodward, April 15, 2002.

81. "Turner Gets Life Term," *Memphis Commercial Appeal*.

82. "No Parole Hope for Leon Turner, Thrice Murderer," *Jackson Clarion-Ledger*, March 23, 1950, 1.

[83.] "State Loses Fight to Send Turner to Electric Chair," *New Orleans Times-Picayune*, March 23, 1950.

[84.] "No Parole Hope for Leon Turner, Thrice Murderer."

[85.] "No Parole for Killer Turner; Juror Tells the Inside Story."

[86.] "No Parole Hope for Leon Turner, Thrice Murderer."

[87.] Ibid.

Chapter 20

[1.] "Leon Turner Gets Life Imprisonment without Hope," *Kosciusko Star-Herald*, March 23, 1950, 1.

[2.] "Justice Went Awry," *Jackson Daily News*, March 26, 1050.

[3.] Letters to the Editor, *Memphis Commercial Appeal*, March 26, 1950.

[4.] Three letters to the editor addressing William Faulkner's response to the verdict were published in the Sunday, April 2, 1950, *Commercial Appeal*. One, by Clayton Stephens of Tupelo, Mississippi, accused the author of bringing up the race issue:

If Turner's victims had been white children, would Faulkner have been so excited about the jury verdict?

If Turner had been a Negro, would Faulkner have written a letter about the trial? I am just as sensitive to the crime as Faulkner, but to inject the race issue into that trial is foolish.

The only sensible approach to the race issue is to give justice to all and not make an issue of a man's color.

To give a Negro special consideration just because he is a Negro is just as wrong as to fail to give him the consideration to which all people are due.

The Negro situation in the South may be good material for a best-selling novel, but as for advancing true brotherhood, it is false.

Faulkner responded one week later in the same forum:

The stand I took and the protest I made was against any drunken man, I don't care what color he is, murdering three children or even only one child. I don't care what color they are or it is.

It seems to me that the ones who injected race issues into this tragedy were whoever permitted or created a situation furnishing free-gratis-for-nothing to all our Northern critics, the opportunity to have made this same statement and protest, but with a hundred times the savagery and a thousand times the unfairness and ten thousand times less the understanding of our problems and grief for our mistakes—except that I, a native of our land and a sharer in our errors, just happened to be on the spot in time to say it first. This should be some satisfaction to a Southerner.

5. Nine months later, William Faulkner was awarded the 1949 Nobel Prize for literature.

6. Editorial: "Publicity Continues Our Way," *Kosciusko Star-Herald*, April 6, 1950.

7. Ibid.

8. "10-Year Sentence Is Given in Last 'Massacre Trial,'" *Kosciusko Star-Herald*, April 6, 1950, 1.

9. "Third 'Revenge' Killer Draws 10-Year Term," *Memphis Commercial Appeal*, April 4, 1950, 1.

10. Interview with Mary Ella Harris Carson, July 11, 2006.

11. "Death Cancels 'Thomas Harris Day,'" *Kosciusko Star-Herald*, April 13, 1950, 1.

Epilogue
1. Interview with Mary Ella Harris Carson, July 11, 2006.

2. Interviews with James Harris, July 11, 2002; and January 1, 2007.

3. "That Night ... I remember," *Jackson Clarion-Ledger*, December 3, 2006.

4. Interview with Claude Woodward, May 15, 2002.

5. "Leon Turner Dies Monday at Parchman," *Kosciusko Star-Herald*, February 15, 1968, 1.

6. Interviews with Inez Braswell, July 9, 2002; and Roy Braswell Jr., July 20, 2003.

7. Interview with Malcom Whitt Jr., June 19, 2002; prison records, Mississippi State Penitentiary, Parchman.

8. Interviews with Melinda Whitt, June 18, 2002; and Malcom Whitt Jr., July 12, 2002.

9. It is fortunate for the present account that he did so, for the appeal required that the Fifth Circuit Court trial transcript be typed and kept in the Mississippi Department of Archives and History (case 37,791). The transcript of the Turner trial, which was not appealed, could not be located in the Attala County records.

10. "Attala Massacre Sentence Upheld by Supreme Court," *Kosciusko Star-Herald*, February 15, 1951, 1.

11. Interview with Malcom Whitt Jr., July 12, 2002.

12. Interview with Melinda Whitt, June 18, 2002.

13. Mississippi Department of Corrections official Claire Papizan, e-mail to author, April 15, 2002.

14. "Three Escapees Face Charges."

15. Clarence Grammer, No. 14497, prison records, Mississippi State Penitentiary, Parchman.

16. Interview with Leflore County Sheriff Ricky Banks, June 1, 2005.

17. See http://www.tv.com/The+Lone+Ranger/Pardon+for+Curley/episode/26239/summary.html?tag=container;episode_guide_list.

18. See http://en.wikipedia.org/wiki/James_P._Coleman.

Acknowledgments

Chronicling the tragic incident that occurred in Attala County over a half century ago required digging up others' long dormant memories, some that are very painful to participants and witnesses of the events. It required their willingness to open their past to the probings of, in most cases, a complete stranger: me. I'll admit to great nervousness the first time I contacted many of these Mississippians, but with very few exceptions, they were warm and gracious in allowing me the opportunity to interview them. They showed that Mississippi hospitality is alive and well in "The Hospitality State."

For you who welcomed me into your homes; chatted with me for hours; and dug up old pictures, newspaper clippings, and family trees; my heart will be forever touched by your kindness. First and foremost is Mary Ella Harris Carson. Despite having suffered a parent's worst nightmare—the violent death of several of her children—this Christian lady long ago forgave the attackers. Her warmth and friendliness put me at ease during multiple visits to her home and numerous phone calls, as I mined her most painful memories. Blessed with remarkable recall, she hid nothing from me. She even encouraged me to write the book, saying that I was the answer to her prayers. Now in the twilight of her life, Mary Ella has my unending admiration.

Her son, James, who as an infant was rushed to safety out of the terrorized house by his mother, was a tremendous help in explaining his large family's roles and relationships (as well as in clarifying his mother's frequent use of ambiguous pronouns).

Also deserving my gratitude for allowing raw memories to be reopened are Leon Turner's half-sister, Annie Mae (Sugar Gal) Levy Johnson, and Leon's half-brother, Archie (Bug) Levy, and his wife, Thelma.

My thanks to the Whitt relatives who were most helpful in sharing their families' backgrounds: Malcom Whitt Jr., Gary and Melinda Whitt, and Don Whitt. A meeting between Malcom Whitt Jr. and Mary Ella Harris Carson took place during the writing of this book, and it was a touching and healing event to witness.

Several lifelong residents of Newport, Mississippi, spent hours sharing their memories, touring old cemeteries, and driving me along the back roads of Attala County Beat 4's beautiful countryside to witness the places where the events of *One Night of Madness* occurred. My sincerest thanks go to Bailey Hutchinson, John Owen Edwards, Bobby Hugh McDaniel, Billie McCrory Nance, "Little Pat" Smithson, and their respective spouses. Other neighbors willing to share their memories included Ollie (Mrs. Clifton) Hutchinson, Dave Ballard Jr., Edward Roundtree, and Thurman Lacey.

Many residents of nearby Kosciusko, where I was born and raised, contributed heavily to the story: Inez (Mrs. Roy) Braswell, whose entertaining and humorous stories about her husband and the old Attala County Jail kept me asking for more; Jeweldean Morgan, who worked at Sheriff Braswell's office; Rick McDaniel, my lifelong friend whose daddy played at the Newport area's house dances, and who has the best memory of anyone I know; Judge John Clark Love; Sallie Wasson; former District Attorney Chatwin Jackson and the men of the

Rib Alley morning coffee club; Dorothy Chunn Bishop and her husband, Sidney; Lloyd Robinson; Eva D. Jones; Nancy Green and "Cooter Bill" Thompson of the *Star-Herald*, who worked for my grandparents and then my parents when they owned the newspaper (and who stayed there more than fifty years); Fifth Circuit Judge Clarence E. Morgan III; Ellen Oaks Pettit; Mary Rutherford Douglas; and former Attala County sheriffs Claude Guess and Marvin "Pop" Lawrence.

My gratitude for their openness also goes to Leon Turner's direct descendants: Suzie Lee Turner Moore Brewer, Leon's daughter, whom I did not know existed until she called me; Dewayne Brewer; and Bertha Armentrout.

Others mentioned in the book or their relatives to whom I am indebted for warmly sharing their knowledge include Dr. Jack Aldridge; John Aldridge Sr.; Flowery Levy; T. G. (Tom) Sadler, former Yazoo County sheriff and Hogjaw's handler; Roosevelt Whitcomb; Helen Roby Ward; Cassel Ward; Annie Bell Harvey; Patty Branch Wigginton; Dal Bailey; and Roy Braswell Jr.

Providing wonderful first-hand recollections of Leon Turner's trial were Leon's defense attorney, Claude Woodward, and jurors Irving Pylate and Charles E. Burns.

Other Mississippians who allowed me to pick their brains include Wade Shipt, Lois Blaine, Ellen Pettit, Faye Allen Smith, Sheriff Ricky Banks of Leflore County, and former Mississippi governor William F. Winter, who as a young pup served in the state legislature with my grandfather, Stokes Sanders.

Much library and records research was required for this book, and I received fantastic assistance from many Mississippians. My gratitude goes to Clinton Bagley and Anne Webster of the Mississippi Department of Archives and

History; former Attala County circuit clerk Sara Reese and her staff: Wanda Faucher, Patricia Cain, and Lula Thompson; Jane T. Bond of the Mississippi Department of Corrections; Shirley Keenum of the Humphreys County Library; John Elsey of the B. S. Ricks Memorial Library in Yazoo City; Betty Williamson and the helpful staff at the Durant library; and Gwen Cole of the Investigative Bureau of the Mississippi Highway Patrol. A special thanks to Ann Breedlove of the Attala County library, who demonstrated her great researching ability on many occasions.

Thank you Bill Minor, dean of Mississippi reporters, for sharing your reporter's memory of the trials. And thanks to Jerry Mitchell, ace reporter from the *Jackson Clarion-Ledger*, for giving helpful advice and encouragement at the beginning of the endeavor.

Thankfully, two dear friends volunteered to read and edit each chapter: Ellen King, former teacher and lover of all things French; and Brenda Eliason, NASA engineer extraordinaire. Ladies, I could not have done it without you. Wonderfully patient and appreciatively honest, you took my struggling words and helped turn them into a cohesive story. Adding the final, professional touch was Bob Fullilove, of the Kosciusko Fulliloves, whose extraordinary copyediting turned them into a book.

I was very fortunate to find a talented mapmaker, Emily Han, in a local school's art program. Amazing Emily drew the maps in the summer before she entered eighth grade.

A huge thank-you goes to my aunt Mary E. McMillan, for allowing me to utilize her home as base camp during the many research trips I made to Kosciusko; and to my brother and his wife, Roy and Beverly, for doing the same during my stays in Jackson. In addition to the hospitality and fun, you saved me lots on hotel bills!

I am deeply grateful to my late mother, Della Sanders McMillan, for her foresight to record the events of the murders and trials in a scrapbook and to my late father, W. W. "Billy" McMillan, for taking the photograph that started it all.

Thanks to my three sons, Josh, Will, and James, who provided needed moral support for their father's project. Will, thanks for providing the original inspiration for this book. Look what you brought forth!

Finally, my love and gratitude go to my wife, who endured seven years of inattention, frustration, and I-can't-do-that-now-because-I've-got-to-work-on-the-book grumpiness that came with my obsession. Her encouragement, advice, and patience were soothing and highly appreciated. Thanks, Teresa, for making every day a dream.

Index

Stokes McMillan is fourth generation born and raised in Attala County, Mississippi. His great-grandfather founded the local newspaper, the Kosciusko *Star-Herald*, which his grandfather and father later published. Presently an engineer with NASA at the Johnson Space Center, McMillan lives with his family in Houston, Texas. *One Night of Madness* is his first book. You can learn more about his work at www.stokesmcmillan.com.